AF412753

# Dreadlock

# Dreadlock

## A Novel by
## Lew Anthony

McCLELLAND AND STEWART

For Rita, who gave up her living room

Copyright © 1981 Michael Shuter Enterprises

All rights reserved

*The Canadian Publishers*
McClelland and Stewart Limited
25 Hollinger Road
Toronto M4B 3G2

CANADIAN CATALOGUING IN PUBLICATION DATA

Anthony, Lew.
  Dreadlock

ISBN 0-7710-0756-6

I. Title.

PS8551.N85D74   C813'.54   C80-094846-7
PR9199.3.A688D74

Printed and bound in the United States of America

# PART ONE
## Home Base

# CHAPTER ONE

## *Wednesday — 4:55 P.M.*

"Jamaica?" Bishop's surprise was unmistakable. "We got some terrific footage from Jamaica today. CBS."

"What's CBS doing down there?" I'd just finished sifting through a file of recent clippings on the place. "Surely not political trouble again?"

"No," he said, amused for some reason. "This was a freak thing. An accident."

"What happened?" I didn't particularly care, but Bishop sometimes listens while I talk shop and you have to be fair about these things.

"Some Kraut tourist killed himself on one of those parasails," he said, laughing.

"And that's funny?" Like most news guys, Bishop affects a callous air that borders on being smart-ass and sometimes crosses the frontier.

"Wait'll you hear how he did it."

"How?" I hadn't called Bishop for a preview of his newscast; I'd called to invite him to join Helen and me for a late steak, and to tell him I was going down to the Caribbean for a few days. Business. Richard Bishop is my next-door neighbour and occasional drinking companion. Also, he has a slight crush on Helen.

He chuckled again. "Good old Fritz Spritz, or whatever his name was, never believed a man could fly, but here he is soaring a hundred feet above the ocean, being towed around by a speedboat. Meantime, here's this '60 Minutes' crew, which is down in Negril shooting a nude cruise for one of Safer's whimsy pieces. Of course, Safer isn't there. He's off in Tahiti or some place."

"What the hell's a nude cruise?"

"What it says, I guess. Bunch of tourists take off all their clothes and sail around, sizing each other up. Hell, Shuter, don't ask me. You're the guy in the travel business."

"Yeah, but not nude cruises."

"That's *your* story. Anyway, the CBS guys're aboard the *Calico Jack*, which is a clapped-out old schooner, shooting a few miles of tits-and-ass that'll never make air. Then, Fritz decides to fly by and ogle the naked ladies. Or the boatman does. Whatever. But something goes wrong. The guy driving the boat screws up. Next thing you know, poor old Fritz slams into the *Calico Jack*'s mast at about thirty miles an hour, and it's *auf Wiedersehen!*"

"Messy."

"Exactly. But the pictures are fabulous. Best accident footage I've seen since Wallenda fell off his tightrope in Puerto Rico. The camera never stopped. Picked up Fritz early, and followed him straight in. They got it all: a lot of screams from the naked ladies, a little blood, a few bits of Fritz, and an eloquent shrug from the idiot driving the speedboat who, by the way, is the damnedest-looking guy you've ever seen. He's got braids a foot long."

"They're called dreadlocks."

Bishop laughed again. "No wonder." He paused. "I'll say one thing for those CBS guys. They're pros, even the ones who don't shoot news. The field producer was on the phone to Rather's shop approximately fifteen seconds after they got ashore this morning. It's not quite noon, so New York decides to take a look."

"And you've already seen the pictures?"

"Big-budget television," he said, envious. "They flew the film to Montego Bay in a puddle-jumper, Leared it across to Miami, souped it, and fed it up north. Naturally, Rather grabbed it but we'll voice-over about forty-five seconds."

"I'd expect it of you," I said, "but I'm a little disappointed in Dan Rather. I thought his news judgment was better."

"What do you mean?"

"It's hardly a world-shaker. Aside from the victim's family and friends, who are presumably in Germany and out of range of the 'CBS Evening News', who cares?"

"I care," he growled. "And so will everyone in the country, when they see the pictures."

"Why?"

"Because it's November. We're all up here freezing our ass while this Kraut's tooling around the tropics, spending his deutschmarks the way we used to spend dollars. And then he gets his. Boy, does he get his!"

"And that's news?"

"Are you kidding, Shuter? It's practically textbook television. Sex, violence, and faraway places."

He agreed to join us before midnight at the House of Chan, where, despite its name, they serve the best steaks in Toronto. I said goodbye, leaving him to his footage, feeds, and satellites – the costly toys of his sometimes childish trade.


Bishop's account of the parasailing accident at Negril left me uneasy. Only a couple of hours earlier I'd learned that one of our passengers had gone missing from Negril and there was a chance she was in trouble. The passenger, Carol Malone, had friends in high places – starting with my boss.

I sat at my standard-issue vice-president's desk, gazing out the rain-streaked windows and thinking about the German tourist. Poor bastard. What a weird way to buy it. Not that there's a good way. But parasailing, far from home? I've parasailed a few times, and it always seemed safe enough to me.

Of course, people get themselves into the dumbest jackpots. I've spent most of my thirty-seven years cleaning up other people's messes – at home, in the cops, and now here, at the airline. It's an endless and often thankless task. But I've always been a sucker for people in trouble, even when it's of their own making, which it usually is. Bishop ribs me about having a Galahad complex. I don't. It's just that I hate to see innocent people in over their heads.

I leaned forward and buzzed Mrs. Innes. It was getting late and I needed help.

"Yes, Mr. Shuter?" Mrs. Innes had worked a long day but her tone was still morning-crisp. She is a marvel of efficiency and thoughtfulness – part machine, part mother.

"See if you can track down Stu Bladon."

While I waited, I thought some more about McGregor's call. The boss had been unusually upset, which meant I'd soon have to gather up my tired mop and battered bucket. That's me: Michael Shuter, janitor. Janitor to a world working an eight-day week – eight days and seven nights.

Predictably, Bladon had jumped at my invitation, and now he was enjoying himself, drinking Directors' Stock, and watching Guy Lafleur, Montreal's superstar. They're both powerful stimulants. Bladon's eyes shone, his heavy shoulders were hunched with tension, his normally expressionless face was set in a tight smile. A good hockey game will bring out the boy in the hardest of men, and Bladon is hard. In his business, they're all hard.

I decided to wait until the end of the period before spoiling his fun.

Bladon, Helen, and I were staring at the ice, watching the play sweep up and down while the crowd roared. Usually the Maple Leafs manage to extend the Canadiens before losing, and the Canadiens always put on a great show.

There was a lull while television sold some beer, and Bladon leaned back, flexing tension out of his shoulder muscles.

"Shuter, you know how to live." His big hand gestured at our surroundings – Holidair's private booth in Maple Leaf Gardens.

"Goes with the job."

He sighed. "No perks like this in the force."

"No, there aren't."

"Of course," he laughed, "if I make commissioner..."

"Hang in. You've got a shot."

Bladon is a good cop, tough and thoughtful. He is also a good administrator and clever politician, a company man. That's what it takes to move up. That, and a clean nose. I was always a lousy politician and my nose was usually dirty. But I'd been a good cop too. Everyone said so. There are still days when I miss it.

"Commissioner? Not a prayer. No connections." He grinned slyly. "Now, if I was the solicitor-general's son-in-law, I suppose..."

"That's very funny."

"You're right, Shuter. I apologize."

"No need. It doesn't bother me. Not any more."

The nepotism stuff doesn't; I earn my pay. But the rest of it bothers the hell out of me, although I try not to show it. After two years, there are still moments when the pain is savage, almost exquisite. They are the unexpected moments, when memory suddenly breaches all the walls I've built. There are so many triggers: a face caught in half-profile, a song on the radio, a raincoat like hers, a scent she'd liked.

"May I freshen your drink, Inspector?" Helen was making a fuss over Bladon, playing hostess. She's good at that, and should be; she flew for ten years before becoming our chief stew.

"The name's Stuart, Mrs. Boyko. And, yes please." He passed her his glass.

"If you'll call me Helen." She beamed, her smile genuine rather than professional. Helen likes big, tough men. She looked at me inquiringly.

"Not just yet." I was nursing my scotch. I had a feeling it was going to be a long night.

Television finished selling beer, and the producer buzzed the referee's beeper, giving permission for resumption of play. The tube runs hockey now; it runs all pro sports. The fans who buy the tickets take second place to the armchair consumers. But they still pack the arenas, paying ever-higher prices to watch ever-slower games. Tonight, the fans were getting their money's worth; the Canadiens were leading 2-0, but every square inch of ice was being fiercely contested.

"How many of these things are there?" Bladon was fascinated by the booth. It is protected from the public gaze by one-way glass, has four comfortable chairs, a small refrigerator, a lockup bar, and a telephone, all behind an unmarked door on the building's second level. We use it to entertain VIPs: foreign tourism officials, resort owners, big wholesalers, bureaucrats, politicians.

"Four, I think. One in each corner."

"Civilized way to watch a hockey game."

Maple Leaf Gardens is showing its age. It was completed in the depths of the Great Depression, a fact that fresh paint and new theatre seats can't overcome. But, along with the Montreal Forum, it remains a national shrine. All societies build temples to their gods, and in Canada the gods have been hockey players and Mammon. If the cathedrals of Victorian England are the great railway stations, the cathedrals of twentieth-century Canada are arenas and bank towers. I prefer the arenas.

The bell sounded the end of the first period, and the teams clumped, sweating, to their dressing-rooms.

"Good game." Bladon was still enjoying himself.

I nodded, trying to decide how to begin, but he was ahead of me.

"Okay, Shuter. What is it?"

I didn't say anything, so he carried on.

"Must be important. Usually, when you want something, you phone and it's two beers and a pub lunch. Tonight, it's the Canadiens and twenty-five-year-old whisky."

"It's sensitive. I need to pick your brain, maybe get a name or two."

Helen studied the Gardens program, pretending not to listen.

"Go on." Bladon was looking at me closely, his drink forgotten.

"Alan Malone."

"The MP for Toronto-Centre? What about him?" Bladon's face slipped into neutral. He was wary, and I could hardly blame him. The RCMP had been burned recently for paying too much attention to the politicians. Hell, the force had been burned recently for just about everything. After years of operating quietly, out of the public eye, the undercover side of the Royal Canadian Mounted Police was up to its funny hat in boiling water, being investigated by just about everyone able to hire a hall and summon witnesses. A federal royal commission of inquiry into RCMP wrongdoing was under way. Various provinces were conducting judicial inquiries. The press was embarked on a spasmodic witch-hunt, with a score of half-baked reporters running around trying to act like Woodward or Bernstein. And much of the country was appalled by the almost daily revelations of illegal activity within an organization which, over the years, had come to symbolize Canada itself. The list of RCMP sins was endless: break-ins, mail tampering, surveillance of politicians, buggings, muggings, arson, perjury. Day after day, senior lawmen took one witness stand or another to testify they saw nothing wrong with breaking the law in order to maintain it. None of it was new to me, of course; it had all contributed to my disillusionment and, ultimately, to my resignation.

"McGregor called from Ottawa this afternoon," I said. "He was in a flap, which isn't like him. He tracked me down at the club, had me dragged right off the court."

"What's bothering McGregor?"

"He ran into Alan Malone in the Chateau Grill. They flew together in the war, and they've stayed in touch. McGregor says Malone's a pretty good guy, rich, into politics late in life because he wants to contribute. An idealist, and you and I know about idealists in politics."

Bladon made a face. "So?"

"Malone's got a problem. Apparently he was shy about bringing it up, didn't want to impose on an old friendship. But McGregor says the man is worried. Worried and embarrassed."

"What about?"

"His daughter. She's gone missing in Jamaica. Ran off with a black guy down there. McGregor seems to feel we're responsible."

Bladon frowned. "Why?"

"Because we sold her the ticket, I guess. She missed the flight home. That was last Friday. This is Wednesday."

"I know what day it is," he said sourly. "What do you mean, missed the flight?"

"Happens more often than you'd think. A kid gets down to the sun, the beer's cheap, the water's fine, the local talent's a change of pace. The next thing you know the kid says the hell with it, and stays. Usually, they come home in a few days, when they're bored. Or broke. Or broken-hearted. But in this case, there hasn't been a word. No card, no call."

"An accident?"

"No. She travelled down with another girl, a nurse named Patsy Baird. They were rooming together, a two-week package at Negril. First week, Carol Malone took up with some local dude. Then she took off."

"How old is she?"

"Twenty-five. No kid. That's what I told McGregor: she's

just another girl who likes black guys. Well, that's okay by me. Certainly it's not the airline's fault. But McGregor says I'm to go find her."

"Sounds routine."

"It should be, although there's not much I can do after I track her down. Get her to phone home is about all."

"Doesn't she have a job?"

"Yes and no. She's an artist, an illustrator. Freelance. She works mainly for ad agencies. Quite good, I'm told. Anyway, she doesn't punch a clock."

McGregor knew quite a bit about Carol. An only child, he'd said. Talented, educated in France, independent-minded, lived alone; an interesting girl. But then, she was bound to be interesting. Dullards never get into trouble; they don't have the imagination.

Bladon tugged his moustache. "What happens when a passenger doesn't show up for a return flight? Do you just bring him back on the next one?"

"Depends. We like to fill all the seats, and in peak season we usually do. Which means that a no-show often has to come back with a scheduled carrier. They've always got seats. Helen knows that drill better than anyone."

Helen smiled, pleased to be included. "Well, we do a count, of course. And if we're short we check the ticket stubs against the manifest. Once we've figured out who's missing we start paging them."

"What good would that do?" Bladon asked.

"You wouldn't believe the trouble the public can get into in airports. They get lost. They get fascinated by the planes. They fall into bars, forget what time it is, try to get on the wrong flights. In Malone's case Baird told our agent in Montego Bay her friend was probably going to miss the flight. So when we were one short it simplified things."

"Do you delay departures when someone doesn't show up and you have no idea why?"

"We can't. I mean, at what point do you cut it off?

Holidair's a fairly big airline. We've got eight 747s and six L10-11s. But we're flying all over the world. Our schedules are pretty tight."

"What's your responsibility?"

"None, legally. If someone misses a flight for a legitimate reason, car trouble or whatever, we're as helpful as possible. It's good public relations. But in peak season there's not much we can do, except refer them to a scheduled carrier. Our tickets are quite specific: it's the passenger's responsibility to make the flight."

"Airline tickets," Bladon said in disgust, "read like my insurance policies."

Bladon was taking a closer interest than I had expected and I wondered why. "Stu, was there a squawk on this? Alan Malone's a Member of Parliament. I mean, he'd know who to call."

He looked at me levelly. "Maybe I did hear something. Nothing official."

"What did you hear?"

"Let me think for a bit, Shuter."


A roar went up in the building. The teams had reappeared for the second period, their uniforms bright splashes of colour against the milky ice. The harsh lights television requires heightened the brilliance of the scene. Visually, hockey has a pristine quality no other team sport can match. It looks clean, even if the game itself is sometimes dirty. The colour contrasts are vivid, the players swift and graceful. At its best, hockey is a sort of high-speed ballet—but too often, these days, it smacks of roller derby.

Bladon was looking at the game again, but I doubted he was concentrating on it; he seemed preoccupied. Helen had gone back to her program, pretending to read a piece on Lafleur.

Helen Boyko is a company woman the way Bladon's a company man—to the core. She is also beautiful: tall, slim, raven-haired, big-chested, fighting an impressive holding action against the calendar. She always smells faintly of orange groves. In her mid-thirties, she's divorced from a pilot who had to be crazy to let her go. She has worked for McGregor for fifteen years, during which time Holidair has grown from a shoestring operation into one of the world's largest charter lines. For the past four years, Helen has been our director of cabin personnel. But her influence is much wider than her title suggests.

Her personal life is something of a cipher. She flirts a lot, but seldom dates. She once told me the pilot had really messed her around, broken her heart, and that she'd never get burned again. There was a time, not so long ago, when Helen and I were both vulnerable, when we might have started something. But there were too many ghosts in the way and the moment passed. We were probably wise: in an office romance there's no place to hide.

Bladon had done his thinking. He swung around in his chair and cleared his throat: "Helen, I hope you won't mind, but I'd like a private word with Shuter."

"Not at all." Her smile was too bright, this time forced. "I need some cigarettes anyway. How long should I take to buy them?"

"Ten minutes, tops. And thanks."

"It's okay." She picked up her handbag, smoothed her skirt, and stepped through the door.

"Beautiful woman, that." Bladon sounded wistful. He has four kids and a wife who keep him broke. His gambling habit helps, too. He bets on everything and is an inveterate buyer of lottery tickets. "Is this place clean?"

"I work for an airline, not Moscow Centre."

"Don't con me, Shuter. You'd Hoover a kindergarten. I trained you myself."

He was right, of course. I have the booth swept occasionally, along with our offices; it's all part of my job. In business, you never know what your competitors will do for an edge and I'd been trained to expect the worst. McGregor, an honest man, was shocked the first time I outlined my plans for a new security system, and explained why we needed it. But he agreed to go ahead, and I'd spent a small fortune since, protecting Holidair's interests and its passengers' safety.

"I'm taking a chance, Shuter, I don't want my balls in the wringer."

There wasn't much I could say. Bladon is SS, the RCMP Security Service – a.k.a. Spook Section. I'd been there too. We both knew the rules. Pal or not, Bladon wouldn't contravene the Official Secrets Act.

"I appreciate it."

"This Jamaica thing," he said quietly. "Watch yourself."

I felt a twinge of alarm. Bladon doesn't traffic in hollow dramatics; there's enough real drama in his workaday world. "You said it sounded routine."

"The Malone girl? I suppose it is, except for the political connection. Malone's headed for the cabinet, and soon. He can get the Prime Minister on the phone quicker than you can get the operator." He lowered his voice some more. "We took a look at Malone. He's straight. Old Bay Street. Money's legit, and lots of it. No bad habits. And he's been co-operating beautifully on this Jamaican thing."

"What Jamaican thing? I'm not with you."

He leaned closer. "There's an operation running down there at the moment. Hush-hush. We've been asked to keep an eye out."

"What is it?"

"Nothing you need to know about to find the girl. It's strictly government-to-government. Actually, PM-to-PM. But we've been briefed and it's serious."

I shrugged. "So what?"

"You read the papers, hang around with Richard Bishop, move in what I understand are known as informed circles. You know the problems in Jamaica. The place is on a knife-edge."

I know the tourists' Jamaica fairly well. Janet had loved the country and we'd holidayed there three times. But I hadn't been back in the two years since she died. Ghosts, again.

Jamaica is a glorious island, but troubled. A holiday-maker's dream: endless sunshine, uncluttered beaches, warm water, good hotels, magnificent scenery. But a nightmare for people in the working world: religious and racial strife, violent political division, hard-core poverty, the worst slums in the western hemisphere, a collapsed currency, and a totally unrealistic economy. When it comes to problems, Jamaica is the Third World in microcosm. For a couple of years, it received so much bad press that tourism virtually stopped. Recently, there's been a recovery. We programmed 1,600 seats a week to Montego Bay for the coming winter, and almost all of them were sold.

"Jamaica's had problems for years," I said. "What else is new?"

Bladon shook his head. "Problems, yes. But this is a full-blown crisis. Shuter, I *can't* tell you. You know that. But this thing could get very heavy. Heavy to the point where everything down there collapses under the weight. And by everything I mean the government, law and order, the works."

"Is it political?"

Bladon put on his best poker face, but said nothing.

"Castro, then?"

Again, no response.

"Okay," I said. "If I don't need to know, forget it. You mentioned Malone was co-operating. With whom?"

"When his daughter didn't come home, Malone called External and asked them to find her. I think he expected the high commissioner himself to lead a search party. Of course, all External could do was make a formal request to the authorities in Kingston. I'm told there was a cursory check, but there wasn't much Kingston could do."

"There never is."

"Wouldn't you know it?" he said gruffly. "Some bright spark at External, an ambitious little bastard on the Caribbean desk, gave Malone a briefing on the operation I mentioned. Hoping to suck up to a future cabinet minister, of course. Ever since, Malone has been trying to square his personal concern with his public responsibilities. It took a couple of heavyweights from the Prime Minister's Office to stop him raising the matter in the House."

Bladon was talking in riddles but I could piece enough of it together: Malone goes to the External Affairs Department with a personal problem, and comes away with some classified information he feels ought to be shared with the public. Enter a couple of senior aides to the Prime Minister; they're powerful people, and smooth – like a good cognac. The aides persuade him to remain silent.

"I don't want to go down cold, Stu. I need a few names."

"We've got two men on station there. Strictly liaison, if you take my meaning. But I don't want you anywhere near them. They haven't been briefed on this one. Almost no one has."

I looked at him sharply. If senior members of the force in Canada were aware of a situation in a foreign country, it was almost inconceivable that the men on station wouldn't know, too. But it was barely possible, so I let it go. "What I want is Jamaican names. Locals. And not just local cops. There's a whole level of society down there that's closed to outsiders. You know, they see us as rich grumblers who drink too much and get sunstroke."

He considered it. "I'll do this much. There's a guy here in town who helps us every once in a while. We did him a favour once, and he's been paying us back. In instalments. Weird guy. A Rastafarian. He's got hair like you wouldn't believe. But he seems to know everybody in Jamaica."

"What's his name?"

"Lucky. Ras Lucky. Real name's Llewellyn. David Llewellyn."

"Where do I find him?"

"He works for some little recording company down near Kensington Market. A dubber, I think it's called. Something to do with the record business. Phone me tomorrow and I'll dig it out of the files. Or, I suppose you could find him tonight."

"Tonight. You can take Helen to dinner without me."

He looked at me oddly. "I'm a married man."

"And don't you forget it."

He laughed but there was doubt in his eyes. "I'm a struggling public servant, not a $75,000-a-year airline vice-president. I can't afford expensive dinners."

"It's $80,000, plus stock, plus expenses." I didn't enjoy rubbing it in, but Bladon hadn't wanted me to quit. "Don't worry. The airline'll treat."

"Shuter, you haven't got a job, you've got an oil well."

"Ras Lucky," I said firmly. "Where?"

"There's a West Indian joint out on College Street, near Bathurst. The JamJam Club. He hangs out there. It's spliff city. About six deep breaths and you're gone. The local cops let it go. It's all part of their goddamn community relations program. Next thing you know, the Toronto cops won't interfere with the hoods in Little Italy on account of gangsters are part of the Italian cultural tradition."

I laughed, but Bladon didn't think it was funny.

"Be cool, Shuter. Don't come on strong at the JamJam. Just mention my name, buy the guy a couple of beers, and tell him what you want."


There was a knock and Helen stuck her head in, smiling uncertainly.

"I gave you boys twenty minutes, but I got tired of hanging around the hotdog stand. Two different guys tried to pick me up."

"It's okay," I said. "We're finished."

Bladon stood to hold her chair while she folded into it, crossing her lovely legs. "I hope you didn't think I was being rude," he said formally, "but my position is delicate. Shuter says you're reliable, so I'll just say this: I've probably told him some things I shouldn't have. But if he finds the Malone girl, the RCMP will not be unhappy."

"Don't explain," she said. "I understand."

While Bladon and I had been talking, the Canadiens had broken the game open. They were leading 4-0, and there were still two minutes left in the second period. With so many franchises in the National Hockey League today, Montreal only comes to town twice a year. It's probably just as well; Leaf fans wouldn't tolerate more frequent drubbings.

I glanced at my watch: not quite ten o'clock, and another period to go. "Helen, I'm going to leave the inspector in your hands."

"I'll be putty," Bladon laughed.

She seemed surprised. "Where are you going?"

"I'm going to find some curried goat."

"You're joking. We're going for steaks."

"You're going for steaks. I've got to meet a guy about Carol Malone. I'll take Bishop, if he's interested."

"All right," she said. "Stuart and I will carry on to the House of Chan. I doubt your goat is going to match their U.S. Prime."

I picked up the phone, dialled the network's number, asked for Bishop, and waited until he came on the line. He sounded out of sorts.

"What's the matter? No news tonight?"

"There's too damn much of it. How's the game?"

"Montreal's killing us."

"Figures. Are we still on for steaks?"

"No. Something's come up. I thought I'd treat you to something a little different. We're going Caribbean."

"Is that anything like going Dutch?" Then he remembered: "Oh, yeah. Your junket to Jamaica."

"Do you want me to pick you up?" His driver's licence was under suspension again; Bishop collects speeding tickets in bulk lots.

"Please. Just come up to the newsroom. We never close." He rang off before I could reply.

Bladon was watching me, a cop again. "I know you and Bishop are close, Shuter. But no scoops, please, or I'll put your ass in a sling."

"I'll tell him about Carol. That's hardly a story for the national news. But I won't say anything about the rest of it. Hell, I don't *know* anything about the rest of it."

"You know enough," he said evenly. "And Bishop can get the PM on the phone even quicker than Malone. So watch it."

"Don't worry," I said, putting on my raincoat.

"I always worry."

We shook hands. "Thanks, Stu. I'll keep you posted. Take good care of Helen. I think she's got her eye on Guy Lafleur."

"He's married," she pouted. "It says so in my program."

"I'm married, too," Bladon said wearily. "Thanks for the hockey, Shuter."

"Our pleasure." I gave Helen a peck on the cheek. "See you tomorrow. You can sign my name at the restaurant."

# CHAPTER TWO

## *Wednesday – 10:10 P.M.*

A cop was standing over my car, studying it. I'd parked illegally on Church Street, just across from the Gardens. So far, he hadn't written a ticket, but he glared as I walked up.

"You shouldn't park here, sir." The Metropolitan Toronto Police are unfailingly polite until you give them reason not to be; then they're no fun at all.

I tried to sound suitably contrite. "The lots were full, officer. I didn't want to miss the start of the game."

"There's a sign." He pointed at the NO PARKING ANYTIME sign, directly overhead.

I nodded gravely and brought out my keys. The rain had stopped, but the wind had picked up. I popped up the gull-wing door, and heard him grunt in surprise.

"Don't see very many of these." He'd made no move to take out his book.

"There aren't many around."

"A Bricklin," he said. "How do you like it?"

I wasn't going to get a ticket. "Fine. It's a little noisy."

He bent over to peer in at the dashboard. "Sharp car. Looks a bit like a Corvette, except for those doors."

"They stole the doors from Mercedes."

I got in and started the engine; it sounded a bit rough. The cop listened for a moment, then frowned.

"My brother-in-law has a Corvette," he said. "He's an asshole."

There didn't seem to be anything to say.

"Next time, I'll give you a ticket." He swung the door down, and stepped back as I pulled away from the curb.

The Bricklin *is* an unusual car. Fewer than 2,900 of them were built before the company went under, taking $22 million of the taxpayers' money with it. That was in the mid-1970s. The car was the brainchild of an American promoter named Malcolm Bricklin, who wanted to be a latter-day Henry Ford and who came to Canada to find a friendly government willing to underwrite his fantasies. The Province of New Brunswick, economically depressed and chronically desperate for industry, helped Bricklin set up shop in an old brush factory in Saint John. From there he launched his assault on Detroit, with the first all-Canadian sports car. That the design and engine were American somehow was overlooked in the early euphoria.

Inevitably, there were problems. The production line was unable to turn out cars fast enough. The car was unrealistically priced, intended to go on the market for $5,000 a copy when it should have been aimed at the luxury trade. Shortcuts were taken, in an effort to speed production and reduce costs. Pieces started falling off the finished cars. The price kept going up. Huge injections of fresh capital were required and, finally, a wiser but poorer New Brunswick government pulled the plug. Bricklin returned to the United States, claiming to be broke, and the car that bears his name became an instant Edsel, a collector's item, one more curiosity piece on the tangled scrapheap of automotive dreams.

But, damnit, the thing worked. When you turned the key the engine started, and you could drive it away. The cop was right, too: the Bricklin *is* a sharp-looking car, with its low-to-the-ground styling, its moulded fibreglass body, its gull-wing doors. I'd bought mine used, a little more than a year earlier, for just under $10,000, and I haven't regretted the purchase, even though parts will never be easy to find.

I switched on the radio and half-listened while Lightfoot fretted about whether a former lover had mentioned his name; an oldie, but indisputably Canadian content. Like the airlines, the radio stations have to satisfy their federal regulators; one Gordon Lightfoot for two Neil Diamonds, one Anne Murray for two Linda Ronstadts. In Canada, there's a rule or regulation covering virtually everything. Even pop music. Canadians are the most regulated people in the free world, and I sometimes wonder if it is really any worse in Russia. Probably. Everyone says so.

I know one thing: I wouldn't have been able to resign from the Komitet Gossudarstvennoi Bezopastnosti as easily as I'd quit the Royal Canadian Mounted Police. As a KGB officer I'd have had to defect. Or they'd have slapped me into Lubianka, pending my certification and the next train east. Getting out of the force was easy, except for the paperwork. Tons of it.

Lightfoot yielded the turntable to Bob Marley and the Wailers, who promptly confessed to shooting a sheriff. The reggae beat started me thinking again about Jamaica. "A full-blown crisis," Bladon had said. There was no doubt the Jamaican government had its problems. All governments have problems. But as long as the sun shines and the Caribbean stays warm, North Americans are going to flock there in winter and Holidair will continue to fly them.

Holidair is a remarkable success story, a tribute to Douglas McGregor's vision and his hard work. Like all the airline geniuses – the Freddie Lakers, the Max Wards, the Juan Trippes, even the Howard Hugheses – McGregor has pursued his dream with a single-mindedness bordering on fanaticism. The result is an airline which today has 5,000 seats, all in wide-bodied aircraft, and flies to every continent.

When McGregor began, after coming back from a distinguished Second World War, he had a single-engine float plane and a small freight contract with a pulp and paper company in the north woods. Then he acquired a DC-3 and moved into the passenger business. Today, the replacement value of Holidair's fleet would be more than $800 million. McGregor simply kept ploughing back his revenues, taking on new debt and growing with the market.

I turned at Bloor Street and drove into the National Television Network's parking lot, choosing a space marked RESERVED FOR E.G. CARRUTHERS VP. Good old Carruthers, whoever he was: probably a murderous infighter in the lethal little wars they're always waging inside television networks. Bishop tells me stories of deviousness and back-stabbing as nasty and Machiavellian as anything I ever encountered in the RCMP.

The door popped open and I got out, turning up my collar against the weather. Cold wet November days are always depressing in Toronto; there's a whole winter of them to come. The rest of the country might think of southern Ontario as the banana belt, but the wind and rain sweeping up from the lake thought otherwise. Shivering, I ran to the front of the building, dodging puddles all the way.

The commissionaire glared at me as I approached his station, a damp intruder. There was dandruff on his thin shoulders and his campaign ribbons looked almost as tired as his eyes. A newspaper lay open on his desk. He'd been drooling over the Sunshine Girl, page three's daily treat for dirty old men of all ages. Maybe it wasn't fatigue in his eyes, after all. Maybe it was regret. He was years past that sort of campaign.

"Mr. Bishop," I said, unbuttoning my raincoat and trying not to look like the Yonge Street Flasher while I did it. "He's expecting me."

The old man shoved the visitors' log toward me with an up-from-under look, an odd amalgam of deference and defiance.

"Ya gotta sign in." His voice was part whine, part wheeze:

evidence of too many disappointments, too many cigarettes over far too many years.

"I know." I scrawled my signature, illegible as always. In terms of real security, the NTN system is laughable. But it is probably all the network needs: a uniform to discourage any drunks or punks who might wander in from the street. Actually, there's not that much to secure. In television, they steal ideas, talent and, occasionally, wives from one another over three-martini lunches at Winston's or the Windsor Arms. High crimes and misdemeanours, courtesy of the American Express card.

The commissionaire checked my signature, then sighed elaborately; I was another idiot who couldn't be trusted to follow simple procedure.

"The time. Ya gotta fill in the time. Here." He jabbed the log with a yellow forefinger. He might have been a long-suffering schoolteacher, explaining yet again the mysteries of the two-times table to the class dunce. I glanced at my watch and scribbled in 22:19. It seemed to satisfy him. "Mr. Bishop's in the newsroom. Third floor, to the left." Class dismissed.

I walked to the elevators, acutely aware that I was in a foul mood. My distemper had nothing to do with rude commissionaires, the weather, or Carol Malone. It sprang from more fundamental sources: boredom and guilt. Lately, I'd been spending less time at my office, more at the Cambridge Club, killing afternoons in the gym. Or playing squash. Or gin rummy. Or snooker. Or swilling twenty-five-year-old scotch and then, half-heartedly, chasing twenty-year-old skirts. You'd think I was training for the *Playboy* pentathlon.

Actually, I had no reason to be bored. There was lots to do. McGregor wanted me to begin acquainting myself with all facets of the airline, not just the security end. But I kept stalling. For the moment, at least, the intricacies of high finance, personnel administration, scheduling, maintenance, marketing, and all the rest of it, held little interest. So I'd been goofing off, and feeling guilty because it didn't really matter. I had job security. I'd married the boss's daughter.

Bishop was sitting at the big central desk in the newsroom, a confused and cluttered place overlaid with tension. It smelled of cigarette smoke and overbrewed coffee. Bishop was stubbing out a cigarette with one hand, and holding a felt pen in the other. He was doodling on a scratch pad. Bishop is a compulsive doodler; his designs are weird and wild, involuntary ramblings that mask the workings of an agile mind. He looked up with a faint smile. "How was the game?"

"The Leafs were a step too slow."

He nodded. "Take a chair. We're a minute, ten over."

Bishop is dark, two inches taller than my six-one but at one hundred and seventy, he's thirty pounds lighter. He is also polite, in an old-fashioned, almost courtly way. It's his small-town upbringing, he says. I had one of those, too, but my manners lost their polish during fifteen years of villains and clowns.

"How's it going?"

"Nothing earth-shattering, but some solid stuff. I may have to drop Afghanistan."

"That's okay by me."

"An NBC crew got caught in a firefight."

"What about the German parasailer?"

"We've had to slash it back to twenty-two seconds. A shame, really. The pictures're out of this world."

"Film at eleven."

Bishop laughed. It's a standing joke in network newsrooms, a putdown of the news programs produced by local stations, where pictures are usually more important than content. At the networks, they like to pretend content takes precedence and sometimes it does. Bishop says the local stations would ignore the outbreak of the Third World War unless there was film of it. Even then the war would take second place to a hometown fire, and the locals' mid-evening promos would say: "Four injured in midtown blaze, World War Three begins... film at eleven on 'Eyewitness News.'"

I enjoy ribbing Bishop about the news business, mainly because he takes it so seriously. The news is supposed to be different every day, but it always sounds the same to me: politicians shouting at one another about jobs and inflation, trouble in the Middle East, a flood here, a fire there, a shoot-out some place else. One night the CBC screwed up its video-tapes and ran a two-week-old newscast in Vancouver. Nobody noticed. Not a single viewer called to complain. Bishop laughs about that but I know it bothers him.

Bishop is executive producer of the National Television Network's nightly newscast, a half-hour program shown across the country at eleven o'clock, local time. He is also my pal. Not that we're really close. No one ever gets really close to a reporter or a cop. But I owe Bishop; he helped me through a dark time.

He was doodling again, trying to accommodate Afghanistan.

"Tell me," I said, "why is it always NBC that has the fun? When was the last time an NTN crew got caught in a firefight?"

"During our last salary negotiations. Don't give me a hard time, Shuter. I can barely afford to send a crew to Montreal, never mind Asia."

"I thought this was the big time."

"Don't start." He's always talking budget and what he could do if he had more money to spend on talent, travel, and technology.

Bishop made his decision: NTN viewers would not see NBC's adventures in Afghanistan. He lit another cigarette, and sighed. "I was looking forward to a steak and seeing Helen. What's this about going Caribbean?"

"I'll tell you later. Anyway, you'll like the JamJam Club."

"The what?" Bishop rarely strays from the mink-and-martini district along Bloor Street.

Jim Nesbitt, the lineup editor, walked up, looking harassed. "Hello, Shuter. What brings you here?" Nesbitt, a balding man in the cruel grasp of middle age, held out a hand.

"Picking up the boss."

"Well, you can't have him yet. We're a minute, ten too long, and he won't decide what to drop."

Nesbitt has spent his entire working life in television. Bishop recruited him from oblivion at the CBC, and he's been making NTN look good ever since. Nesbitt is a technical wizard who also has the rare ability to line up a newscast, to craft a solid half-hour with pace, style, and a logical flow. Night after night, once Bishop decides which stories to carry, and in what general order, Nesbitt packages them into a slick program which nails the viewers right to their easy chairs.

The ratings show it, too. NTN is Canada's newest nationwide network, and still a distant third behind CBC and CTV in the overall battle for viewers. But it is beginning to come on, especially in news and current affairs. Bishop runs the news department with verve, on a comparative shoestring. Smoke and mirrors, plus a lot of prayer, says Nesbitt, who is used to the lavish budgets of the publicly owned CBC. Whatever NTN's technique, it's working; Bishop has the big boys at CBC and CTV looking over their shoulders and well they might. Bishop is only thirty-one, but around the eyes he's old enough to be down in Florida on a pension.

"I thought Bishop was supposed to be a legendary decision-maker," I said to Nesbitt. "At least he tells me he's a legend."

Nesbitt chortled. "The last good decision he made was to hire me. And the only legendary thing about him is his expense accounts. He spends more on lunches than we spend on news."

"Then how come he always sticks me with the tab?"

"I was thinking of you earlier, Shuter," Bishop said, getting even. "We're leading tonight with your old firm."

"What now?" I looked at him bleakly. Just as I'm intrigued by the news business, Bishop is fascinated by police work. He is addicted to thrillers, and leads a rich fantasy life in the pages of whodunits and spy novels.

"Ransacking medical records again," he said. "Mental patients. It's quite incredible."

Nesbitt shook his head. "No wonder you got out, Shuter. The cops are worse than the crooks." He turned to Bishop. "What goes?"

"Afghanistan."

"Pity. The pictures are good."

In television news, every second is precious. Reporters will kill for extra air time. It makes their job easier; telling a complicated story in only a minute, and relating the script to film is a hard thing to do. Extra air time also feeds the reporters' egos, which tend to be large; air time to a television reporter is like smack to a junkie.

Nesbitt tore the Afghanistan page from his script, and did some arithmetic on a pocket calculator. "Maybe a few seconds light, but we should be okay."

"Looks okay, Jim," Bishop said. "Should be a good show."

Nesbitt gathered up his papers and hurried off to the control room.

"Good guy," I said.

"The best." Then Bishop laughed. "Of course, his news judgment could be better. He wanted to lead the show tonight with the cost-of-living figures. They're up again. They're *always* up again. It's his CBC training. I told him we'll lead with the cost of living the first time the figures are *down* significantly."

One of the staff began adjusting wall monitors, turning up the sound. The CBC was coming out of a current affairs show, CTV's movie was winding down, and NTN's sit-com was running out of gas, although the laugh track was doing its best to disguise the fact.

At eleven o'clock another battle in the unending ratings war was joined. Simultaneously, from the monitors:

"'The National,' with Knowlton Nash..."

"Lloyd Robertson, Harvey Kirck, with the 'CTV National News'..."

"Direct from network headquarters in Toronto, it's the 'NTN Nightly News', with Victor Davis and, tonight, reports from..."

Bishop believes in pizazz; also in stealing good ideas from CBS.

Within seconds, I was confused by the competing voices. Both CBC and CTV were leading with the cost-of-living figures as part of a general whine about the economy. NTN, meanwhile, was rolling footage of computer cards and Mounties; no one I recognized.

Bishop was taking notes, muttering to himself, finding fault with all three shows. They looked to be running smoothly enough to me. When NTN and CTV were into commercials and the CBC was in the middle of a long and confusing report about fish quotas, Bishop relaxed slightly and lit another cigarette.

"Those things are going to kill you," I told him, for perhaps the hundredth time.

"No," he said sourly, "Victor Davis is going to kill me."

The NTN anchorman had become tongue-tied at one point, stumbling over his introduction to a report while the newsroom staff groaned and began predicting a re-feed. Although the news is shown live in the east, it is taped for the western time zones. When there's a major screw-up, the program is done again at midnight, Toronto time, when it goes live to the Central time zone and is taped for eleven o'clock in both the Mountain and Pacific zones. If there's a screw-up in the re-feed, the whole thing's done again at one A.M. in Toronto. As Bishop says, it's a good thing NTN doesn't serve Hawaii; the news could take all night. Every time the news is re-fed, it costs more than $7,000 in studio, overtime, and transmission charges. Bishop does not like re-feeding; $7,000 will buy quite a few decent lunches.

"Richard," I said, keeping my voice low so the staff wouldn't overhear, "was there anything on the wire out of Jamaica today? Aside from the parasailer, I mean?"

"No," he said, "I don't think so. What sort of thing?"

"I'm not sure."

"A story?"

"Not yet. I'll tell you later."

"If there's a good story in Jamaica, I don't want to be reading it in my *Globe and Mail*." He went back to his doodle; NTN's two-minute commercial break was almost over. "I think Susan Quill's still here. Why don't you talk to her?"

"It would be a pleasure, but why?"

"She claims to be our Caribbean expert. God knows, she spends enough of my phone budget talking to that part of the world."

"Where is she?" I'd met Susan Quill once or twice before, but hadn't seen her in the newsroom tonight.

"Probably in her office, in a snit because I bit her standup. She was too long with a so-so piece about a Gay-Lib demo at City Hall."

Standups are the little sermonettes with which television reporters usually close their stories. They're known in the trade as payoffs, a chance for reporters to appear on camera. Frequently, they add little information to a report, and Nesbitt once told me that dropping them is usually the easiest way to save seconds.

"I didn't realize your reporters had their own offices."

"They don't, normally," Bishop chuckled, "but Susan got a big offer from the CBC. I couldn't match the bucks, but I did have some surplus office space. She likes to work on her own."

Susan Quill's office was little more than an ambitious cupboard. She was sitting at a cluttered desk, reading from a file of newspaper clippings. When she joined NTN from a small newsroom in western Ontario she was as green as Ireland, but Bishop worked hard with her and now she's a star.

Grey eyes sparkled behind St. Laurent glasses. Her dark-blonde hair was tied back with a ribbon that matched her eye colour, and she was wearing a white turtleneck and a grey-flannel skirt. Susan Quill is a good-looking young woman: big white teeth, long straight nose, trim bust, very shapely legs.

"Hello," I said. "Mike Shuter."

"Sure, I remember. The Mountie." Her voice had a husky quality that just avoided being overtly sexy; on television it sounded mature and confident.

"Not any more. Am I disturbing you?"

"It's okay. I'm just doing a little research."

"You're working late."

"It beats watching television."

I knew she was single, but surely she had a boyfriend. Maybe he worked nights, too. "Bishop suggested I drop by."

"A story?"

They're all so hungry for stories. "No, nothing like that. I'm going to Jamaica for a few days and I was wondering if anything new was going on down there. Bishop says you're the ranking authority."

"Jamaica. Lucky you. Did Richard say that?"

I nodded. "He called you his Caribbean expert."

"Then why doesn't the cheap bastard give me a raise? Or send me on a trip?"

"I didn't know young ladies swore."

"Then you don't know young ladies." She laughed; a nice laugh. "What can I do for you?"

"That's a leading question."

"I'm a leading lady."

"So everyone says. Suzie Q."

She made a face, but was still attractive. "Jamaica," she said, lighting a cigarette. "The country's broke, of course. But it has been for ages. The government has things pretty well under control, although violence is simmering all the time."

"What about the Cubans? Are they stirring things up again?"

"No. Not really. They haven't been all that active. A school or two, a couple of tacky housing projects. Castro's as broke as the Jamaicans. He's costing the Russians millions of rubles a day."

"And the Rastas? What about them?"

"They're not the terrorists most people believe. Actually, most of them are very gentle, though their beliefs might seem strange to you and me. I mean, after all, they think Haile Selassie is God and that his death is a fiction of the western press. You know: 'Jah lives.' And they call the Queen the 'Whore of Babylon.' But their religion isn't any more illogical than Christianity. Or Buddhism. Or any of them."

"Don't tell me the burnin' and lootin' Bob Marley sings about is a fiction of the western press, too?"

She shook her head. "Sure, there's some violent Rastafarians. You should see Trench Town. A terrible slum. You'd be violent too. The slogan's everywhere these days: 'The poor can't stand no more.'"

"Do you know a local place called the JamJam Club?"

"The JamJam? Sure. It's on College Street. A Rasta hangout. Lots of grass."

"Don't tell me you smoke dope," I said, smiling.

"Mr. Shuter," she said in a weary tone, "everybody smokes dope."

I sighed. "I guess that's the difference between twenty-five and thirty-seven."

"I'm twenty-six." Susan carried her age like a regimental banner; she was another foot-soldier in the war between the sexes. "A lot of old men in their thirties smoke dope, too."

I let that go. "Is the food at the JamJam edible?"

"It's not bad, if you like salt fish and ackee, which I do."

"What about curried goat?"

"Maybe not that."

We both laughed.

"Are there many Rastafarians in Toronto?"

"Quite a few," she said, frowning. "A thousand, maybe more. All together there are something like 150,000 West Indians here. No one knows for sure, because so many are in the country illegally. But most of the West Indians in Toronto are Jamaicans, and a significant percentage of the Jamaican population is Rasta."

"Do you happen to know a local Rasta named David Llewellyn? They call him Ras Lucky."

"No, I don't." Her face clouded over, and she gazed at me sceptically. "What's all this about? The JamJam? Ras Lucky? I thought you were going on holiday? Is there something going on? A story?"

"No."

"Well, you don't sound to me like a man who's going on vacation. You haven't asked about a single beach. Or bar."

"That's why I'm going to the JamJam," I said. "One of the guys was telling me about the place, thought I might like to get in the mood for my trip. He knows this Ras Lucky, and suggested I talk to him, get the names of a few hot spots in Ocho Rios."

"I prefer Port Antonio." She was looking off into the middle distance, probably recalling her last visit. "It's less touristy."

"I may go there, too."

"That's right. I remember now. You work for an airline."
She looked wistful. "I wish I could get some sun."

"Tell you what. When I get back why don't we go to the
JamJam some night? You can have some ackee and pretend
you're in Jamaica."

"Big deal," she said; but then she smiled. "Actually I'd like
that."


Bishop was chairing an informal meeting at the news desk.
Nesbitt looked upset. Most of the rest of the staff looked
weary. Davis looked faintly apologetic, his noble brow
furrowed.

"I wouldn't re-feed just for the stumble, Victor," Bishop
was saying as I walked up. "But we up-cut you on the cost-
of-living story, we rolled the wrong goddamn tape on Suzie
Q's piece, we went to black for four seconds coming out of
second commercials, and we had a graphic upside down. All
in all, a fuck-up. And that's not even mentioning the fact that
on two occasions we went to wide shots when we should
have been in tight."

It was the director's turn to be apologetic. "Most of that's
my fault." He was very young, very earnest.

"It happens," Bishop grunted. "Just get it right at twelve."

I waited for Bishop to gather up his clipboard, say good
night to the staff and collect his jacket and topcoat.

We stopped in the lobby to sign out. The commissionaire
was a model of good humour and efficiency. There was no
sign of the Sunshine Girl. "Good night, Mr. Bishop," he said
pleasantly. Bishop is a comer at the network; in television,
even the security guards keep up with office politics.

# CHAPTER THREE

## *Thursday – 12:15 A.M.*

A small neon sign announced the JamJam Club to what I'm sure was a largely indifferent world: JAMJAM – WEST INDIAN FOOD – FULLY LICENSED. The club was up a narrow flight of stairs, over an Italian tailor's shop and a Greek travel agency. Toronto is a city of 2,500,000 people who come from some place else, and College Street west of Spadina Avenue is ethnically mixed: Chinese, Portuguese, Greeks, Italians, East and West Indians all jumbled together, along with a few WASPs too old or too poor to move on.

During the drive across town, I'd briefed Bishop on Carol Malone's disappearance, without telling him anything of what Bladon had said. As I'd expected, Bishop wasn't particularly interested; since Carol had come to no apparent harm, she wasn't worth a mention on the national news, despite being the daughter of an MP.

We left the Bricklin on a side street near the club, and climbed the JamJam's stairs. The door was locked, which was odd for a restaurant. We could hear the syncopated beat of a reggae band, and I had to knock several times before anyone came to see who we were.

"Yes, mon?" The voice crackled through a small speaker above the door. A peep-hole opened, and we were inspected by a yellowish eye.

"Is the kitchen still serving?" I asked.

"You wan' to eat?" The eye blinked. Slowly.

"We're hungry."

"Okay. Welcome to de JamJam." The eye went away, and a circuit-breaker clicked the lock open.

I pushed on the door, and we stepped into the club's gloom. The yellow eye belonged to a huge West Indian who weighed at least 300 pounds. He was wearing a wool toque and a leisure suit made from what looked to be old flour sacks. It stretched taut across his vast belly. A gold tooth gleamed dully from the front of his mouth as he smiled a Caribbean welcome.

"You been here before, mon?"

"First time."

"You can hang de coats dere," our host said, indicating an unattended cubicle. "My name Matthew. De manager."

"Mike Shuter," I told him. "This is Richard Bishop."

Matthew nodded, happy about something. "You gen'men wid de police?"

"No, man." I shook my head.

"Doan care," Matthew said. "Jus' wondered, is all."

We abandoned our coats, and I glanced around, getting my bearings. There was a small bar along the left wall, being tended by a heavy black woman who wore a thick grey cardigan over her shoulders. Enormous breasts surged out of the top of her red evening gown, which looked to be about three sizes too small around the waist and hips. Five young blacks lolled along the bar, each nursing a bottle of Red Stripe, the best-selling beer in Jamaica. They all wore their hair long, in dreadlocks: Rastamen.

Farther into the room I could see a cluster of small tables, a tiny dance floor, a bandstand and a gaudy jukebox. The walls were decorated with signs advertising Red Stripe and Panther condoms. Somebody's idea of a joke; in Jamaica, Panther signs are everywhere. There were also a few Jamaican Tourist Board posters, their white beaches, green palm trees and impossibly blue seas incongruous on College

Street in November. Pots and pans clattered behind french doors which obviously led to the kitchen.

There were about thirty people in the club, all of them black except for us and a table of bored-looking girls in the far corner. One of the girls was up, feeding the jukebox, bending over to study the selections. She had a voluptuous rear end, encased in tight denim. A few of the patrons were eating, and a lot of them had been smoking: the sweet smell of marijuana hung over the club, as sharp and unmistakable as woodsmoke on a clear fall day in the countryside.

Matthew led us to a table in the middle of the room, produced two grease-spattered menus, and asked what we'd like to drink.

"Red Stripe," I said.

"Scotch," said Bishop, who refuses to compromise on some things. "Chivas, if you have it."

Matthew seemed only half-pleased with our order. "Got Johnny Walker, is all."

Matthew ambled to the bar. One of the young Rastas said something to him, and Matthew shook his head.

Bishop was studying the menu, not bothering to mask his distaste. "The things you get me into, Shuter."

"Have some salt fish and ackee. It's delicious. The Jamaican national dish. It's strange. They use Newfoundland cod in their national dish, and a local fruit that's poisonous if you eat it at the wrong time of the month."

Bishop shuddered. "You're kidding. Why don't they use their own fish? There must be fish in Jamaica."

"They prefer cod. It used to be their only source of salt."

He considered it. "I guess it's a fair trade. The Newfies' national dish seems to be rum."

Matthew arrived with our drinks. The jukebox was blaring out a tune from Peter Tosh's album "Legalize It," the ganja lovers' incessant advice to the government in Kingston. A couple of Jamaican guys were dancing with two of the girls.

Matthew bent over to recommend the curried goat. I

ordered salt fish and ackee for two, which brought another gleaming smile. Then I put a hand on his shoulder and brought his ear closer.

"Is Ras Lucky here tonight?"

Matthew looked at me doubtfully. "You know Lucky, mon?"

"No," I said. "But I'd like to talk to him."

Matthew stood there, wondering what to do. I took out my wallet and found a business card, one that says I'm a vice-president of Holidair. "If he's here, would you please give him my card and ask him to join us."

"I'll see, mon." Matthew moved slowly to the kitchen. A few moments later, he came out, walked across to a table near the jukebox and spoke to a man who was eating alone. Matthew gave him the card, and the other man studied it. He seemed puzzled, and kept glancing toward our table.

"Who's this Lucky?" Bishop asked.

"Bladon suggested him. I need a few names. Apparently, Lucky knows everyone in Jamaica."

Our man finished his meal, then pushed away from the table and stood. He was tall, perhaps six-three, and slim as a straw. His hair was very long, hanging in coils to his shoulders. There was an air of dignity about him as he came toward us. He looked to be about thirty years old but the gloom and his beard made it hard to be sure.

"Which de vice-president?"

He was holding my card gingerly between thumb and middle finger, as though afraid he might crease or smudge it.

I stood, aware that people, including the Rastas at the bar, were watching us. "Are you Ras Lucky?"

"What a vice-president want wid I?" His voice was soft, laced with suspicion.

"Inspector Stu Bladon suggested we have a talk," I said, watching his eyes go blank. "This is a friend of mine, Richard Bishop."

Bishop stood and held out his hand, which Lucky accepted without enthusiasm.

"How do you do?" Bishop said.

Lucky ignored him and turned toward me again.

"You wid de police, mon? I and I doan like de police 'round here." He raised his voice a bit and glanced around the club; I got the impression the line was for the benefit of the Rastas at the bar.

"No man, we're not cops." I motioned him to a chair and he sat down, his face utterly expressionless. "Have a beer."

He nodded, and I signalled to Matthew, who was standing at the corner of the bar, watching.

"What you do wid de airline?" Lucky asked. He continued to ignore Bishop, who'd begun to doodle on his paper place mat.

"I solve problems."

"What kind o' problem?"

"Any kind of problem that comes up."

He studied me for a moment. "You a hard one, mon?"

I didn't say anything. Matthew arrived with Lucky's beer, putting it down slowly, loath to move away.

"Thank you, Matthew," I said firmly. "That's all for now." When Matthew returned to the bar, I told Lucky I was off to Jamaica to find a missing girl and I hoped he'd give me an introduction to some people who might help. Bladon would appreciate his co-operation; so would Holidair.

"Could you get I a ticket home?" Lucky was cat-quick to see an opportunity.

"Any time you want to go," I said. "You'll fly as our guest."

He nodded, but his face was still expressionless. "Dis girl. What she got to do wid I?"

"Nothing. She's just a Canadian girl who went down on holiday, met a Jamaican guy, and forgot to come back."

"Happen all de time. Canadian girl like de Jamaican men."

He nodded at the girls near the jukebox and smiled. His teeth were very even, very white. He took a long swallow from his bottle, then set it down carefully on the formica tabletop. "Who she go off wid?"

"I don't know. Someone she met at Negril. She was staying at the Negril Beach Village, with another Canadian girl."

Lucky thought about it for a while. "A Rastaman?"

"We think so." Patsy Baird had told me on the phone that Carol's friend wore his hair long.

He thought some more. "Okay, mon. You get down to Negril you find de doctor. Dem call him Doctor Black. Him a silly Rasta, but you mention I. De doctor know everyt'ing dere is to know. Maybe you get him one ticket, too."

This was going to become expensive. "Maybe," I said. "Who else, in case Doctor Black isn't around?"

"At de Negril Beach Village see Ras Daniel. Him singer dere. Mention I. No problem."

Obviously, Lucky felt his name would work wonders in Jamaica; I hoped he was right.

"What about Kingston?" I asked. "Maybe the man comes from Kingston. Most Rastamen do."

"Simple t'ing," he said. "You go de Reggae World. It a record shop downtown. Ask for Winston Llewellyn, brother to I. Winston know everybody."

"Does he work at the Reggae World?"

"No, mon. Him just dere. You find him, no problem. When you go down?"

"Maybe tomorrow, maybe the next day."

Lucky looked at me shyly. "Maybe you takin' down a big Tide for I. Give it to Winston, for I and I's sister."

"A big what?"

"Tide, mon. Soap flake. Dey hard to get in Babylon."

"Oh, sure, I'll do that."

He smiled again. "Maybe I call you one time, 'bout de ticket. Winter soon come."

"My number's on the card."

He looked at the card again, put it carefully in his shirt pocket and stood. "Have a lively time. It warm in Babylon. Not like T'ron'o."


"Doctor Black!" Bishop snorted, when Lucky reached the bar. "Ras Daniel! Brother Winston! Shuter, you've got to be kidding. Or he is."

Matthew arrived with our food, two heaping plates of cod and ackee, plus rice and beans. He put a bottle of Pick-a-Peppa sauce on the table, and wished us good appetite. I ordered another round of drinks, and tucked in. Bishop approached his plate cautiously, taking tiny tastes of everything before swallowing. I think he was worried about being poisoned by out-of-season ackee.

"Try some of this," I said, handing him the Pick-a-Peppa sauce. "It's so much better than HP or A-1 you won't believe it."

Bishop took the bottle and studied it. "Look where it's made." He pointed at the label: Shooter's Hill, Jamaica, W.I. "They've got a town named after you down there."

"Different spelling."

"Naw," he said, pouring some sauce on his plate. "One of your dumb ancestors screwed up, that's all. Dropped the double O and replaced it with a U. A social climber, probably. Preferred Nancy Mitford to Ian Fleming."

While I ate, I kept an eye on Lucky. He was at the bar, apparently arguing with the Rastas, who'd been watching our table ever since he'd joined us. They did not look friendly. After a while Lucky shrugged, said good night to Matthew, and put on his coat, a heavy wool pea-jacket. He adjusted a large-brimmed, black felt hat to a jaunty angle and went through the door.

Reggae continued to blast out of the jukebox. Two of the

girls were dancing by themselves, moving to the rhythm of Toots and the Maytals while their girlfriends nodded and swayed, sitting down.

It was past one o'clock, the legal closing time, but no one made a move to cut off the bar. One of the Rastas ordered another beer, and proceeded to roll a monstrous spliff, which he lit casually and offered to his friends. They all had a hit or two, and I heard one of them say dreamily: "Dat good herb, mon."

Bishop had finished his food, which seemed to surprise him. We ordered another drink and talked about Carol Malone for a while; then about our jobs; finally, about women.

"What's the story on Susan Quill?"

"A good reporter," he said. "Fearless on the phones."

"Does she have a boyfriend? Or live with someone? Or what?"

"She lives with two Siamese cats. Baba and Wawa, after you know who."

"Cats?" I'm not very fond of cats.

He nodded. "A few of the staff have pitched her, of course, but she keeps her private life pretty much to herself."

Aside from the cats, Suzie Q sounded worth further investigation. "I think I'll take her out some night."

Bishop grimaced. "Come on, Shuter. Stick to the stews and the downtown dolls and do yourself a favour. A girl like Suzie Q will screw up your square cop's head even worse than it is now."

"Why do you say that?"

"Because I know these things. And I know those girls. You'll never understand women like Quill. They live in a different world. Your trouble is, you go around thinking you're Fletch, when in fact you're Lew Archer. Different generations."

While I'd been talking, the crowd had thinned. The Rastas had wandered off into the night, as had most of the other patrons. The girls, though, were hanging tough. Probably they had been to Jamaica, developed a taste for the local men, and gone on the prowl back home. Likely we'd flown them down and back.

Matthew brought me the bill and we got our coats. Bishop congratulated Matthew on the food and promised to come back. Matthew grinned, his gold tooth flashing as we bade him good night.


"Got a match, mon?" The voice drifted out of the shadows by my car. The street was dark and empty. The rain had stopped but the mercury had dropped. I peered into the murk, trying to see who was there.

"Sure," I heard Bishop say.

Then I saw them: the five young Rastas from the club.

I moved quickly around the car to the curb side. Beside me, Bishop was fumbling for his lighter, but I had already made up my mind.

"Watch yourself!"

"What?" Bishop sounded confused. He is simply not cut out for rough work.

I took the one with the knife first.

"Hi," I said pleasantly, stepping in close and kicking him in the groin.

He screamed, but I was already wheeling, moving in tighter on the one with the length of pipe. I kept spinning through a 360-degree turn and caught him in the face with an elbow smash. I felt teeth break, and heard a gurgling sound.

The remaining three rushed us. I couldn't see any other weapons. One of them grabbed Bishop and I heard him grunt in shock, then cry out.

I needed a quick decision over my pair. I butted the first one in the face and he fell back. I grabbed the second by his dreadlocks, pulled him toward me, and chopped him across the bridge of the nose with the heel of my hand. Not hard enough to kill, but he'd remember me for a while; a broken nose takes weeks to mend.

Bishop was wrestling awkwardly with his Rasta, whom I kicked in the seat of the pants. The kid was more startled than hurt. He turned in confusion, and Bishop smacked him on the back of the head with an overhand right. The kid stumbled forward. I wondered whether Bishop had broken his hand.

As fast as they'd struck, they fled, wounded, into the darkness.

A prowl car had turned the corner, catching the tail-end of what had been a twenty-second street brawl. Two cops got out cautiously.

"Hold it right there!" one of them said. He sounded nervous.

"Good to see you!" I gasped. I'm in shape, but this sort of thing always leaves me breathless for a few moments; it's the excitement, not the exertion.

"What's goin' on?" The other cop sounded older, more sure of himself.

"Muggers," I said. It would have to do.

"Let's see some ID."

Bishop was still trying to catch his breath. He had a small cut on his face and his topcoat was torn. I handed the cop my driver's licence and a business card. He studied them for a moment, then handed them back.

"What happened, Mr. Shuter?" He'd turned polite.

"I think they were looking for an easy payday."

"Niggers!" He spat into the gutter.

"They were black," I agreed.

"Could you describe them? Would you recognize them again?"

Bishop started to say something, but I cut him off. "Not a chance. It's dark, and so were they."

The older cop laughed and the younger one joined in, more confident now.

"Well," said the older one, "you seemed to handle it. Do you want to come down and sign a complaint?"

"It's late," I said. "We're tired. And the kids have learned a lesson. We may as well let it go."

The cops seemed pleased; it would save paperwork. They watched while I unlocked the car and opened the doors. "A Bricklin," said the younger cop. "You don't see many of those around."

"No," I said curtly, hoping to avoid a replay of my conversation outside the Gardens.

"Take care," said the older man, as I started the engine. The cops pulled in behind and followed for four blocks before peeling off, probably in response to a radio call. Well, that's what the Toronto police promise to do: "To serve and protect." It says so on their cruiser doors.

When Bishop had recovered most of his breath and all of his dignity, he began to growl. "Goddamnit, Shuter! Why didn't we go file a complaint?"

"And be up half the night? Waste of time. The cops never catch kids like that."

"Matthew would know them."

Of course, he was right. But I didn't want the local cops nosing around the JamJam. Bladon would have a fit. "Maybe."

"One of them had a knife." He sounded shocked by the very idea.

"Yeah."

"So what did they want? I can't believe it was money."

I stopped for the traffic light at Yonge Street. A few lonely souls stood huddled outside Fran's all-night restaurant, with nowhere to go at two in the morning. Occasionally, a car rolled by, cruising; a lot of guys have come out of a lot of closets in Toronto lately, but they still have trouble finding warm places to spend the night.

"Well, Shuter?"

"I don't know. But it must have had something to do with Ras Lucky."

"I don't understand."

"Neither do I." I swung north on Yonge, toward home. I was weary and my elbow was throbbing.

Bishop was sucking a knuckle and staring out the side window. "I haven't been in a fight since school."

"It shows."

"You really are a tough bastard, aren't you?" He sounded almost sad about it. "You handled those guys the way Spenser would have."

"Who?"

"Spenser. A private eye from Boston. Really tough."

"I struck first. If I hadn't, it might have gone the other way."

"No," he said slowly. "It wouldn't have."

"I've had a lot of practice." It came out almost as an apology.

He fell silent for a while, then began chuckling. "I was going to give the guy a light."

"You gave him a sore head instead."

"Yeah." He went back to sucking his knuckle.

We drove the rest of the way in silence. I swung into my driveway and switched off the engine. Bishop said he'd see me tomorrow, and he went into his house while I went into mine. Home: it's where you go when no place else is open.

# CHAPTER FOUR

# *Thursday—2:35 A.M.*

Rosedale is a delightful place, even in the middle of the night. A mature residential district in the heart of Toronto, it is criss-crossed by ravines and shaded by huge plane trees, bare now in November. It is an area of gracious mansions, smart new townhouses and large front lawns, perhaps the ultimate urban luxury. Rosedale's streets meander charmingly, following no logical pattern; occasionally, I still become lost only a few hundred yards from my house. In recent years, developers have been buying up the old mansions, either to do lavish conversions to luxury flats or to pull them down and put up half a dozen terrace houses like mine.

I bought the house after Janet died. It was an emotional tribute to her memory, the fulfilment of a promise. She had wanted a new house in the midtown area, and we were looking when she fell ill. We lived in a cheery two-bedroom flat, which had all the amenities, but she'd wanted a garden and extra space. Even though housing in Toronto is expensive, money wasn't a problem. My police pay was never going to let us live like the Rockefellers or the Eatons, but Janet made a good salary as a Crown attorney and there was always her father, rich, in the background.

When Janet was dying, and knew it, she told me about the insurance. I sat in the hospital, holding her hand, trying not to cry, while she talked softly about our house, our garden, and how, because of something she'd done before we'd met, I would be able to afford it. "Promise me," she'd said, "promise me you'll get the house."

Janet had carried a quarter-million-dollar term policy on her life, in addition to her standard employee coverage. She'd bought the term policy because it was relatively cheap, because a college chum had gone into the insurance business, and because she had wanted to protect her father's substantial investment in her education. Then we met, fell in love, and were married. Without telling me, Janet changed beneficiaries and kept up the premiums. When her estate was settled, it amounted to a little more than $350,000. It was mine, and about one-millionth of what I'd pay to hear her laugh one more time.

I closed the deal for the house on what would have been her thirtieth birthday, then went down to McGregor's penthouse and cried like a three-year-old. He sat there, concerned and embarrassed; the Scots dislike overt displays of emotion. But he sensed I was close to cracking up. The SS was into areas I hadn't known existed when I first joined the force, and I was up to my neck in dirty tricks. It wasn't what I'd become a Mountie to do, but it was what Mounties were doing. Unhappiness at work and a broken heart are a strong parlay, and a few weeks later McGregor persuaded me to resign and join him at Holidair. I haven't regretted the decision. Not really. But it's strange how things work out. I am pleased enough with the house; but it really belongs to Maria, the cleaning lady who comes in three days a week, and to the happy gang of Japanese gardeners, who descend on the property for an hour every once in a while to work on its tiny lawns and flower beds. I have tremendous affection for McGregor, as well as loyalty to Holidair; but work, to me, will always mean the cops. Very strange, how things work out.

If I bought my house for emotional reasons, Bishop bought

his for financial ones. It is all he can do to carry it, but his house – a twin of mine – is a sensible and growing investment. It is the cornerstone of his masterplan to amass a cache against the day when the news business lets him down. He says it eventually lets everyone down, and he has vowed not to become another timid employee, protecting a pension and paycheque. We all see hell in our own ways, and that's his vision of it: a salary trap.

I was bone-tired, but I didn't go straight to bed. I poured myself a giant slug of Remy and put a Neil Young tape on the sound system. I sat in the dark watching the fish, restless in the night as they patrolled their big tank, secure from predators. Young was keening about a town in North Ontario. I'd come from one of those. I thought about Sudbury, and my father, who'd put a lifetime into the mines. And I thought about digging for Carol in the white sand of Negril. And about escaping the mines via the Mounties. And about the years of digging through the dirt of other people's lives. Somehow, you never escape the mines. "Helpless, helpless, helpless," Young sang. My thoughts were jumbled, but I knew how he felt.

I finished my cognac, shut off the tape machine, said good night to the fish, and climbed the stairs. My elbow still throbbed, but I fell asleep almost immediately.

The phone woke me. It had been ringing a long while.
"Good morning." McGregor.
"Time is it?"
"Eight. Did you have a late night?"
"Yes." He must be in Ottawa. "Where are you?"
"Malton. I took the first flight out. We should talk."
"Where?"
"My place. Sam will give us breakfast."

"Give me an hour."

With a groan, I rolled out of bed. My elbow was still sore; a bruise was developing. I went to the window, and looked out over the garden, toward the ravine. It was raining again. Or maybe it was the same rain. I needed more sleep, but there was no time.

I forced myself to do my exercises: situps, pushups, kneebends, the works. I broke a sweat quickly, the Red Stripe and probably the ackee bubbling out of my pores. Puffing, I stepped into the shower and let the hot water run off me like the cares of the rich.

Twenty minutes later, dressed in a sports jacket and a pair of slacks, I was making coffee and feeding the fish. I am growing fond of them, although I can't say why; they're not exactly cuddly pets. The fish were Helen's idea. She said the house needed some life: plant and animal, as well as human. I'm out of town too often to be fair to a dog, and even cats need care. But the fish have proved easy company. Maria always feeds them too, which means they're living about as well as fish can live.

I drank a glass of orange juice and sat with my coffee at the kitchen table, reading the *Globe*. After glancing at the sports and the stock market listings, I turned to the front section, leafing through it quickly. A small heading on the foreign page caught my eye:

CALGARY PAIR DIE

IN JAMAICA CRASH

and I read the brief item beneath it. A single-engine plane had exploded moments after taking off from Boscobel Airport, near Ocho Rios, killing the pilot and two middle-aged tourists from Alberta. There were few other details: Jamaican authorities were still investigating, preliminary guesswork blamed a fuel leak, the pilot was a veteran commercial operator who took visitors on sightseeing flips.

First the German parasailer, now the Calgarians: Jamaica was being hard on its tourists this week. Dark thoughts

56

intruded. Bad news was supposed to arrive in groups of three. I hoped Carol wouldn't close in the triangle.

After a second cup of coffee, I rinsed my cup and glass and put on my raincoat. There was no sign of life at Bishop's but I was sure he was up. He's always on the phone to his newsroom by nine, and by then he's got a firm grasp on the day and on how his staff should spend it.

The morning traffic was bad, of course. I was tucked in behind a lady in a Datsun and we were barely moving. She was bent over her steering wheel, staring past her wipers at the jam of southbound cars and trucks. It only seems to take a few drops of rain to paralyze the city during rush hour. For some reason, Toronto drivers can't cope with wet streets.

The Datsun lady kept riding her brake. On dry pavement she probably drove like Gilles Villeneuve. If she'd taken the subway to work this morning, she'd be at her office by now: having a cup of coffee, flirting with the boss, gossiping, maybe even working. Instead, she was worried about the time, and riding her brake.

It's crazy. The taxpayers spend hundreds of millions of dollars developing one of the world's best rapid-transit systems, then insist on driving their cars downtown every day. And what happens downtown? Parking tickets happen. And dents. Lots of dents. The extortionists who run Toronto's parking lots seem to think life is one big demolition derby. Theirs is the only business I know in which the operator accepts something of value for safe-keeping, specifically denies any responsibility for keeping it safe, abuses it, and still demands an outrageous fee. I looked closely at the Datsun, and sure enough, its right rear fender was bashed in. I could see the dent clearly, red with embarrassment in the constant glare of the brake light.


McGregor's penthouse in Harbour Square overlooks Lake Ontario and Toronto Islands to the south, the city skyline to the north. Sam Chung met me at the door, all smiles. He was holding a book, but then he's always holding a book – when he's not holding a skillet in his kitchen or a croquet mallet on the court at Massey College.

"Good morning, Michael! It looks absolutely wretched outside."

"Good morning, Sam," I said, taking off my coat. "It *is* wretched. The rain keeps starting and stopping. I drove here in heavy traffic and a rage."

"An interesting syllepsis," he said, taking my coat.

"A what?"

"Syllepsis. A figure of speech, grammatically correct. A single word brings together two constructions, each of which has a different meaning in connection with the word. It's a relative of the zeugma, but of course a zeugma involves error."

"Oh," I said. Sam is always doing that to me.

He speaks the Queen's English the way Her Majesty probably wishes she did – magnificently, with a rich but not fruity Home Counties accent. Of course, he had a superb tutor: Laurence Olivier. Sam Chung learned his English from the great actor's recordings of Shakespeare's plays, having spent thousands of hours listening and practising alone, reading and listening some more – in a lumber camp. Today Sam is probably without equal in Canada as an authority on English grammar and literature. His opinions are sought by a few erudite members of the academic world, whose company he enjoys. Sam is modest. He steadfastly refuses to publish his monographs on Shakespeare, the novels of Dickens and Trollope (he can't abide Trollope), the poetry of Keats and Shelley (he regards Byron as little more than a nineteenth-century hack), or the "entertainments" of Graham Greene. But learned men who have read Sam's work believe it ranks with the finest English literary criticism. Sam Chung is McGregor's cook.

They first met in the north when McGregor was flying freight contracts and Sam was cooking in the camps. After

McGregor's wife died in the late 1950s, he asked Sam to move into his house, I think as much for company as for Sam's culinary skills. Janet was away at school and McGregor was lonely.

So was Sam; he's been lonely most of his life. Sam Chung is a sojourner, one of the last Chinese to enter Canada before Parliament passed the infamous Oriental Exclusion Act in 1923, a craven attempt to appease a jittery white labour force in British Columbia. During the following twenty-five years, a pathetic total of fifteen Chinese and Japanese were admitted to Canada, joining the 100,000 Orientals already in the country legally when the act was passed.

McGregor still talks angrily about the way Sam, and thousands of other Chinese men, paid the $500 federal head tax to get in, and then found themselves trapped – cut off by an ocean and a cruel piece of legislation from their families and friends. There were almost no young Chinese women in Canada, so Sam, like most of the bachelor sojourners, never married. But he survived and, remarkably enough, loves Canada today with a passion few native sons can match.

Sam once told me he forgave and understood the politicians who had been responsible for his lonely sojourn. They were only following the lead of the United States, which had passed its first exclusion act in the mid-1880s and which even the Orientals agreed was a bastion of freedom and decency. Nations set immigration policies according to their self-interest, but he was mildly perplexed by the restrictions imposed by his beloved Britain and by the vast and nearly empty Australia. But one had to be fair. "I doubt Peking would approve your application to settle in China, Michael," he'd said, smiling. "We Chinese are notorious racists."

Although he is at least ten years older than McGregor's sixty-two, Sam looks a decade younger than the Scotsman. Their relationship is one of companions, rather than master and servant. It is one of the pleasures of my life to watch them play *mah-jongg*; they play for blood, and with consummate skill. Of course, the Scots and Chinese have much in common: both societies are organized into clans (*tongs*), are hard-working, shrewd, and thrifty. So it's not surprising that McGregor can play killer *mah-jongg*; the wonder is that Sam Chung never took up the bagpipes.

"Morning." McGregor came striding into the living room, all business, and looking fresher than I felt. He is wiry and fit; he keeps his iron-grey hair short, and wears blue suits and white shirts like a uniform.

"Good flight?"

"Bumpy. We bucked a weather system all the way."

We moved to the dining room, where Sam had laid two places. McGregor's penthouse is magnificent: three bedrooms, three baths, study, living room, dining room, kitchen, and terrace. It is carpeted throughout with a deep blue pile, exactly the colour of a high September sky.

I paused to inspect a new painting, a tugboat battling heavy seas under thunderclouds.

"Do you like it?" McGregor asked. "It caught my eye. The artist's a young man from Halifax, Ross McCulloch. I think he may have talent."

McGregor has a substantial collection of Canadian paintings: the Bobaks, Harold Town, Graham Coughtry, Bob Markel, the Group of Seven, Chris and Mary Pratt, and others, including many younger artists whose names have yet to become familiar. Many of his paintings, especially those by better-known artists, were acquired years ago for a song. But he doesn't collect art to make money. In fact, McGregor has an odd rule: if someone he likes admires a painting, he will sometimes sell it for the amount he paid originally, often a tiny fraction of its current value. There's one condition: the painting must not be resold. He once sold a Tom Thomson to a Montreal travel agent who'd been admiring it. The selling price was $125. Months later, McGregor was astounded to see the painting in a Toronto gallery window. He marched in off the street, confirmed its authenticity, wrote a cheque for $17,000, and took the Thomson home. He never spoke to the travel agent again.

"Well," he said, sitting at the table, "we seem to have a problem."

I nodded. "I know you and Malone are friends, but why the red alert? I can't recall when I've heard you so upset."

McGregor looked almost embarrassed. "I know. But Alan's very worried. He once did me an enormous favour, and I'll help him any way I can."

"What did he do? Save your life in the war?"

"No. Not that enormous. But when I needed him, he was there. That was years ago, when I was changing over to jets. He showed me how to find the money."

"How?"

"He took Holidair public, very successfully." McGregor paused, and his voice grew softer. "I didn't know Malone's family well, but he often talked about Carol. Mind you, she was just a child then, but she was an only child—like Janet."

I didn't say anything.

"If Holidair can help him avoid losing even a moment's sleep over his daughter, we will," he went on. "And anyway, you've been slacking recently. I thought a trip would do you good." Not much gets past McGregor.

"What am I supposed to do when I find her?" I doubted he'd authorize a spanking.

"Tell her that her parents are worried. That they don't give a damn whether her boyfriend is black, blue, pink, or purple. That they love her and expect her to be an adult, which means being responsible and not leaving her family wondering whether she's all right."

"Okay." They were sensible instructions; over the years, I'd had more than enough of the other kind.

McGregor sat quietly for a few moments. Then he sighed. "There's a less altruistic reason for us to help Alan Malone. A business reason. He is one of the few men in Ottawa who understands what we're talking about in this de-regulation debate and he's a member of the Commons transport committee. We can't have too many friends there. Of course, he's highly intelligent. Most of them up there are nitwits."

It's his pet theme: the ineptitude of politicians, the thrust of government into almost every area of life, the hobbling of the private sector by rapacious bureaucrats and their vacuous political masters. McGregor is almost quaint in his rugged individualism and, with Max Ward, our chief competitor in the charter market, has waged a fierce battle against the Canadian Transport Commission and its welter of rules and regulations.

"It's curious," I said, "that I'm off to Jamaica now. Apparently there's a major flap on down there."

He looked at me sharply. "What flap?"

I briefed him on what little Bladon had told me, including Malone's dealings with External Affairs and the Prime Minister's Office. McGregor sat motionless, but there was concern on his face.

"That explains something, at least partly. The Jamaican High Commissioner and I had dinner last night. A private affair, which he initiated. He was quite cryptic, but he seemed most anxious for me to give assurances that we are firmly committed to our Jamaican program this winter. He asked me, point-blank, not to cancel flights."

"Cancel flights? We couldn't afford it. We're loaded with Jamaica."

"I know. We've already sold more than 20,000 seats."

Sam arrived with ripe melon and coffee.

"What would you like for breakfast, Michael? Perhaps a mushroom omelet? I have some excellent sausage, too."

"Sounds fine, Sam."

McGregor wanted only hot rolls and preserves, and Sam bustled off, muttering under his breath. He worries constantly about McGregor's diet.

"What else did the High Commissioner say?"

"He said he hoped Holidair would not be intimidated by the scare stories being whispered by his government's political opponents."

"Had we heard any scare stories?"

"Nothing at all. Until now. But Bladon's warning is disturbing. Very disturbing."

I frowned. "It's been a bad few days for tourists down there."

"In what way?"

I told him about the accidents.

"It's so fragile," he said.

"What is?"

"Public confidence. It only takes an incident or two to stampede people. Or one major accident. Look at the DC-10. A perfectly good aircraft, although I thank my stars I didn't buy any. After Chicago, I doubt the DC-10 will ever fully recover. You know, it's ironic: Detroit can kill 100,000 people a year and no one thinks twice about it, but let aviation lose a few hundred and it's page one for days."

"It's the drama factor," I said. "There's no drama in car accidents."

McGregor looked at me bleakly. "It's the same thing with destinations. If people suddenly get the idea that it's not safe somewhere, Jamaica for example, it's almost impossible to get them to go. That's what's so troubling about Bladon's crisis. If Jamaica starts showing up on the front pages again, tourism will stop dead. And if that happens, who knows? Jamaica has to have tourism to survive."

"It may have something to do with the Rastas," I said, pouring myself some coffee.

"Why?"

I told him about the JamJam and the street fight. McGregor listened grimly, alarm and outrage etched on his face.

"Why would five young toughs attack you and Mr. Bishop?"

"It doesn't make any sense. Maybe they thought we were in the dope trade or something. Poaching on their territory."

"Rastafarians," McGregor mused. "That worries me. Most of them are gentle enough, but some of them, quite frankly, are terrorists. If the Rastafarians are threatening to make trouble again, no wonder the government's worried."

Sam returned with our breakfast, and stood beaming while I tasted the sausage and omelet and pronounced them first rate.

"You always have a good appetite."

"When you're cooking, Sam."

"I detect flattery, but as an old man I accept the compliment. Who knows whether there will be another?"

McGregor buttered a hot roll, and gazed at a point somewhere over my left shoulder. "Do you remember the Holy Thursday Massacre? Back in sixty-three? A bad time. Several police were killed and a few Rastas. Just outside MoBay. That was the start of it. And it didn't take long to put the wind up everyone. Some of my friends had houses on the North Shore. After the Holy Thursday Massacre they began selling out."

"That was a long time ago."

"Yes, but the problem has existed ever since. The government still has the gun laws. The legislation has been modified but Gun Court remains – on the South Camp Road in Kingston. A forbidding place. Any Jamaican caught, even with a few bullets, can be locked up for life." He paused. "Anyway, the Rasta movement's been growing, and so have the government's economic problems. The Rasta cult really took off when Selassie visited in sixty-six. They thought he was God. Poor little devil, he seemed quite shaken by it all. Tens of thousands of Jamaicans, mobbing the airport at Kingston, bowing down to him in prayer. As I recall it, the Rastas were a bit disappointed in their God; he was too short."

We were silent for a few moments. Then McGregor cleared his throat. "I want you to get cracking on this. What are your plans?"

"Right now, I'm off to see the girl Carol travelled with. Then I guess I'll get to the office and organize a flight."

"I'll put someone on it. I'm not sure when our next flight goes to MoBay. Our programs have become so complicated I can't remember them the way I used to."

"I can always fly scheduled."

"Yes, but Holidair is better."

McGregor is a company man, too. Of course, it's his company.

Patsy Baird, a dumpy-looking girl in her mid-twenties, was a nurse at Wellesley Hospital. She lived in a small one-bedroom apartment in the Village Green, a mid-town cluster of high-rise buildings with a high percentage of young tenants. A cautious girl, Patsy asked me to slide my ID under her apartment door. Finally, I heard chains rattling.

"Hello, Mr. Shuter. Sorry about all the precautions, but there's a lot of weirdos around."

"You can't be too careful," I agreed, although I doubted anyone would molest Patsy. She was overweight and wore her mousy hair cropped short.

"Sorry I couldn't see you yesterday," she said, "but I'm on nights this week, and had to get ready for work."

"I gather your holiday wasn't much fun."

"It was okay. But I was worried about Carol."

"Yes," I said, looking around. Her apartment was sparsely furnished, but immaculate. There was an uncomfortable-looking sofa along the side wall, and I headed for it. A few plants, the mandatory stereo system, two wicker chairs and a bricks-and-boards bookcase filled with paperbacks completed the living room. There was no carpet.

"Would you like a coffee? I've just made some fresh."

The coffee was strong but good, and I told her so, which brought a smile. At least her teeth were beautiful.

"You say you were worried about Carol?"

"Yes. She likes to have a lot of fun, you know. And she's sometimes a bit thoughtless of others. But she's not usually this irresponsible."

"Have you known her a long time?"

"We went through high school together."

"I thought she studied in France?"

"That was later, when she wanted to be an artist. I went to nursing school and she went to Paris." Patsy sounded mildly hurt by the injustice of it all. "Anyway, we've stayed friends. I work odd hours, you know, and Carol works pretty much when she pleases. I wanted a holiday, but I didn't want to go by myself. So I asked her, and we booked with Holidair."

"And stayed at Negril Beach Village?"

"Yes. It's really nice. The hamburgers are good."

"What happened?"

"Well, Carol met him." Patsy bit her lip. "At first, it was kind of fun. He's a terrific dancer. But Carol started to get involved."

"Was she sleeping with him?"

She nodded again, savaging the lip this time.

"I suppose he had some good herb?"

She seemed startled. "Yes. Lots of it. Carol likes to smoke. I guess I do too."

"Everybody seems to," I said, thinking of Susan Quill.

"Anyway, Carol said she was going exploring, packed a few things in her flight bag, and took off with him."

"And that was the last you heard?"

"That's right. Really, Mr. Shuter, I'm worried. This just isn't like Carol. She's a bit scatterbrained, but she's not completely silly."

"The guy," I said. "Can you describe him, give me his name?"

"He had an odd name," she said, getting up from her chair. "Cudjoe. He was called Cudjoe."

Patsy was rummaging in her bag. "My pictures came back yesterday. I've got quite a few of Cudjoe."

She handed me a thick envelope of colour prints, and I started shuffling through them.

"That's Carol," she said, pointing.

I was astonished. Carol Malone was a raving beauty, a tawny blonde with green eyes – centrefold stuff in a bikini: large breasts, wasp waist, flared hips, long dancer's legs.

"And that's Cudjoe," Patsy said, pointing to a huge black man with wild dreadlocks. He was standing with a possessive arm around Carol. They were on a beach.

"How tall is Carol?"

"She's tall. About five-seven or so. Quite a bit taller than me."

If Carol was five-seven, Cudjoe was at least six-foot-six. He had broad shoulders and a washboard belly. He was wearing a pair of khaki cut-offs. He looked like a powerful, powerful man. Certainly, he was no beach boy, hanging around and hoping to score with a tourist.

"Could I keep some of these for a few days?"

"Yes, of course. Are you going to find her?"

"Yes. With these pictures, it's no problem. You'll be talking to her in a day or two."

As if on cue, a phone began ringing. Patsy went into the bedroom while I sat staring at the picture. If Patsy was right, Carol would not willingly have stayed out of touch this long.

"It's for you," said Patsy, sounding surprised. She stood aside to let me enter her inner sanctum. Perhaps optimistically, she had a queen-size bed, neatly made. With its blue spread it looked like a lonely stretch of sea.

"Shuter," I said into the phone.

"There you are, you sonuvabitch!" Bladon.

"What?"

"I'm going to break your back!" Seething.

"What's the matter?"

"Meet me in the coffee shop across from my office. You've got five minutes."

"I'm busy. What's the problem?"

"Not on the phone."

"Then no coffee shop."

"Ras Lucky," he said tightly, "ran out of luck. They found him four hours ago. Hacked to pieces. The local cops say it looks like a ritual killing."

# CHAPTER FIVE

## *Thursday—11:20 A.M.*

The coffee shop was in a hotel noted mainly for the strippers and hookers who work in its dingy basement cocktail lounge, only a few steps from the snazzy new headquarters of RCMP "O" Division. The everyday denizens of the area are winos, pimps, pushers, thieves, and crazies. The decision to locate "O" Division HQ on Jarvis Street was supposed to help revitalize a blighted area; instead, it helped demoralize a police force. The local cops are forever laughing about the formal complaints they receive from the Horsemen who can't seem to cope with the drunks in their parking lot or the smashed wine bottles on their front steps. But winos and litterbugs are outside federal jurisdiction.

"You're in trouble," Bladon said, as I joined him at a table. His mouth was set in a thin line and a little knot of muscle bulged along his jaw. "Everybody's flapping across the street."

"What happened?"

Bladon leaned close, almost whispering.

"The locals found David Llewellyn's body in an alley, just after dawn. He'd been dead only an hour or so. The medics say he was tortured, then snuffed. It's not pretty, Shuter. At least three different knives were used, maybe more. Machetes, they think."

I felt Sam's breakfast churning. A waitress shuffled up, chewing gum. I shook my head and she went away, resuming a desultory conversation with a tart who was waiting at the counter, hoping to turn a morning trick. Life goes on.

"Why, for God's sake?"

Worry pushed some of the anger from Bladon's face. "Lucky belonged to narcotics. Bill McNicholl's raising absolute hell."

McNicholl was in charge of the drug squad, a very tough cop.

"I warned you to be careful," Bladon went on. "And what did you do? You came on heavy at the JamJam, and got McNicholl's best snitch dead."

I shook my head. "Is that what Lucky was? A nark?"

"An unwilling one, but effective as hell. McNicholl had him over a barrel, so naturally he saw the light. Remember the yacht-load they busted down in Nova Scotia? That was Lucky. And all the hash pressed into record albums they grabbed in Montreal? Lucky again. The guy was magic."

Like all police forces, the RCMP relies heavily on informers. A good snitch is ultra-valuable, prized by the cop who runs him; he can be a passport to promotion. If Lucky was one of Bill McNicholl's star snitches, somebody was going to catch hell.

"Stu, I did exactly what you told me. And Lucky was helpful. But your name did it. If he was McNicholl's, how come he knew you?"

"Because I used him once or twice on political stuff. There's a lot of heat on this Jamaica thing, Shuter, and last night it made sense to put you onto him."

"I know who killed him."

Bladon stared at me. "Who?"

"Five little bastards in dreadlocks." I gave him the full report, ending with the arrival of the local cops outside the JamJam.

70

"Goddamnit, Shuter! Now there's no way I can keep you out."

"Stu," I said impatiently, "I haven't got time to get tied up in a local murder investigation. I've got to get down to Jamaica."

He shook his head. "You'll be lucky to stay out of jail. Here's how McNicholl's going to see this. The guys who attacked you are in the trade and we're starting to hurt them a bit, make the odd big bust. They know we must have someone on the inside. So they suspect Lucky. They're watching him. Then you show up, with cop stamped all over you. They brace Lucky, and he tells them you work for an airline. They're sceptical, but it just could be. So they decide to ask you a few questions."

"Damnit, Bladon, one of them had a knife and another one was swinging a piece of lead pipe."

He nodded. "Maybe that was just for visual effect. But you go straight into your Bruce Lee number, and they know. Shuter, they just *know*. No desk-jockey from the executive suite of a goddamn airline is into the kind of tricks you probably showed them. So what do they do? They go away, they smoke some dope and they think cop. Then what? They go find Ras Lucky, have a little chat with him. Somewhere along the way, he breaks. Probably about the time they cut off his third finger. And he says, 'Okay, okay, I been snitchin',' and they say, 'So long, Lucky, see you in Babylon.'"

"Have you told McNicholl anything?"

Bladon shook his head. "The thing's still breaking. I just picked it up at the office, and started looking for you." He paused. "Nobody across the street wants the force involved. McNicholl wants to leave it to the locals and that's fine with me. He's already told them we hadn't been using Lucky lately. But if I tell McNicholl I sent you out to see Lucky last night, he's got to tell the locals."

"Can't you pull rank?"

"Yeah," he said glumly, "I can pull rank. But I can only do it so often. You know how it is. Bad for morale, we're all Mounties together, all that crap."

"How about this?" I said. "Go see McNicholl. Tell him about Carol Malone. And me. And Lucky. And the JamJam. But use the old national security gaff. You've still got the Jamaica operation running."

Bladon shook his head. "No go. McNicholl already knows about the Jamaica situation. I briefed him myself."

So there was a drugs tie-in! There had to be. Otherwise, SS would never have briefed narcotics.

"Look, Stu, if you're right, Lucky's days were numbered anyway, and McNicholl would know it. Now that doesn't make me happy about it. I'm just as angry as you are. I don't like people who help me getting hurt. But the fact remains: I've got to find the girl. You said yourself it might help."

"What do you think? Can you track her down?"

"I'm a cinch." I told him about my talk with Patsy, and showed him the snapshots.

He studied them for a few moments. "Great-looking girl. The guy looks like a handful, though."

"Hell, I've even got his name. Cudjoe. It shouldn't take me a day."

Bladon looked at me sharply. "What did you say his name was?"

"Cudjoe. Why? Do you know him?"

He shook his head and gazed out at the traffic, apparently wondering what to do. "All right," he said tightly. "We'll play it your way. But be quick, and don't screw up. I've got a lot of balls up in the air right now and two of them may be mine."


I walked to my car with a small fire burning in my belly, stoked with anger over Lucky's brutal death and worry over

Carol's silly life. A few stubborn leaves were blowing in the gutter. Like them, I was being buffeted by forces outside my control; I only hoped I wasn't at the end of *my* life cycle. As Lucky had said with eerie accuracy: "Winter soon come." Soon enough, for all of us.

I knew one thing: the fact McNicholl had been briefed meant ganja was involved. I couldn't imagine why a drug problem would be important enough for the Jamaican Prime Minister to get in touch with his counterpart in Ottawa, but I was going to find out.

Jamaica, of course, is overrun with marijuana. Almost everyone on the island uses it, or has. But that's becoming true of Canada too. I'd always managed to avoid the narcotics beat, but I knew enough about it. The total value of the illicit drug trade in Canada has climbed to more than three billion dollars a year, most of it marijuana and hashish. The stuff cascades into the country despite the best efforts of cops like McNicholl. That's free enterprise for you; if the demand is sufficient and the profit potential great enough, the entrepreneurs will find a way. What happened in the United States with booze during Prohibition is happening all over the world with dope today.

Until recently, Jamaican ganja was regarded as low-grade smoke by the heads of North America, who thought of Colombian as their Directors' Stock and Mexican as their Chivas Regal. But the Mexicans have been cracking down on the trade and most of the Colombian shippers are so rich now that they've retired in luxury, believing the reward/risk ratio is no longer acceptable.

Ganja has been wafting into the vacuum, and building a reputation—chiefly because of improved cultivation. The Jamaican authorities have been trying to keep the pressure on, but their small police force is unequal to the task.

Lucky must have been a mule or a small importer when McNicholl turned him. As a snitch, he was risking his life. No matter how mellow marijuana makes its users, the men who run the industry are as murderous as the old-time bootleggers·


Holidair's offices take the twenty-seventh and twenty-eighth floors in a tower at Bloor and Yonge Streets, and we're going to need more space soon. As one of four vice-presidents – the others worry about sales, finance, and operations – I'm entitled to a fancy office and a bright secretary. I could manage without the big office, but I'd be adrift without Mrs. Innes.

"You've had a lot of calls," she said, as I stopped at her desk. "Inspector Bladon phoned several times..."

"I've just left him."

"...and Mr. Bishop called twice."

"I'll call him."

She handed me a thick file. "I've prepared a dossier on Jamaica."

"When did you put all this together?"

"I came in early."

"You're a beautiful woman, Mrs. Innes."

"I also found this." Mrs. Innes has little use for blarney. "*Toronto Life* did an article on Carol Malone as part of their series on successful young women in the city."

I glanced at the piece, a mini-profile accompanied by a colour picture of Carol at a drafting board. According to the magazine she was a rising star in commercial art circles. She lived alone, spent a lot of time at 21 McGill, which is the best women's club in the country, and earned a substantial living. She also skied.

"It doesn't say anything here about her penchant for black lovers and marijuana."

"Of course not," Mrs. Innes sniffed. "*Toronto Life* is a family magazine. Mr. McGregor's been asking for you, too."

"I'll see him in a while. I need you to do an errand. Can you go across to the supermarket and get me the biggest box of Tide they make?"

I went into my office to phone Bishop.

"Shuter, what the hell's going on?"

"What do you mean?"

"You know perfectly well what I mean. That guy we met. There's a story and you're holding out."

"I've been told one or two things in confidence. Can you understand that? In confidence?"

"Can you understand this? Last night I meet a man in a tacky bar and today he's dead. The police say he was a dope dealer. Susan's out on it now, but we're getting nowhere. You're supposed to be my pal and you're telling me nothing."

"There's nothing to tell."

"Wouldn't Travis McGee tell Meyer? Wouldn't Nero Wolfe tell Archie? Is there a connection between David Llewellyn's murder and Carol Malone? Or should I ask her father?"

"Do your piece on Ras Lucky's death, if you think it rates the national news, but leave the Malones out of it."

"Why should I? There's obviously some connection."

"I think you'll find it was just coincidence."

"I don't believe in coincidence," he growled. "Anyway, Susan knows about our meeting with Lucky. You told her yourself."

I'd forgotten. "Head her off."

"Why?"

"Because if you don't, Holidair and NTN will be invaded by big men with flat feet, looking for clues."

"So what?"

"I want to find the girl. The cops can wait."

Bishop sighed. "Okay, Sir Galahad, I'll hold off. But I'm not sure I'll be able to keep Quill on the leash."

"Who's the boss there, anyway?"

"Sometimes I wonder."

I told him I'd see him later. Damnit. If Quill said the wrong thing at local headquarters, the Mounties were going to be neck-deep in the Llewellyn case, and I was going to be right there with them. The last thing anyone needed right now was a lot of public speculation about drugs and death, Jamaica and Carol Malone.

Helen Boyko was in McGregor's office, having coffee and talking about the Malone problem. "There you are," she said. "I've just been organizing your flight. We have a morning departure to MoBay. Nine o'clock."

I looked at McGregor. "Look, maybe I should go now. Otherwise I may not get away at all."

I told them about my morning.

"My God!" said Helen.

"Do you think there's any connection between this man's murder and Carol?" McGregor asked.

"Yes, but I'm not sure what. I've told Bishop it's just coincidence but he doesn't buy it."

"I don't know," said McGregor slowly. "It's hard to see how there could be any connection."

I outlined Bladon's theory. McGregor listened carefully, then made a decision: "Cruel as it sounds, the local man's murder is beside the point here. Our objective is Carol. You'll be nearly as far ahead arriving at MoBay early tomorrow afternoon as you would be if you got in tonight. There's nothing scheduled going down at this time of day, anyway. You'd have to charter a Lear."

"That would be okay with me."

"Fly with us," he said, closing the matter.

I turned to Helen. "I'll need some money. Better make it five thousand American. Nobody wants the Canadian dollar these days."

"I'll send someone down to the bank."

"Also," I said, "see if you can organize a car for me at MoBay. Something fairly tough. No Toyotas or Fiats or anything like that."

She nodded. "I'll twix Johnson."

"Who's Johnson?"

"Herb Johnson, our agent in MoBay," said McGregor automatically. "A good man."

Helen went off to see to my requests and McGregor stopped pretending. "I don't like any of this. Are you going to be all right? I mean, I can get the Jamaican authorities cracking. I've got more influence down there than the whole Canadian government. They're not flying twenty thousand tourists to Jamaica this winter."

"I'll be okay. But I'm sick about Llewellyn."

He picked up Patsy's snapshots and gazed at them pensively. "It's peculiar. A young woman does something thoughtless, and I get you involved. The next thing we know there's some kind of crisis and now a killing."

"Yes, it's peculiar."

He studied the snapshot again. "I don't like the looks of this man; and it's got nothing to do with his colour."

"That's another peculiar thing," I said. "When I mentioned Cudjoe's name, Bladon reacted. But then he said he'd never heard of the guy."

"Perhaps he's not being altogether frank."

"Probably not. He's usually playing some angle. But what can we do?"

"We can be careful," he said. "Can't we?"


Mrs. Innes had acquired the Tide. I sat at my desk for a while and did some paperwork until Helen came in with my cash.

"Here. It's a lot of money."

"I'll try not to lose it." I don't like to be short on the road and I often run into situations where credit cards are useless.

Helen sat down and crossed her legs. "The boss is pretty upset."

"He's worried about the girl and so am I."

"Do you want me to come by tonight and help you pack?"

"By all means, come by. But I can pack for myself."

"And arrive a mess of wrinkles. It's bad for Holidair's image."

I laughed. "Boyko, aren't you ever off duty?"


"I just wanted to say," said Alan Malone, speaking from his office in the House of Commons, "that Mrs. Malone and I are grateful."

"Not at all," I said, turning down the stereo. "It's part of my job."

"Mac tells me you are one of the most capable fellows he has ever known."

"McGregor exaggerates."

"Mr. Shuter, I'm sixty-one years old. Carol is twenty-five. Attitudes have changed so fast. My wife and I have tried to be flexible, supportive...." His voice trailed off.

"I'm sure she's okay. I'll get her to call you."

"Patsy Baird has told us a bit about the man Carol is with," he said, in a firmer voice. "Probably not everything. These young people stick together. But I don't mind saying that we are heart-broken, not because of any racism but because he sounds so unsuitable. Carol is a well-educated young woman who, rightly or wrongly, has become used to certain standards of comfort and sophistication."

At least he wasn't trying to fudge the situation. "I wouldn't worry about it too much, Mr. Malone. It's probably just a passing fancy."

"There's something else, Mr. Shuter. I know you're experienced, but I will feel better if I know you won't take unnecessary risks."

"I never do."

"Jamaica is going through a difficult period just now. I am not at liberty to discuss the specifics, but it is only fair to suggest that you proceed cautiously."

"You mean the ganja crisis?"

"I beg your pardon?" He was surprised.

"I am aware," I said carefully, "that there is a matter of grave official concern, and that it involves drugs. I don't know the details. Yet."

"Mac said you were resourceful."

"I'm also aware that you can't discuss the situation. But I'm grateful for the warning."

"Perhaps we'd better leave it at that," he said. "Good luck, Mr. Shuter. And God speed."

I poured myself a tot of Directors' Stock and put a Jimmy Buffet tape on the machine: "Changes in Latitudes, Changes in Attitudes." Appropriate stuff. Would Alan Malone's attitudes change if he moved to the tropics? It was doubtful. Intolerance seems to increase with age.

I sipped my whisky while Buffet delivered his musical report on American expatriates who run off to the banana republics. With my assurances to everyone that I'd have no trouble finding Carol, I was almost as bad as the conmen Buffet was singing about. Certainly, I was less confident than I pretended; the trail was at least ten days cold.


I knocked together a fridge-and-freezer supper for Helen: some slices off a side of salmon smoked by Nova Scotia's incomparable Willy Krauch, a couple of marinated venison steaks, a salad, and a bottle of claret. Then we took our coffee and brandy into the living room, where I told her about Malone's call.

She was sympathetic. "It must be very hard for him. And his wife."

"Yeah. Miscegenation may be acceptable intellectually but it rarely is emotionally."

"*What* may be?"

"Miscegenation. One of Bishop's four-dollar words. Interracial sex."

"Oh. Is that what's worrying Mr. Malone?"

I shrugged. "He says not. But you know that old line about would you want your daughter to marry one? Yeah, I think that's a big part of it, although a man like Malone would never admit it."

The phone rang. It was Bishop, inviting us next door.

"You're off early."

"They can get it together without me once in a while," he said. "I've got a treat for you. Two treats actually. Susan is here and, by the way, she's cool on that other thing – our meeting with Lucky."

"Good."

"And the second treat is some footage I had the library dig up. You might call it vintage Rasta."

"We'll be right over." I hung up and turned to Helen. "You escape the dishes. Maria can do 'em. Bishop wants us to drop by."

We carried our drinks next door and Bishop waved us inside. "I've got brandy," he said, looking at our snifters.

"We'll get to yours," I said.

Helen and Suzie Q hadn't met before, and while Bishop made the introductions I wandered over and studied his electronics wall again. There were four television screens, three of them normal-sized Sonys, the other a seven-foot Advent. There were two video-tape cassette players – a Beta-Max and a VHS unit. There were several tape decks, reel-to-reel units, AM-FM receivers and a turntable. Floor-to-ceiling shelves sagged under his vast collection of albums, tapes and video cassettes. The whole house was wired, with speakers in almost every room. Television has perks, too.

"All the toys, eh?" said a throaty voice behind me. Susan had walked up carrying a glass of white wine. Without her glasses, she looked even younger and more attractive than she had the night before.

"He claims he needs this stuff for his work."

Susan laughed. "Richard is a television junkie. He's a

print convert, and they're the ones who usually get hooked the hardest."

"He's a thriller freak, too. I don't know where he finds the time."

"And what about you? What turns Michael Shuter on?"

I looked down at her and grinned. "The usual. Good booze, good food, good hockey, the occasional bad woman. I'm your typical, garden-variety Canadian."

Susan wrinkled her nose, but whether in distaste or amusement I couldn't tell. Before she could respond, Bishop came up. "All set, Suzie?"

"Ready."

"What this is, Mike, is some black-and-white footage of Haile Selassie's state visit to Jamaica in 1966. Classic stuff. I had it put on a cassette today." He nodded to Susan, who began fiddling with knobs and buttons.

Grainy images flickered on the seven-foot screen. While the tape rolled, Bishop and Susan took turns ad-libbing a voice-over; the footage had background sound, but no commentary. It began with shots of huge crowds at Palisadoes (now Norman Manley) International Airport in Kingston. Rain scudded across the runway, and high winds tugged at umbrellas and dresses. "Here," said Susan. "This is the moment the Rastas gained a thousand instant converts." The camera panned along the runway and picked up an approaching jet, which suddenly glinted as the sun burst through to a roar from the crowd. "They believed Jah ordered the clouds away," Susan said. It *was* a trifle eerie: by the time the Ethiopian Airlines 707 stopped in front of the terminal, the airport was awash in sunlight.

"Too bad it's not in colour," said Bishop. "Watch what happens now."

Workmen had pushed a staircase out to the Boeing and a carpet was being unrolled. A guard of honour from the Jamaican Defence Force stood rigid, and a score of dignitaries awaited the emergence of His Imperial Highness. But security was inadequate, and there was a sequence of confused pictures, the camera swinging wildly, trying to capture the scene as hundreds of civilians broke through police lines and surrounded the plane.

"Bloody shambles," Bishop laughed. "Old Highly Suspicious didn't know what to do."

The Boeing's door swung open and there was another surge of noise.

"Look at him," said Susan. "Scared to death." The emperor suddenly appeared, in full uniform, at the top of the steps. He waved uncertainly. The camera zoomed in on his face. The man looked confused, unsettled by the wild scene below. A few Rastas tried to scale the side of the steps. The police intervened and punches were thrown. Through it all, the honour guard stood at attention, eyes front.

"There he goes," said Bishop. Selassie suddenly turned and scuttled back into the plane, a tiny god in full retreat before his avid worshippers.

The confusion continued for a while; then the film jumped to the door again.

"It took them almost an hour to restore order and persuade him to come out again," Bishop said. "Can't really blame him. It must be unsettling to travel half-way around the world and be greeted as a god."

"He knew," said Susan. "He knew all about the Rastas. He just didn't know about Jamaican efficiency. Selassie was used to the protection of the Ethiopian Imperial Guard, which used to be one of the best military units in Africa. Giant men, with spears and lion's-mane anklets. Compared to them, the Jamaican security forces were a joke."

Selassie appeared again in the door. Police had cleared the crowd and he hustled down the steps, shook hands hastily with the governor general and Prime Minister, climbed into a limo, and sped off to the safety of King's House. The tape clicked off.

"Poor little man," said Helen.

"After a shaky start," Susan said, "the trip was a personal triumph for the emperor. He made a lot of friends and the Rastas made a lot of converts."

When it was almost eleven o'clock, Bishop began to grow restless, anxious to see how his troops had made out and what the other networks had. Helen wanted to watch the news too, but Susan said she would prefer to inspect my house.

"You in the market for a house?" I asked.

"On my salary? You're joking. I'm just curious to see what your M-C-P-S is like."

"My what?"

"M-C-P-S," she said, grinning. "Male chauvinist pig sty."


"They're beautiful," Susan said, watching the fish. She'd had the two-dollar tour and was sipping a glass of wine. I'd been mildly annoyed by the clutter in the dining room and kitchen. Not that I'm compulsively neat; far from it. But for some reason I wanted to make a good impression on this woman.

"Your cats would like them."

She was surprised. "How do you know I've got cats?"

"I used to be a detective. I've been checking up on you."

"I'm not sure I like that," she smiled.

"Bishop told me. Don't worry, Suzie Q. No obscene phone calls, no peeping through your shutters. I may be a male chauvinist pig, but I'm a straight male chauvinist pig."

She was laughing now. "I'm sure you are."

"Do you like the house?"

"Very much. Richard said you bought this place because of your wife."

"Something like that."

She asked me about Janet, putting her questions in a straightforward manner, which was a relief. I get fed up with false sympathy. But Susan was easy to talk to; of course, that's her stock-in-trade. After a while, the door opened and Helen and Bishop breezed in.

"Not a bad show," he said, pleased. "The CBC screwed up. Lost their audio for about fifteen seconds. Nesbitt'll be buying drinks."

"It's nearly midnight," said Helen, yawning. "I've got to go."

"Me too," said Susan.

Helen collected her coat and gave me a kiss on the cheek. Bishop said he'd see me in the morning – perhaps. At the door, Susan Quill smiled good night and held out a hand. Her hand was cool.

# PART TWO
## Eight Days and Seven Nights

# CHAPTER SIX

## *Day One (Friday) – 7:35 A.M.*

A three-paragraph item in the *Globe*'s sports section completed the bad-news triangle. A delayed dispatch from Port Antonio reported a strange accident: the Wednesday-morning drowning of a member of the U.S. Olympic swim team. He'd been holidaying in Jamaica, and apparently had suffered cramps while scuba-diving in the Blue Lagoon, where Errol Flynn used to cavort between swashbucklers. The victim's coaches and teammates back in the States were at a loss to explain how a world-class swimmer could drown.

I sat at the kitchen counter and sipped my coffee, irrationally relieved that number three hadn't involved Carol. It was certainly odd: the German parasailer, the Calgary sightseers, and the U.S. Olympian had died at approximately the same time, while engaged in typical pursuits at three different resorts.

Would anyone else even notice? Probably not. I had Jamaica on my mind, and anyway I'd half-expected the third accident. Most people are superstitious without knowing why. I'm superstitious in a reverse kind of way, a legacy of my childhood. Man cannot accept that he's master of his fate. It's easier to blame or credit external forces for shifts in personal fortune, and an amazing number of people prefer to ascribe such shifts to the supernatural. It's a throwback to the dark days of ignorance, shamans, and sorcerers, but the durability of ancient taboos and beliefs is remarkable.

My father, a practical man in most matters and fearless of anything on two legs, was almost neurotic in his superstitions. He carried a rabbit's foot into the mine every day. He would turn on his heel and walk around a city block to avoid a black cat. He used to cross his fingers and touch wood whenever he heard anyone say anything optimistic. And just in case the ancients had it wrong, he led the family to church every Sunday, hedging his bets. None of it helped. His lungs went anyway. I was fifteen when he died, the rabbit's foot tucked beneath his pillow, and I've deliberately flouted the conventional superstitions ever since: walking under ladders, opening umbrellas before going out of doors, things like that. Also, I avoid churches.

The *Globe*'s report on Lucky's death was long on speculation, thin on detail. The Metro cops were "pursuing several lines of inquiry"—headquarters doubletalk which meant they were stuck. David Llewellyn had been "known to police" and the paper said he'd been in the dope trade. Well, you can't libel the dead, and it was true, anyway. Lucky's slaying, the paper went on, was the result of a gangland squabble—a "settling of accounts," to borrow the delightfully understated phrase used by the Montreal cops to describe underworld hits in their town. There wasn't a hint of RCMP involvement, which meant Bladon and McNicholl were keeping the lid on.


Toronto International, popularly known as Malton after the village it has overwhelmed, is northwest of the city. It is Canada's busiest airport, used by dozens of carriers, big and small. The international airlines all want to fly to Toronto, which is booming, but the federal government requires many of them to turn around at Montreal, which is not. The reasons are political. For one, Ottawa is committed to propping up Quebec, because otherwise *La Belle Province* may simply wander out of Confederation, something no one this side of the lunatic fringe wants to happen. For another, Ottawa is trying to cover its ass, having blown a billion dollars building a second Montreal airport, Mirabel, which no one wants to use. By forcing foreign carriers to fly into Mirabel, and requiring many flights originating in Toronto to stop over there en route to Europe, the federal government is able to cook the traffic books. But everyone knows Mirabel is a boondoggle; the airport has even adopted a white elephant as its official symbol.

There are two terminals at Malton, and Holidair is fortunate to operate out of Terminal One. It is an architectural gem, efficient for passenger and carrier alike. The building is circular in design, which minimizes the distance people and baggage must travel to and from flights, and it contains several layers of parking, which is handy if you can find a space. Originally, the intention was to repeat the design as often as traffic increases warranted. But the Department of Transport changed its mind when it commissioned Terminal Two, a vast warehouse where Air Canada is the principal tenant. No one likes Terminal Two; it's too big. Jack Nicklaus would need a driver, a three-wood, a seven-iron, and two putts to get from one end to the other. Passengers are sent off on route-marches, clutching boarding passes when they ought to be issued with maps. Nevertheless, Terminal Two is busy, handling almost a million passengers a month, and the trend is up.

The Holidair area was crowded. In addition to my flight, we were loading a 747 for Hawaii and an L10-11 for Freeport, and the three departure times were bunched, which puts extra strain on the ground crew. I followed my porter up to the Jamaica line, gave him two bucks, and prepared to shuffle along with everyone else. But Helen had been on the phone, and one of our reps spied me.

"Good morning, Mr. Shuter!" Double-keen, he began

wrestling with my luggage. "We'll stow these aboard. Mrs. Boyko said you'd likely be in a hurry at MoBay."

"Thanks." I sneaked a look at his ID, a Polaroid Identikit tag bearing his picture and the name Tony Abruzzi. "Are we full this morning, Tony?"

"Not quite. It's still a little early for Jamaica."

"Then you'll have a breakfast for me?"

He grinned. "Are you kiddin'? It's not every day we get the brass."

Reluctantly, he allowed me to carry my briefcase and the Tide while I followed him to the counter. He issued instructions about my bags and handed me an envelope containing a ticket, which I didn't need, and a boarding pass, which I did. The security people get upset if you don't have a boarding pass.

Most of the Jamaica-bound passengers had already passed through security and were in the departure lounge. Tony asked whether I wanted to go to the VIP facility we share with several other outfits operating out of Terminal One, but I said I wanted to go to the duty-free shops.

He nodded and checked the time. "Right. You board at 4-B, in about twenty-five minutes. But don't worry. We won't leave without you."

"If I'm late, you'd *better* leave without me. Otherwise McGregor'll fire us both."

I strolled along to the duty-free area, which was doing a brisk trade despite the hour. For all but the most seasoned travellers, airports tend to warp time. People who normally wouldn't dream of having a drink before five P.M. can be found knocking them back in airport bars at ten in the morning. Not in Toronto, of course; in Ontario the bars can't open until noon. But I've often noticed the phenomenon elsewhere. The Age of Aviation is three-quarters of a century old, but there's still an aura of adventure about flying, a sense of breaking free—not so much from the "surly bonds of earth" as from the strait-jacket of social convention. Our passengers lose their inhibitions—both sexual and alcoholic—far more often than we lose their luggage.

I wanted to buy a token for Gilly Byles, owner of the hotel where I planned to establish headquarters in Negril. It's not easy to buy something for a man like Byles; he already seems to have everything. But finally I decided on a bottle of vintage Armagnac, a change from the Appleton's twelve-year-old rum he usually drinks after dinner.

Duty-free shopping is sometimes a bargain for tourists, always a bonanza for the entrepreneurs who get permission to run airport shops, and often a pain in the neck for airlines. Quite apart from the question of why the mere purchase of a ticket on an international flight should enable anyone to avoid taxes on liquor, tobacco, and other products, there is the question of security. The big problem is booze on long flights; the passengers have it with them in the cabin. It's a problem no one wants to tackle first because of the competition factor, but drunks at 35,000 are a potential menace.

Like most charter operators, Holidair runs a free bar during flights. But I've given our cabin crews strict orders to regulate the flow. After the first couple of rounds, service is deliberately slowed. Because the drinks are free, people are prepared to wait a little longer. However, the scheduled passenger will buy one or two from the stews, then start in on his own. There are rules against it but they are almost impossible to enforce; a cabin crew of sixteen can't keep an eye on more than 400 people, packed close in high-backed chairs. One possible solution: a voucher issued by the duty-free shop at the point of departure and honoured by the shop at the other end. But that would involve a delay for arriving passengers, and in the airline business delay is almost as dirty a word as crash.

The security guard gave me an odd look as she inspected my boarding pass and placed the Tide and my briefcase on a short conveyer belt passing through a scanner. Unless the Tide people had included some deadly prize in their package, I was clean; there was nothing in the briefcase except Mrs. Innes's dossier on Jamaica and a manila envelope containing fifty U.S. $100 bills. I'd debated briefly whether to bring a gun, but a gun seemed a bit drastic for a job like this – crisis or not.

I walked through the metal detector without tripping the alarm, nodded good morning to the constable who was watching for the tell-tale red light, gathered up my hand baggage, and headed for the departure gate.

Since the hijacking fad, the public has become used to security at airports. There are layers of it, some obvious. Everyone's into the act: the RCMP, the Department of Transport, Customs and Immigration, the airlines themselves. The customs people are the sneakiest, watching for smugglers not only during the actual inspection but before and after it as well. They use a variety of secret observation points, as well as plainclothes types, to monitor arrivals' behaviour. More than one smuggler has come to grief after clearing inspection, because he wore too broad a smile or hugged his case too protectively. Sabotage and terrorism are a bigger worry than smuggling and harder to defend against. Part of the problem is on-the-job boredom: it's not easy to stay sharp, day after day, when you're looking for an enemy who may never come.

Our ground hostess wanted to pre-board me, and it was easier to go along than resist. She led me onto the aircraft and solemnly handed me over to the cabin crew. It made me feel incapable, a nuisance, as though I were an especially irksome child. The purser, an attractive woman in her early thirties, who kept twisting the simple band on her fourth finger, offered to take me up to the flight deck to meet the crew but I declined, saying I was tired and they were busy. I took a seat in the front row, snapped on my belt, and waited for the other passengers.

They were a mixed lot, as always: mainly couples, quite a few girls travelling in pairs, a few lone wolves. Three weeks ago, Carol and Patsy had taken this flight. I could imagine the wolves then – ogling Carol, speculating, wondering where she was going to stay, plotting an end-run around Patsy. A beautiful girl goes through life with a bull's-eye on her back. But Carol had proved an elusive target for the holiday swains from Canada; she'd gone Caribbean, all the way.

After takeoff, I declined a drink, accepted a breakfast, and began reading Mrs. Innes's file. She had xeroxed pages from several books and periodicals, organizing them under subheadings: Geography, Politics, Military, The Economy, Tourism, History, and so on. A lot of the material was familiar but I spent an hour skimming it.

Jamaica is the third largest island in the Greater Antilles, after Cuba and Hispaniola. It covers 4,400 square miles and measures 150 miles east and west, fifty-one miles north and south at its widest point. The interior is rugged, peppered with long-dead volcanoes. The northern and southern coastal plains are latticed with streams and rivers. Indeed, the country's name is thought to come from the ancient Arawak Indian word, *Xamayca*, meaning "land of springs." Population is just over 2,000,000, 750,000 of whom live in Kingston. More than 90 per cent of the people are descended from African slaves imported by the Spanish and British. Jamaica is a constitutional monarchy, a member of the British Commonwealth, and essentially a two-party state. The People's National Party and the Jamaica Labour Party dominate the legislature, both espousing social democracy. The people take their politics as seriously as Maritimers do, occasionally lapsing into violence in their partisanship. Both parties are nervous about the Rastafarian cult, which claims to be a religion but which has many trappings of a nascent political movement. The Rastas, meanwhile, express contempt for the conventional politicians. Law and order are maintained by the Jamaican Constabulary Force – 5,000 regulars, augmented by 4,000 auxiliary police – and the Jamaica Defence Force – 2,500 men serving in land, air, and sea units. The economy, originally based on bananas and sugar, is chronically weak. Principal products today are bauxite and tourism. Nearly 200,000 tourists were expected to visit the island this winter, most of them Canadians and Americans. But Jamaica is developing a following among the Europeans too. Germans, Austrians, Swiss, and British are starting to holiday there in large numbers, attracted by the bargains their relatively hard currencies can buy. By New World standards, Jamaica is an old country, discovered by Columbus and settled early in the sixteenth century by the Spanish. Down the years it has been under several flags: the Spanish, the Union Jack, the Jolly Roger, and its own since Independence in 1962.

The purser came by, asking whether I'd like a drink before lunch. She seemed so anxious to get me something that I ordered a bloody mary. So far, the flight had been training-manual smooth. The captain had been on the blower, reporting we had a strong tail wind and would be arriving fifteen minutes early. Perfect.

I picked at my lunch—chicken Kiev, lemon pie—and drank a split of Pouilly-Fumé; everyone else was offered an indifferent Bordeaux, so Helen must have been fairly detailed in her instructions. I filled in a landing card and currency declaration form while we overflew Cuba, lying green and brown and poor in the sun. Then, a few minutes after one o'clock, we began to lose altitude and the seat-belt sign came on.


The purser off-loaded me first, carrying one of my bags down the steps and smiling proudly when I complimented her on the flight. A neat black man, wearing a white shirt and a Holidair tie, was waiting with a porter on the tarmac. He volunteered a strong smile and a limp hand. "Welcome to Jamaica, Mr. Shuter. I'm Herb Johnson."

"Hi. Mr. McGregor sends his regards."

Johnson seemed to grow two inches; McGregor's name

has a powerful effect, even in the most remote outposts of his empire.

The sun was directly overhead and dazzling, bleaching out the cream-coloured exterior of the terminal. The air was heavy with humidity, a radical change from the chill damp of Toronto and the controlled comfort of the Jumbo. There were only two other jets on the ground – an Air Jamaica 727 and an Eastern Airlines DC-9, loading for Miami. You can't make any money on the ground. Our aircraft would be turned around in seventy-five minutes, refuelled and re-loaded for the flight back to Toronto. Tonight at nine-thirty, the same plane would take off for Gatwick and tomorrow morning would deadhead to Frankfurt to bring a load back to Montreal.

Sir Donald Sangster International Airport is a one-runway facility, the port-of-entry for tourists bound for the North Shore resorts. Since my last visit, a new arrivals concourse had been built and it was optimistically huge. Johnson and I trudged along an endless corridor. Not for the first time I wondered whether the world's architects had reached a secret agreement that airline passengers ought to be sent off on long hikes to get their circulation going again, after several hours in a narrow seat.

"Did you manage to find me a car?"

"Yes, sah! A Mercedes sports model. Very nice."

"Surely not from Hertz?"

"No," he grinned. "I borrowed it from a friend. Mrs. Boyko said you wanted power. It belongs to a chap who owns a hotel here in MoBay. He bought it for his girlfriend but she ran off with another man. You can keep it as long as you want."

The immigration officer accepted my landing card and currency declaration without comment, then became fasci-nated by my passport, thumbing through it page by page, inspecting the various stamps. "What is the purpose of your trip?"

"Business."

"How long will you be in Jamaica?"

"I'm not sure."

"We'll make it for three months, then." He found a new page and stamped it. "Welcome to Montego Bay."

Aside from a platoon of porters and an abnormally large number of soldiers and police, the customs hall was fairly quiet. But the Holidair passengers were starting to trickle through and the place would soon be humming. A three-piece band was tuning up in one corner, shepherds from the various hotels were steeling themselves for the inevitable questions and complaints from arriving guests and the steward at the Appleton's stand was filling plastic glasses with rum punch, complimentary for all arrivals.

The porter hefted my bags onto the inspection table and the customs man, who knew Johnson, asked whether I was carrying any firearms. When I said I wasn't, he beamed and chalked my cases, waving me on.

The car was a white convertible with red upholstery, about $45,000-worth of unrequited love. "Who'd she run off with?" I asked. "Adnan Kashogghi?"

"No," Johnson laughed. "A tennis teacher."

He helped stow my bags, the Tide, and the bottle of Armagnac in the trunk, tipped the porter, and handed me the keys.

"Is there anything our office can do for you?"

"Not at the moment, thanks. I'll yell if I need help."

I folded my jacket, put it on the passenger's seat and started the car. At the airport gates, a half-dozen soldiers lolled about in camouflage kit. They looked bored and uncomfortable. I swung right and set off for Negril, the sun warm on my face. It was almost like being on holiday.

# CHAPTER SEVEN

## *Day One (Friday) — 3:40 P.M.*

The Coconut Cove is a good hotel, right on the beach. It is a collection of well-appointed apartments, some of them on two floors, nestled among the palm trees that line Negril's seven-mile stretch of white sand. Janet and I had stayed here and found the accommodation first class, the food good, and the service friendly, if a bit casual — claims not every Jamaican hostelry can make. The hotel has a central service core which includes a small gift shop and a cozy bar, as well as an indoor-outdoor dining area.

Gilly Byles met me in the lobby, seemed pleased and surprised by the Armagnac, and offered me an immediate drink. But I wanted to get organized, so once I'd registered and deposited most of my cash in the safe I went along to my suite. My bags were already inside, and the air-conditioner had been running all day. There were fresh flowers in the living room, as well as a bottle of Chivas Regal and a bottle of vodka. I looked in the fridge and discovered a dozen bottles of Heineken and a half-dozen splits of Veuve Clicquot, which isn't Krug but isn't bad. I was glad I'd brought the Armagnac.

Upstairs, I unpacked and took a shower to banish the dust and sweat of the road. Then I put on a pair of trunks, went down to the living room, and opened a beer. It was cold and delicious, almost indistinguishable from the Dutch original.

Heineken is brewed in Jamaica under licence by Desnoes &
Geddes, the bottlers of Red Stripe. I took the beer onto the
balcony and sat watching the swimmers and sunbathers
enjoy the good life, far from home.

The sea was calm, shimmering in the late-afternoon sun.
A soft breeze nullified some of the humid, eighty-degree
atmosphere, and propelled a half-dozen sailboats across the
bay. A half-mile off shore a black-hulled schooner lay at
anchor; it had to be the *Calico Jack*, whose spar had claimed
the parasailer. Palms rustled overhead and bees were working overtime among the hibiscus, oleander, and bougain-
villaea blossoms.

I finished the beer and went back inside, locking the balcony door. The sea looked too good to resist. Because old
habits die hard, I put the Do Not Disturb sign on the front
doorknob and quickly rigged a simple burglar alarm. I found
a couple of threads, wet them lightly with saliva, and stuck
them to the door-jamb, one a hand-span from the top, the
other a hand-span from the bottom. Standard tradecraft.
Even amateurs will often notice the top one, and pros will
always find them both; but no one can replace them exactly,
without leaving some kind of a mark or scratch.

The sand felt good between my toes and the water was
like a salty bath – warm, buoyant, and soothing. Tiny fish
schooled in the shallows, slivers of silver darting around my
legs. I wondered whether they'd agree to trade places with
my fish, whether they'd choose security and regular meals
over freedom. It's a deal more and more humans seem
willing to accept, but I wasn't sure about fish.

Before I'd been in the water two minutes, I was approached
by a young Jamaican, who wanted to sell me some ganja. He
claimed to be able to deliver anything from a couple of spliffs
to a couple of tons. The beach hustlers in Jamaica can be a
nuisance: within a quarter-mile, a stroller is likely to be
offered everything from a dope deal to a coral collection,
with handicrafts and a flour-bag shirt thrown in. The beach

at Negril is like a main street with movable shops, except the merchants aren't paying much business tax. Given the wide availability of ganja, it's hard to believe the Jamaican authorities are serious about curtailing the trade. Bill McNicholl's boys would have a grand time at Negril; they'd make more collars than the Arrow shirt people.

I escaped the young agribusinessman by stretching out in a crawl and powering straight out to sea. I'm a strong swimmer, if not particularly stylish, and I churned steadily for about four minutes, stopping when I became weary. I flopped over on my back and floated, content under a flawless sky. The sun was lower now, but still warm. I looked in toward the green line of palm trees; except for the people on the beach there were few signs of civilization. Jamaica has been clever in controlling development at Negril, refusing to allow buildings to rise above the treeline. If the place is not quite unspoiled, it is far from being ruined the way Miami Beach has been. Perhaps that's the chief advantage developing countries enjoy: a chance to learn from the mistakes of the industrial world.

I floated for a while, then rolled over and headed toward shore. It was time to go to work.


The Coconut Cove's beach bar wasn't doing much trade. Two middle-aged couples were getting happily smashed on rum punches. Two good-looking young women, brown in bikinis, were trying to make their drinks last until sundown. The bar had a cassette player and the bikinis were listening to Marley's "Kaya" album, sniggering while he sang about sharing the shelter of his single bed. I eased onto a chair in the shade of the bar's thatched roof, and caught the steward's eye. The name "Thomas" was stitched on his jacket, and he seemed glad to see me. He slapped a cardboard coaster on the bar and stood, almost quivering, at attention. "Good afternoon, sah!"

"Not bad." The warm breeze was towelling my back, and I was thirsty.

"What is your pleasure, sah?" Thomas sounded as though he'd done some time in a British regiment. The Empire may be gone, but traces remain, echoes reverberate.

"Heineken, please."

He swept the cap from a bottle, poured the beer into a frosted glass, and set it before me with a flourish. The head was exactly an inch high. Sid Oland would approve; he's a fifth-generation brewer, and as serious and fussy about beer as any oenophile is about wine. Oland once told me that the most subtle flavours in a beer burst to the top of the foam the minute it's poured, lingering on the drinker's taste buds while he finishes the brew. Also, a one-inch head keeps the other flavours locked in. In any case, this beer tasted good after my swim and I said so, which seemed to make Thomas's day. He couldn't have looked happier if his surname was Desnoes or Geddes.

He moved away to make more punches for the middle-aged couples, taking great care in the mixing. The bikinis declined a refill, a decision Thomas accepted stoically. Marley wailed on about a misty morning, and I finished my beer. Without asking, Thomas produced a second Heineken and a fresh glass. Definitely my kind of bartender.

"Were you in the army, Thomas?"

"Yes, sah!" He was at attention again, rock-still, a soldier in mufti on a tiny parade square. "West Indies Regiment."

Thomas appeared to be in his late forties, wore a close-trimmed moustache, and kept his hair short. He had a strong jaw and alert eyes. There was muscle under his white jacket.

"That was a while ago."

He nodded. "Before Independence."

I knew that the West Indies Regiment, now disbanded, had had a distinguished record in both world wars. When Jamaica seceded from the West Indies Federation, dooming

100

it, Kingston set up the Jamaica Defence Force. The JDF has an air wing and a coastal patrol unit, as well as regular troops, and is used mainly for internal security. Like its regimental predecessor, the JDF is heavily influenced by British military tradition and procedure. Britain still provides the bulk of Jamaica's military aid, although Canada trains JDF airmen.

"Enjoy the army?" I asked, already knowing the answer.

Thomas beamed. "Yes, sah! I served in the JDF, too."

I introduced myself and we talked for a while about army life. Thomas had served a total of twenty years, including an early stint as a steward in the officers' mess, and retired with the rank of sergeant. He had a small pension, but prices climbed every month and civilian jobs were scarce, so he was glad to be tending bar at the Coconut Cove.

Occasionally our conversation was interrupted by guests who came by to order drinks and carry them back to their chaises. The bikinis finally finished their drinks, gathered up their paraphernalia, and strolled up to the hotel. A few moments later, the middle-aged couples stumbled after them, doubtless off for a sobering nap so they could get smashed again at dinner. Life in the tropics may be slow and easy, but you need a champion liver to survive it.

"Alone at last," I said with a smile.

Thomas frowned uncertainly. "Sah?"

"I wonder if you can help me. Do you know a guy named Cudjoe?"

"Who?" The frown dissolved into a stare.

"Cudjoe. I don't know the rest of his name. He's a big guy, six-six, may six-seven. Long hair. About thirty."

"Are you jokin' with Thomas, Mr. Shuter?"

"No."

"A duppy? You think I know a duppy?" He seemed delighted by the notion.

"What's a duppy?"

"A ghost, sah. Of course, I don't believe in them, but many folks around here do."

"Why a ghost, Thomas?"

"Cudjoe has been dead for over two hundred years."

It was my turn to stare. "Two hundred years? Don't be silly. He was in Negril this month. I've got a picture of him up in my room."

"If Cudjoe was here this month, it must have been his duppy."

"I don't understand."

"Cudjoe was the chieftain of the Maroons," he said patiently. "Slaves who ran away toward the end of the Spanish time in Jamaica. I have been told that the name Maroon comes from the Spanish word *cimarron*, which means 'untamed.' Under Cudjoe, the Maroons defeated the British army again and again. We used to study their campaigns in the regiment. They say the Maroon wars were the first sustained guerrilla action ever faced by British regulars. They lasted about seventy-five years, until the middle of the 1730s. The British had little chance because Cudjoe never allowed the Maroons to be trapped in a full-scale battle. He always attacked from ambush, and made camp in difficult terrain. Cockpit Country, and in the Blue Mountains, near Kingston."

"They kept the British at bay for seventy-five years?"

"The Maroons were good fighters. Eventually, the authorities decided to sue for peace. The Maroons were granted their freedom and their own land."

"Your Cudjoe sounds like quite a guy."

Thomas considered it. "He was a good general, sah. But he drank too much, and many feel the treaty he signed was a betrayal. The British used the Maroons to keep the slaves down. They were like a police force. Some folks still resent it."

"Well, Thomas, that was a favourite technique of the British colonists. They did it in India, in Africa..."

"I know, sah. But this is Jamaica. The Maroons remain apart from the rest of us."

"The Cudjoe I'm looking for is no duppy. He's flesh and blood, and a lot of it. I think he's a Rastaman. He wears dreadlocks."

Thomas shrugged. "It is a fashion. Not everyone with locks is a Rasta."

"What about a local Rasta named Doctor Black?"

"Everybody knows Doctor Black, sah."

"Where would I find him?"

He looked at me doubtfully. "I do not wish to pry, but it is unusual for newly arrived guests to be seekin' out local folk. Is Doctor Black in some trouble?"

"I have a message for him from one of his friends in Toronto."

Thomas thought for a moment. "Sometimes you find him on the beach, sometimes in town. He's a coral carver. Many tourists buy his work. But if I may, sah, do not pay his askin' price. He is used to bargainin' with folks."

"I'd like to talk to him."

"At this time of day, you could try Miss Brown's tea room. In town. Anyone can show you. But just have a Red Stripe at Miss Brown's. Do not try her tea, unless you wish to drift for a few hours."

"What's wrong with her tea?"

"Nothin' is wrong with it. But she makes it with mush-rooms."

I signed my bar tab and stood, stretching. My trunks were almost dry. "I'll see you tomorrow, Thomas."

"Walk good, sah," he said, managing not to salute.

The tea room was a dilapidated shack in the middle of town, itself an aggregation of run-down shanties and shops which hadn't changed much since I'd last seen it. The boom in Negril tourism obviously had yet to filter many dollars down through the local economy. Either that, or a fortune awaited some enterprising paint salesman. I put on my best tourist's face and marched up the short path. A half-dozen men and women were standing outside a service window, eating meat patties and drinking Red Stripe or tea. The door was open and I stepped into a tiny front room. There was a counter with four stools, three of them occupied by Rastas. One of them was zonked. A barefoot woman, wearing a print dress and a head scarf, was behind the counter. She smiled at me uncertainly while a naked little boy tugged at her skirt.

"Miss Brown?"

"Miss Brown not here at de moment."

"Actually, I'm trying to find Doctor Black."

The young woman darted a look at the three Rastas, one of whom waved an indifferent hand and looked up with mild interest. "You want some coral, mon? Very nice. I make a good price for you."

"Maybe."

Doctor Black was wearing a khaki safari jacket over washed-out jeans and a pair of new-looking Ponys. He began producing pieces of black coral from his pockets, setting out his wares with the practised moves of a Toronto street-hawker.

"Very nice lion head." He handed me a carving about half the size of a golf ball. It was exquisite. The lion wore an expression of benign wisdom and, given its place in the natural order of things, understandable self-confidence. Rasta carvers love lions, the symbol of Jah.

"How much?"

Doctor Black gazed at me thoughtfully, trying to measure my wallet. "Hundred dollar American."

"That's a lot of money." I put the carving back on the counter.

"Dat head a lot o' work." His voice was soft and low. He held up the piece, admiring it.

The young woman bustled about opening Red Stripes and passing patties through the window. Occasionally a patron ordered mushroom tea, a greyish brew that, depending upon its strength, could make a person mellow or crazy.

104

Mushroom tea is legal in Jamaica, presumably because the authorities regard it as no worse than rum or whisky. The zonked Rasta was grooving happily on it, moving slowly to some private rhythm. The third man nursed a beer, paying no attention to my negotiations with Doctor Black.

"Is he okay?" I asked, indicating Mr. Zonk.

"Him fine. Him jes' had some tea." He grinned again. "You want some tea, mon? You feel good wit' it."

I shook my head. "Can I buy you a beer?"

"No, mon. Buy some coral."

"Why are all your pieces dark?"

"I work only wit' black coral. Dat why dey call I Black. Dis de only place in de worl' where black coral grow. It expensive, 'cause de diver got to go down maybe t'ree hundred feet to fetch it up."

"Why do they call you 'doctor'?"

"I use a knife jes' like a surgeon." He passed the lion's head back to me. "It wort' a hundred."

I inspected some of his other pieces but I liked the lion best. What the hell. I could always give it to Susan Quill. She liked cats.

"Okay, Doctor. A hundred for the lion, and another hundred for a half-hour of your time."

His smile dissolved and his friend looked up, surprised: $200 U.S. is a lot of money in Negril.

"What you want, mon?" Doctor Black seemed leery of such a windfall.

"A talk. David Llewellyn gave me your name in Toronto."

"Ras Lucky? Why Lucky givin' you de name of I?"

"Because I asked for his help."

"When was dat?"

"Thursday. The morning he died." I said it quietly, and kept my face expressionless.

He stared at me uncomprehendingly. So did the other Rasta and the young woman. For some reason, her child chose this moment to begin wailing. Mr. Zonk bopped on, oblivious.

"Died? Lucky?" Shock moved Doctor Black's voice up an octave and several decibels. There was a hush among the patrons outside.

I waited.

"What you want, mon?" Now he was whispering, and there was pain in his eyes.

"I want to ask you about Cudjoe."

He shook his head and rose abruptly, gathering up his carvings. He left the lion's head on the counter and I picked it up, handing him a $100-bill.

"Ras Lucky a friend to I. You come, mon." He nodded goodbye to the young woman and moved toward the door. I followed, aware that the people outside were watching us closely. Behind me the little boy continued to cry.

Doctor Black got into the Mercedes without comment. He looked troubled, almost ill. After a few moments, he said quietly: "How Lucky die?"

"He was murdered. Machetes."

"In Canada? Dat impossible."

"It happened."

"Who kill him?"

"A gang of young Jamaicans. Rastas."

He shook his head violently, his locks swishing through the still air. "Not Rastas, mon! Not Rastas."

"Where to? Rick's?"

"Doan matter. Who are you, mon? How you know Lucky?"

"My name's Shuter. I work for an airline in Toronto and I'm looking for one of our passengers. Lucky said you could help."

"Shooter? Like a gun?"

"No, man. S-h-u-t-e-r."


Rick's café is on the far side of Negril Bay, at the western-most tip of the island. It is popular among the artists, middle-echelon jet-setters, and jaded New York fashion models, who were flocking to this part of Jamaica long before the beach area was developed. Built on a rocky cliff thirty feet above the sea, Rick's features a big open bar under a thatched roof. During the high season the place is packed but now there were only a half-dozen customers, waiting for the sun to go down. Rick's is world-famous for its sunsets, less well-known for the local divers who entertain patrons by falling off the cliff.

I acquired $20-worth of blue plastic drink tokens and Doctor Black and I took chairs, facing west. He ordered a scotch, knocking it back in two gulps. I signalled the bartender to bring him another. "I thought Jamaicans drank rum."

"It depend, mon. I learned whisky in Philly."

While I drank a Heineken and Van Halen did their heavy-metal thing over Rick's sound system, he told me he'd gone to the States when he was in his early twenties. He had an aunt in Philadelphia, and he found a job there as a construction labourer. But he hated the Pennsylvania winters and he missed Jamaica, so he came home and began carving full time.

"It not Market Street," he said with a grin, indicating the tropical splendour around us, "but it not bad."

The sun was about to set, and we fell silent, watching. The Caribbean glowed in golds and reds out beyond the blue. Even Doctor Black, who could watch a Negril sunset every day, seemed moved. Only about four minutes elapsed from the time the sun's lower rim dipped below the horizon until it had completely disappeared. Watching it, I could understand why the ancients had worshipped earth's star.

Doctor Black turned from the view and looked at me bleakly. The pain was back in his eyes. "Tell I 'bout Lucky."

"I only met him once. But I liked him. Your friend was into some heavy things in Canada, and one of them fell on him."

"What heavy t'ings?"

"Ganja."

"Nothin' heavy 'bout herb."

"The law says there is."

He made a sour face. "Dey should legalize it. Doan hurt nobody."

"It hurt Lucky."

"Why you askin' Ras Lucky 'bout I, anyway?"

I told him in more detail about my job, Carol, and why I wanted to find her.

"Why you mention Cudjoe?"

"That's who the girl is with." I reached into my pocket and took out the snapshots. He looked at them, but said nothing.

"Do you know Cudjoe?"

He didn't reply.

"Where do I find him?"

Again, he didn't answer. Instead, he drained his glass and signalled for another. The silence stretched out ominously.

"I doan mess wit' him," he said finally. "Cudjoe, what dey call in Philly, a heavy dude."

"So what? I'm not going to mess with him. I just want to talk to the girl."

"Stay clear of Cudjoe, Shuter. And his women."

"Is he a Rastaman?"

Doctor Black snorted. "Him hardly even Jamaican. Cudjoe raised in Detroit city."

This seemed so unlikely that I laughed. "Well, Detroit's a kind of Babylon, too."

"Cudjoe no Rasta. Him no friend to I an' I. Ganja de only t'ing Cudjoe and I agree on. Him a trader, maybe de biggest in Jamaica."

"Listen, it's important."

"Don't ask, mon. Maybe it better you doan find him. You look like a hard one, Shuter, but you not ready for Cudjoe. Nobody ready for him."

Further discussion seemed pointless; he wasn't going to draw me any maps. I held out a folded $100-bill.

"No, mon. Keep de money." He kept his eyes down.

I reached over and tucked the bill into his jacket pocket. "It's getting late. What do you say we go?"

"You go. I stayin' a while." He tried to smile, but didn't quite make it.

"I'm at the Coconut Cove if you change your mind."

"Walk good, Shuter."

I left him in the gathering dusk, with his whisky and his conscience.


Night was closing in fast, the way it does in the tropics. I parked the car and went up to my suite. No one had been nosing around. I put on a beige linen suit, splashed some vodka over ice, and asked the switchboard to get me Toronto.

Sam Chung answered on the second ring.

"The boss home, Sam?"

"Ahh, Michael! What a splendid connection! You might be in the next room."

"Yeah. Well, I'm not."

"Mr. McGregor is in his study. Are you enjoying the Caribbean?"

"So far so good. I've had a swim and bought a piece of coral."

"Coral, you say?"

"A lion's head. It's quite good."

"Fascinating," said Sam. "Coral, of course, is a calcareous substance. It consists of the continuous skeleton secreted by many tribes of coelenterate polyps for their habitation and support. It can be quite beautiful. The largest known accumulation of coral is the Great Barrier Reef off Australia, and it is a little-known fact that ..."

"Sam! Will you put me through to McGregor, please?"

McGregor came on, sounding calmer than he had in the past couple of days. "How's it going?"

"Not much to report, although there is definitely some kind of flap on. Security was tight at Sangster and there was a roadblock on the Negril highway. There's no sign of Carol yet, but I've established that her boyfriend is something of a villain. A dope dealer from Detroit."

"That doesn't sound good."

"Frankly, I expected something of the sort. Carol's probably one of those kids who think there's something romantic about the guys in that business."

"Did you have a good flight?"

"It was okay."

"Only okay? What was wrong? Were the meals all right? Was..."

"Take it easy, Douglas. It was all terrific."

He hung up with a grunt, and I asked the hotel switchboard to connect me with NTN.

Bishop sounded grouchy, too. "Well, the traveller's pal. What happened, Shuter? The sun go down?"

"Spectacularly. Why?"

"You're on the phone, not lolling on the beach, so it must be after dark."

"I've been working. What's up?"

"Unemployment's up. To eight point three per cent, seasonally adjusted. Of course, Nesbitt wants to lead with it, but I've got a perfectly good prison riot running out in British Columbia."

"Anything new on Lucky?"

"Susan has been nosing around the West Indian community, but we haven't got an angle. The story just doesn't rate nationally. The Toronto papers are having a field day, though. They've been raging on about Metro's night of the long knives and the murderous men making millions in the marijuana market. Gawd, but the *Star* loves alliteration!"

"Okay," I said. "Hold the fort."

He broke the connection with a click that echoed 1,800 miles down the line.

# CHAPTER EIGHT

# Night One (Friday) – 8:55 P.M.

One of the hazards of travelling alone is you tend to log a lot of bar time. The trick is to pace yourself. Man is a social beast and bars tend to be sociable places – warm, secure from dragons, and offering the prospect of companionship. They also offer good things to drink.

By the time I walked into the Coconut Cove's cocktail lounge, most of the guests were already in the dining area. But a handful of dawdlers were keeping the steward company, including the two young women I'd seen at the beach bar.

I ordered a vodka martini, extra-dry with a twist. While the steward was stirring it, I inspected the women, more from force of habit than curiosity. They were attractive, wearing casual clothes that showed off their holiday tans. There was no sign of husbands or boyfriends, which suggested they'd travelled on their own, a slightly more sophisticated version of the Carol-and-Patsy expedition.

Unattached women used to be an oddity at holiday resorts, but today they represent almost a quarter of the market. Equally important, they stimulate travel by unattached men. McGregor, a Presbyterian, is loath to admit it, but sex has all but overtaken sunshine as a sales aid in our business. The Pill and the rise of the independent woman have had nearly as much to do with today's travel boom as the development of the low-cost package and wide-bodied aircraft. If the Pill gave women the opportunity to enjoy a rich sex life without fear of pregnancy, the Pill-on-holiday has given them the chance to act out their fantasies free from emotional responsibility. On balance, it's been a positive development, although from time to time the new morality clashes unhappily with old conventions and people, usually the immature ones, get hurt. Carol, perhaps, would turn out to be a case in point.

My martini was cold and sharp, and it started my salivary glands pumping. I glanced along the bar and caught one of the young women looking at me. I held her eye, we both grinned, and I raised my glass.

"Good evening."

"Hi!" she said brightly. "Having fun?"

"Always."

"Lucky you."

Susan Quill had used the same phrase when I'd told her I was off to Jamaica.

"May I offer you ladies a drink?" Another good thing about bars; they help break more ice than they serve.

"That would be nice."

I signalled for fresh daiquiris, picked up my martini, and moved along to join them.

"Mike Shuter. From Toronto."

"I'm Linda Ames," said the one who'd been doing the talking. "This is Vicki Sullivan. We're from Bahston."

Linda had jet-black hair and a light dusting of freckles over a turned-up nose; her brown eyes hinted at mischief. Vicki had dark red hair and blue eyes; she also had a figure that would have kept Paul Revere home nights and the American colonies British. Both women appeared to be in their late twenties, and neither wore a wedding band.

"I saw you on the beach," said Linda, smiling. "Muscles." She struck a Charles Atlas pose and patted her biceps.

"Enjoying your holiday?"

"It's been great," said Vicki mechanically. "The hotel and beach are super."

"We haven't met any men," Linda pouted. "Everyone seems to be in twosomes."

Vicki glared at her friend. "Linda, we agreed. We wanted to be left alone."

"You said 'not bothered'. You didn't say anything about solitary confinement." Linda grinned up at me. "Anyway we go home on Sunday."

"To Bawston," I said, not getting the New England accent quite right.

"So tell us what it's like to be oot and aboot in Tuhronna, eh?" Linda said.

Except for recent *émigrés* from Glasgow, I've never heard anyone say "oot" or "aboot" in Canada, although Americans insist that's how we talk. But Linda was pretty close with her pronunciation of Toronto and dead-on with the "eh," so I said: "That's not bad. Have you spent some time in Canada?"

"Just Montreal. For the Olympics. But a friend of mine is a Canadian. From Ontario. We used to laugh at each other's accents. He played for Bahston College, had a try-out with the Broons." She frowned at the memory. "He didn't make it."

We chatted for a while about Boston, Toronto, and hockey. Like so many New Englanders, they were hockey fanatics. Their idea of a dream date was a Bruins game, followed by dinner at Jason's.

"I saw Bobby Orr there once," said Vicki in the wistful tone other women might reserve for Robert Redford or Rod Stewart. "He was having a steak with some of the players. It's a shame he can't play any more."

We were still discussing Number Four's miserable medical luck, and his remarkable career, when Ivan, the maitre d', came into the bar.

"Good to see you again," he said, shaking my hand. "It's been a while."

"How have you been?"

He shrugged. "Busy. Endless staff problems."

"Come on, Ivan. This place almost runs itself."

"There are days, Mr. Shuter," he said, smiling at Linda and Vicki, "when I think Coconut Cove is straight out of *Don't Stop The Carnival*."

I offered him a drink, but he declined. "Maybe later. Aren't you having dinner?"

"Shortly," I said. "By the way, have you still got the horses?"

"Of course."

"Can you book me one for morning? Six-thirty?"

"Consider it done."

Linda was looking at me sceptically. "A horse? Can you ride one?"

"Can he ride?" Ivan laughed, turning to go. "Mr. Shuter used to be a Mountie."

For some reason, Vicki and Linda were amused by Mounties. They launched into a series of one-liners about Rose Marie, Nelson Eddy, the Yukon, Eskimo pies, King of the Royal Mounted, and whether I always got my man.

"I always get mine," Linda chuckled.

Enough. I reached into my pocket, found a Canadian $50-bill and put it on the bar, face down. The scene on the back was an artist's depiction of the RCMP Musical Ride — thirty-two lancers on horseback, forming a circle.

"See there?" I said, pointing. "That's me, dead centre. Me and Giddy."

"Giddy?" said Linda.

"My horse. As in giddyup."

They peered at the bill doubtfully.

"The Musical Ride," I went on. "Calgary Stampede, nineteen sixty-three."

They studied it some more. "It doesn't look like you," said Linda, finally.

"The guy was a lousy artist."

Our drinks were nearly finished and I was starving. Before the level of repartee could sink any lower, I invited them to join me for dinner. Linda accepted promptly but Vicki seemed reluctant.

"Were you really in the Musical Ride?" Linda asked. "I saw it on television once. It was terrific."

"I was just kidding."

"But you were a Mountie?"

"For more than fifteen years, during one of which I practically lived with a horse. As I remember it, he lived better than I did."

"Giddy," she said, smiling.

"Actually, his name was Max."

"What do you do now?"

"I work for an airline."

They regarded me with heightened interest. To them, the airline business was glamorous; almost as glamorous, I suppose, as rock music or pro hockey. People have strange ideas about airlines and the men and women who work for them, ideas involving romance and freedom and intrigue associated with faraway places. In truth, there's very little glamour, romance, freedom, or intrigue. Travel can be as boring as an assembly line, if you do it all the time; ask any member of the jet set – or any stewardess.

Standing at the entrance to the dining area with a good-looking woman on either side, I felt a bit like Hugh Hefner, who seems incapable of appearing in public without being wrapped in a thick security blanket fashioned out of *lapin*. While we waited for Ivan, several of the guests looked at us curiously, including the two middle-aged couples I'd seen at the beach bar. They were wrecked again, giggling foolishly and grumbling about the quality of the wine. One of the women was wearing a tiny maple leaf pin. Vicki and Linda seemed not to notice them, but I shuddered; they were the type of Canadian tourists who've been giving Americans a bad name around the world for years.

The night was flawless. A half-moon glowed pale in a black sky salted with stars. The on-shore breeze continued to blow softly, but the air was still warm. On the terrace, three or four couples were dancing to a group called Silly and the Children of Jah.

Ivan led us to a table for four, helping Vicki and Linda settle into their chairs. He distributed menus, which they examined without enthusiasm. I sent him off in search of a bottle of Puligny Montrachet, and smiled at Linda: "Aren't you hungry?"

"I guess so. The food's good here, but it's a bit bland."

"They have to cater to the North American palate."

"Well," she smiled, "I'd give my arm, if not my all, for a Big Mac."

"You sound like Patsy," I said, laughing.

"Is that your wife?" She sneaked the question in casually with an ease born of long practice.

"No. A girl I know."

Linda decided not to push it. "Oh."

A waiter arrived with the wine and an ice bucket. I asked what the chef had in the kitchen, and he pointed impassively at the menu; veal *cordon bleu*, for God's sake, and roast pork.

"What else have you got? What are *you* having for supper tonight?"

He grinned as understanding dawned. "Chef makin' some Stamp and Go, sah! And there's some Run Down."

"With the bananas in?"

"Yes, sah!"

"Sounds good. We'll have the Stamp and Go, some pumpkin soup, bammies, and the Run Down with rice and peas."

"Very good, sah!"

Linda and Vicki were staring at me, lost. "What was all that about?" Linda asked.

"Stamp and Go is an appetizer. Cod fritters. You'll like them. Pumpkin soup is a national delicacy and bammies are thin breads made with casava flour. Run Down is fresh mackerel, cooked with green bananas in coconut milk and

116

Jamaican spices. Rice and peas, of course, is really kidney beans and rice."

The meal was delicious. Linda ate heartily, although her friend just pushed food around her plate. Linda and Vicki worked in the claims department of a New England insurance company, did a fair amount of travelling and were starting to wonder whether their careers were worth doing without a husband and a houseful of kids somewhere in the suburbs.

I asked the waiter to bring us fresh fruit and Blue Mountain coffee. Vicki, who hadn't said much during dinner, pleaded a headache and asked to be excused.

"You two have fun. I'm not feeling very well."

I offered to walk Vicki back to her room but she wouldn't hear of it. "No, no. I'm okay. Enjoy your coffee."

When I sat down again, Linda's mood turned serious. "I hope you're not upset. Vicki's usually a lot of fun, but she's kind of depressed right now. She just broke up with a guy." She shook her head slowly. "You know, love gets people in more trouble than almost anything, except maybe cars."

"Cars?"

"Everybody gets into trouble with cars." She paused. "Are you married, Mike?"

"I was. My wife died."

"Oh, I'm sorry." People always say they're sorry; it's such a dumb word.

"Did you love her very much?" And women always ask that question. What do they expect? A denial?

I didn't say anything. We sat in silence, listening to the music. I thought of Janet, and the fun we'd had on our last visit to Negril: swimming, scuba-diving, spear-fishing, tennis, early-morning rides, making love. Something must have showed in my face, because I became aware of a small, warm hand covering mine, squeezing it.

"Are you okay?" Linda asked softly. Then: "Hey! It's okay."

"I'm fine." I looked at my watch; Ras Daniel awaited.

"Linda, I have to go next door, to Negril Beach Village. It's business, I'm afraid. But if you'd like to come along, we could have a nightcap."

She beamed. "I'd like that. We went there one night, but Vicki wasn't in the mood. It looked like fun."


Negril Beach Village is a big development aimed at swinging singles and cost-conscious young couples, a kind of vacationers' supermarket, offering a full range of facilities and services. A guest can spend his entire holiday – as well as his entire budget – on the premises. Carol and Patsy had chosen well, although Carol had also chosen to stray. Of course, Negril Beach Village's facilities and services stop short of ganja by the pound and six-foot-six studs from Detroit.

During our stroll I told Linda a bit of the Village's background. Despite its superb location and amenities – tennis courts, a huge pool, a secluded beach for nude bathing, vast drinking and dining areas, riding trail, comfortable if functional bedrooms – Negril Beach Village fell on evil days shortly after it opened. Jamaica was in the throes of political turmoil and violence, tourists were sometimes subjected to robbery or rape and there was an avalanche of negative publicity overseas. Hotel occupancy plummeted and resorts either closed or changed hands with bewildering frequency. The Jamaican government, an original investor in Negril Beach Village, eventually took the place over – lock, stock and rum-barrel. Then it turned to Canada for help.

A Toronto advertising man named Alan Murphy, a hard-drinking and highly creative Irishman, was brought in as a consultant. Murphy proposed a Club Med-type approach, to be marketed under a single word – hedonism. A poster, showing a naked female torso, wearing a strand of the plastic shark teeth the resort uses as an exchange medium, appeared all over North America. Thousands of young people saw it, and decided that hedonism was exactly what they wanted to experience on their next holiday. Negril Beach Village became a brilliant success, spawned several imitators, and helped lead Jamaican tourism out of the doldrums. Holidair, among others, was grateful for the recovery, a fact Murphy never lets me forget and one reason why he shows up so often on my expense accounts.

Linda and I had walked along the road and up the driveway, instead of taking the beach route. The buildings' exteriors were bathed in floodlights and the open-air lobby was bustling with young people. Most wore swimsuits and T-shirts or cutoffs and loose-fitting football jerseys. There are no dress rules at the village.

I bought thirty-six shark teeth for $20 at the front desk and we headed for the bar. It was on the far side of a huge dining area built around a dance floor. A few kids were dancing and a few more were eating; the charcoal grill was operating at full throttle. At the bar, a mob was downing everything from fancy cocktails, with names like Sloe Screw and Wet Dream, to Red Stripe. A five-man reggae band was blasting away from a stage. Every few moments there were shrieks from the pool, where a volleyball game was under way.

"This place is too much!" Linda laughed over the din. "It's like a Cape Cod beach party without the beach."

While we waited for a bartender to work his way toward us, we nibbled banana chips, deep-fried and tasty. The place was moving booze like the Bronfmans—by the carload. Finally, we managed to order a daiquiri and a Heineken from the harried barman.

"Is that Ras Daniel?" I asked, when he came back with our drinks.

"That's Daniel. A great singer, mon!"

I handed him my string of shark teeth. He counted off five, then moved away to mix four brown cows for four bronzed fillies, who definitely didn't need them.

Linda and I found a table where we could watch the

whoop-up and see the band. Daniel and De Lions were working hard, alternating songs I'd never heard with reggae standards made popular by Marley, Tosh, Toots, and Jimmy Cliff.

I drank some Heineken, and studied Ras Daniel. He was tall, looked strong, and wore well-pressed pale-blue slacks and a gaily-coloured sports shirt. His hair, almost light-brown, bounced in coils as he moved across the stage. The Lions were well turned out, too. They all wore dreadlocks, and they were good musicians. Daniel had a strong voice and put a lot of emotion into his songs, most of which were anguished laments or angry social commentary, always leavened by an almost childlike optimism that life would some day be better.

When the set finished, there was a surge of applause, which Daniel acknowledged with a bow, a wave, and a promise to be back shortly. I asked Linda to excuse me, left her half the shark teeth, and walked up to the singer.

"Ras Daniel?"

"Yes?" He turned slowly to see who I was and what I wanted.

"I was a friend of David Llewellyn's. He said you might be able to help me with something."

He frowned. "What do you mean 'was'? Help you with what?"

A few of his fans were listening, so I said: "Perhaps we could have a word in private."

We chose a table where no one could overhear. I introduced myself and told him about Lucky. If anything, Ras Daniel was even more upset than Doctor Black had been. His eyes clouded and he seemed to move off to another time, another space. It occurred to me that perhaps he was praying.

Finally, he spoke. "But why? Why was he killed? Ras Lucky was a fine man, a true follower of Ras Tafari."

"He was also in the ganja business. I think that's what cost him his life."

Grief distorted his handsome features. "It's not the ganja, Mr. Shuter. It's the greed it brings to some people."

Daniel spoke English almost as well as Sam Chung; albeit with a Caribbean lilt. When I asked him about it, he said bitterly: "No big t'ing, mon. I bin spendin' lotta time down de schoolhouse."

"Now you sound like Doctor Black."

"Do you know the Doctor?" he asked, reverting to standard English.

"I met him today. A nice guy, but he wouldn't talk about Cudjoe."

"Cudjoe?" Daniel's face turned stony. "Cudjoe the trader?"

I nodded.

"That ignoramus!"

I sketched in the Carol Malone situation. Daniel listened carefully, asked several pertinent questions, and, when I'd finished, nodded briskly.

"I remember Carol. It would be hard to forget her. She is extremely beautiful, for a white girl. A very good dancer. I remember her friend as well. She was too fat, but nice."

I gave him the snapshot of Cudjoe and Carol. "That was taken here on the beach."

He inspected it solemnly, then returned it.

"Let me tell you about Cudjoe. He is an American, although his mother was born in Jamaica. He is what his American brothers would call a 'bad-ass'. It might be easier to understand his anti-social behaviour if he were from a Harlem tenement or a cold-water flat in Chicago. But Cudjoe is from a middle-class background. His father is a retired foreman from the Ford Motor Company. But he sneers at the disadvantaged, makes gibes at Rastamen, and wears dreadlocks to mock us."

"Why do you suppose a girl like Carol would go off with a man like Cudjoe?"

Daniel sighed. "Why indeed? Cudjoe is very smooth, I'm

afraid. He can be amusing, and he can display a certain rak-
ish charm when he wants to win someone's approval. Also,
it takes two to play a duet. Sometimes, North American girls
come to Jamaica anxious to take up with a local man.
Usually, it is harmless enough, but sometimes people are
wounded. Some of the Jamaican boys are left hurt and
puzzled by these girls. But sometimes it is the girls who are
hurt."

"So, where do I find him?"

"Not around Negril. He only comes here occasionally to
pick up white girls. He seems to prefer them for some
reason."

"Where, then?"

"Ocho Rios. I'm not sure where he lives, but Cudjoe is
usually on the North Shore."

It was a start. We sat there, not saying anything for a few
moments. Then Daniel cleared his throat. "Am I correct in
assuming you will go to Ocho Rios?"

I nodded. "Tomorrow morning. Why?"

"Because I'd like to go with you. I have some free time.
The band always has Saturday and Sunday nights off, but
this week we're off until Wednesday. There's a reggae concert in Kingston Monday night and we've been invited to
perform."

It was tempting. With his local knowledge, Daniel might
prove useful. But I'm used to playing a lone hand. "It's a nice
idea, Daniel, but I get paid for this sort of thing. I've run into
guys like Cudjoe before."

He studied me, then grinned: "I believe you have."

"It could get heavy."

He shrugged. "I played two years on the senior rugby side
at the University of the West Indies."

Rugby is no game for creampuffs, not that Daniel looked
anything of the sort. Still, I was surprised by the university
reference; the guy was a reggae musician, a Rastaman. "Is
that where you learned such perfect English?"

122

"There, and at home. My mother is a teacher. And my father was a solicitor. He is now a member of the Court of Appeal."

"What did you study at college?"

"I have a degree in philosophy."

A philosopher, for God's sake. What was he doing here? "Why do you want to come to Ocho Rios?"

"Three reasons," he said. "First, I may be able to help. Second, David Llewellyn was my friend. And third, I do not like Sweets Jefferson."

"Who?"

"Cudjoe's real name is Jefferson. Sweetness Jefferson. In Detroit, they used to call him Sweets. But nobody laughed."

Neither did I, although the temptation was enormous. What an assignment! Tracking down a six-foot-six villain whose momma named him Sweetness! It was the most unlikely name I'd heard since Wonderful Mons broke into the Canadian Football League.

"Okay, Ras Daniel. You're on for Ocho Rios."

Linda looked angry. I'd only been away twenty minutes and she knew it was business, so she had no reason to be upset. In the meantime, she'd found a friend – a beefy-looking blond guy, who was sitting across from her.

"Sorry," I said, as Daniel and I arrived at the table. That dumb word again.

But she wasn't upset because of me. Just the reverse. "Oh, Mike! I'm so glad you're back!" Linda glared at Mr. Beef, whose smile mutated into a scowl as he looked up at us. He was drunk.

"Who's your friend?" I said to Linda.

"Well, I...I don't..." She looked at me helplessly, then shrugged.

"Go avay!" said Mr. Beef. "Ve are haffing a personal discussion here."

"We are doing no such thing!" Linda snapped. She looked furiously at Mr. Beef who got up, flexing his Vic Tanny muscles. So far, we hadn't drawn a crowd; the fun-seekers at Negril Beach Village rocked on.

I smiled at Mr. Beef. "Apparently you've upset my friend. I'm sure it's just a misunderstanding. Why not come up to the bar and I'll buy you a drink?"

"Go avay!" he repeated thickly. "And take the *schwartzer*. The *fraulein* and I do not vish to be disturbed."

"*Komm hier, Komrad*," said Daniel, who was just full of surprises. "*Wass ist los? Willst du kein Bier haben?*"

Mr. Beef looked at Daniel contemptuously, then spat. "*Rauss, schwartzer!*"

Daniel seemed unperturbed, but he probably witnessed a half-dozen incidents a month triggered by the always volatile mixture of too much booze, too much sun, and too much exposed young flesh.

"Look, Fritz," I said, no longer bothering to smile, "you're making me angry and insulting my friends. Now say good night nicely, take your beer, and screw."

He started it from somewhere in left field, a looping swing his gym instructor had probably promised would make for a one-punch fight. As it happened, his gym instructor was right.

I didn't want a lot of noise; the incident was embarrassing, and utterly pointless. So I stepped inside, slipped his haymaker, and seized his throat with my left hand. I dug in hard on either side of his larynx. He gasped, and his other hand came clawing up. Still clutching his throat, I took his other hand in my right and groped around until I had his thumb bent in a come-along hold. Steadily, I increased the pressure until his eyes began to water.

"Don't make me break it, Fritz."

The fight sagged out of him. His eyes were streaming. The thumb-hold will get through even to the worst drunks.

"Excuse me for a moment," I said to Linda, who appeared

to be in mild shock. "Perhaps you'd order me another Heineken, and offer Ras Daniel something."

Grinning broadly, Daniel settled into a chair.

"Come along, Fritz," I said drawing him forward. Holding his thumb with one hand, I draped my other arm around his shoulder and steered him toward the bar. Except for his tears and the stiff outrage in his bearing, we might have been bosom buddies, discussing the previous night's conquests. I marched him to the edge of the pool. The volleyball game had run out of steam, and there were only a few stragglers left. He started to struggle again, but a little more pressure put a stop to that.

"Next time," I said softly, "I'll hurt you. Now cool off."

I didn't look back to see whether he could swim any better than he could fight.


Linda was smiling nervously when I returned. "Are you all right?"

"Sure. He just had a few too many."

"He was being gross. I didn't know what to do, so I just waited for you to come back."

"Don't worry about it. Nothing's damaged."

"Except his dignity," Daniel laughed. "You should have seen his face when he splashed off to his room."

I grinned wryly. "How many languages do you speak?"

"I speak only love," he said. "In English, French, German, Jamaican, and music."

Daniel said he had to go back to work and we arranged to meet in the morning. Linda and I sat for a while, listening to the music. The crowd at the bar was beginning to dwindle, although the reggae fans and the determined drunks were hanging tough. Linda reached across and took my hand.

"You did that very well."

"I don't get off on rough stuff." It was the truth; it's one thing to knock villains around, quite another to manhandle randy drunks – but sometimes there's nothing else you can do.

She studied my face for a few moments. "Let's go back to the hotel."

This time we took the beach route. Linda carried her sandals in one hand and put her other arm around my waist as we walked down the grassy slope. At the bottom, we stopped on the sand and stood close, watching the moon flash silver on the water. Somewhere in the distance, a dog barked.

She sighed and murmured: "It's lovely, isn't it?"

Slowly, deliberately, I turned her face toward mine, bent down, and kissed her. She gave a little moan and then her mouth began to move under mine. Her breath was hot and her lips tasted faintly of bananas. Her body was hard and I could feel her strength as she clung to me. Finally, reluctantly, I broke off the kiss.

"It's been a very pleasant evening." Ahh, Shuter! You're such a smoothie, a real silver-tongue.

Linda chuckled deep in her throat. "It's not over yet, but you'll have to catch me!"

She spun out of my arms and began running toward our hotel, laughing. I suppressed the urge to hare after her. Instead, I stayed where I was for a few moments. Then I began walking along the beach, at a pensioner's pace.

She was waiting in the shadows by Thomas's bar.

"So," she said, feigning chagrin, "you caught me."


The threads were still in place. I turned on a lamp and moved to the fridge while Linda looked around the living room.

"Would you like champagne?" I asked.

"Are you having some?"

"Yes."

"Me too, then." She had completed her inspection. "This is nicer than our room. What's upstairs?"

"What do you think?" I popped open two splits of Veuve Clicquot and poured the wine into a couple of chilled glasses.

"Do you know what that awful man said he wanted to do to me?"

"What?" I handed her a glass and offered a silent toast.

"Exactly what I'm going to do to you – after I've had a shower."

"What's that?" I teased.

She grinned lewdly. "Why, fuck you for hours, of course. He wasn't very subtle and neither am I."

In spite of myself, I burst out laughing. It is a reflection of my age and small-town origins that I am mildly startled whenever I hear women use four-letter words. These days, I am startled quite often.

"There's nothing funny about it," Linda said sternly, starting up the stairs. "Bring the champagne."


Later, lying in the dark and sipping tepid wine, she began to giggle softly. The sweat was almost dry on our bodies and our breathing had returned to normal.

"What's so funny?" I leaned across and kissed one of her breasts, biting gently on the small, pink nipple, feeling it stiffen under my tongue.

"That's nice," she sighed. "I was just thinking about tomorrow morning."

"It's already tomorrow morning."

"No. I meant about your horse. Can you believe it? I'm jealous of a horse I don't even know."

I nibbled some more. "I don't follow."

"That horse is in for a treat..." She giggled again, then began to writhe, her legs scissoring.

"Mmm?"

"...because you're great in the saddle!" Abruptly, she reached down for me and, shifting lower, began planting warm wet kisses on my chest, then my belly. "Now, can we please have another musical ride?"

"Just as soon as you've fixed my lance."

CHAPTER NINE

## *Day Two (Saturday) — 6:45 A.M.*

The phone was insistent and it was downstairs. Half-awake and double-shaky, I rolled out of bed, knocking over an empty champagne bottle. Soft light filtered through the thin curtains, offending my eyes. Somewhere outside a bird was being unnecessarily noisy. So was the phone. With a curse, I tottered down to answer it.

"Mistah Shutah?" A woman's voice.

"Yeah."

"Front desk, sah. It's six forty-five."

"Yeah?"

"The groom's been waitin', sah."

"Oh, yeah."

"Shall I tell him you'll be comin', sah?"

"Yeah. Tell him, tell him Mr. Shuter soon come."

"Soon come." There was a smile in her voice. "Yes, sah. I'll tell him."

There was no sign of Linda. She must have sneaked back to her room before dawn; probably she hadn't wanted to run a mid-morning gauntlet of guests and staff in her evening togs.

I could use more sleep. Why hadn't I told the front desk to cancel the ride? I climbed the stairs and ruefully contemplated the rumpled bed; two more hours wouldn't hurt. Before I weakened, I forced myself to settle into my exercises.

129

Despite the abuses of the past twenty-four hours, despite the travel and the Heinekens, despite the lovely Linda's delightful demands, nothing snapped or stretched; my body wasn't damaged. An amazing piece of equipment, the human body.

Twenty minutes later, showered and feeling slightly better, I was walking across the road toward the stables. I was wearing trunks, a T-shirt and tennis shoes but already I was warm. In the early-morning light, everything was fresh-looking and lush. At least twenty shades of green were discernible in the trees, shrubs, and grass. Flowers sparkled in their dew. Later in the day, under a high sun, the subtleties would be lost to the human eye. A talented painter might capture the glory of a Jamaican morning, but I couldn't do it justice in words.

The groom, Nigel, was waiting by the small paddock. "Mornin', sah!"

"Well, what have you got for me? Something on its last legs?"

He grinned, shaking his head. "I saddled Molasses, Mistah Shuter. She's a good mare, eight years old and sure-footed."

He disappeared into the stable. I leaned against the paddock rail and chewed a blade of grass. I was hungry. Sex is not only good for the circulation; it's good for the appetite. I decided to keep the ride short and have a long breakfast.

Nigel emerged leading a good-looking beast. Molasses was dark brown and there was some desert in her background. A hunter from the look of her; certainly she'd never pulled a milk-wagon.

"Molasses, sah!" He was proud of her.

She looked at me with a wary eye, wondering whether I was going to be another incompetent tourist, yanking her head back and forth and trying not to fall off.

I patted her neck and stroked her nose and after a few moments she relaxed. I checked the cinch and bridle, then swung up into the English saddle. I sat there for a minute, letting her get used to my weight. Then I gave her a touch with my tennis shoes. She moved off at a brisk walk, satisfied that I could stay aboard.

We walked along the road toward town for about a quarter-mile, then swung through a field toward the sea. The beach was virtually deserted. Sensible people were still in bed with their lovers or their hangovers. A solitary jogger came toward us and seemed to inspire Molasses. She broke into a trot without being asked, hooves splashing in the wet sand by the water's edge.

Negril Beach extends almost unbroken for seven miles. But where brooks run into the sea, trees grow right out into the water, and riders or beachcombers must choose between wading almost waist-deep or picking their way through dense brush. Molasses seemed to like the sea, so we waded at the barriers.

I asked her for a canter and she responded immediately. We bounced along past the Negril Sands Club, a beach bar where Janet and I used to linger. A few yards farther on, three teenage boys lolled, waiting to go out to the reef to hunt for kingfish, snapper, bonito, jackfish, or anything else they could hit. Their spearguns stood upright in the sand beside a small home-built rowboat in need of a paint job. They waved as we romped by.

After another quarter-mile or so, I slowed Molasses to a walk. We waded around another tree break, and I was glad I hadn't weakened and gone back to bed. The sea air had cured my headache.


Like Al Stewart's dreamgirl in "The Year of The Cat," they came out of the sun, running like a watercolour in the rain. But they weren't wearing silk dresses; they were wearing dreadlocks and waving machetes.

Both riders were coming hard and they didn't look friendly. Who were they? And what did they want? An early-morning chat? I wasn't particularly keen to find out. In trunks and a T-shirt, I was defenceless against machetes.

They were less than a hundred yards away now, yelling like Comanches and riding like Roy Rogers on one of his better days.

I wheeled Molasses around and she moved smoothly up through the gears into a full gallop. Her ears were laid right back and her hooves thundered across the sand. I looked over my shoulder, like Sandy Hawley with a comfortable lead over the field. Our lead wasn't that comfortable and they were closing it. Molasses was no match for stallions.

We approached a tree break only about fifty yards ahead of the Comanches. Molasses didn't hesitate. She swung away from the shoreline, charged straight up the bank, and crashed through the bushes. She sailed over a fallen tree and a small brook, clearing them like a Grand National champion. Then she burst out of the underbrush and hit the beach again. I didn't even have to steer.

We'd gained a little but Molasses couldn't keep this up. The sand stretched out before us; there was no help in sight, no place to hide. They were gaining again and I began to think we'd be better off taking our chances across rough ground.

As we neared the Negril Sands Club, I could see the teen-agers standing, staring at what must have been a ludicrous spectacle. They were shouting something but I couldn't hear over the noise of Molasses' hooves. I saw a slim chance, and I'd have to get it right the first time.

I steered Molasses toward the rowboat and leaned over, holding the saddle tightly with one hand. As we flashed by, I grabbed one of the spearguns. Mercifully, I didn't drop it. It was a wicked-looking affair with a long bolt. It seemed to be in perfect working order.

Right, then. Now we'd see what they were made of.

Holding the speargun low, I tugged on the reins but

Molasses didn't want to stop. She probably thought I'd gone crazy. "Whoa!" I shouted, pulling harder, and this time she obeyed.

Sensing a kill, the machete men stopped too, preparing to administer the *coup de grâce*.

Keeping the speargun out of sight, I snapped its nylon line. Then I wheeled Molasses around.

They broke into a trot, raising their weapons. Molasses was trembling. I touched her with my heels and she bolted forward. Gripping her with my knees, I reached down and primed the speargun. Then I let out a war-whoop, which startled her into a full gallop.

It startled them, too.

They were trotting but I was charging, like John Wayne in *True Grit*. The distance closed fast and one of them began to hesitate. But the other came steadily on, looking determined.

At twenty yards I raised the speargun, aiming at the lead rider. Fear twisted his face as he realized what I was doing. His machete wavered but it was too late for evasive action.

Then, with a curse and a prayer, I squeezed the trigger.

The bolt caught him in the shoulder. Blood spurted and he screamed, dropping his weapon.

I was already turning the gun around, gripping it with both hands like a club. In a blink, we were on the other one, just out of reach of his machete. I hit him a solid whack on the head. He screamed too. They were great screamers, these cutthroats.

Molasses and I wheeled around, ready for another charge. But they'd had enough. So had Molasses, God love her. She was covered with lather and her chest was heaving. Together, we watched them flee across a field.

I had been pumping adrenalin by the quart and I began to tremble. Would John Wayne shake? Never. But here I was, covered in goose-flesh under a tropical sun, shaking like a ten-A.M. vodka drinker.

I dismounted and we walked along the beach until we

reached the abandoned machete. As I bent over to pick it up, Molasses shied; she'd seen enough of machetes for one morning. Taking the big knife by its handle, I threw it as far as I could. It arced out over the water, blade flashing in the sun, and disappeared with a small splash.

"Hey! Mon!"

The teenagers, who had been distant witnesses to our weird jousting, were running toward us. "Hey, mon! My gun!"

I swung into the saddle again and waited. They stopped a few yards away, not wanting to get too close to a crazy man.

"Here." I tossed the speargun to the one who seemed most worried about it.

"But de shaft, mon! It gone! Dey cost money!"

True enough. "What's your name?"

"Trevor."

"Okay, Trevor. My name's Shuter and I'm at the Coconut Cove. Come by the desk and there'll be some money for you."

"But, mon..."

I touched Molasses with my heels and we trotted off. Neither of us felt much like answering questions.

Nigel ambled out as we came into the yard. I dismounted, patted Molasses, and handed over the reins. He looked suspiciously at the traces of lather but made no comment. Molasses snorted with pleasure when he slid the saddle from her back.

Finally: "A good ride, sah?"

"Thrilling."

He nodded uncertainly, and stroked the horse. "Thrilling, sah?"

"Yes," I said firmly. "Look, Nigel, I'd like you to do something for me. Come over to the hotel in an hour. There'll be an envelope at the front desk. You'll find a hundred dollars in it."

He looked at me doubtfully; a hundred dollars was more than he earned in a month.

"Half is for you. The rest is for Molasses. Apples, sugar, whatever she likes. It should keep her in treats for a year. Will you do that?"

He beamed. "Yes, sah!"

"You were right. She's a very good horse."


I stood under the shower and tried to make sense out of it. The horsemen had to be part of Cudjoe's operation; no other explanation was possible. But why attack me? And how did they know where to find me? Obviously I was being watched. But it had to be long-range surveillance; I'd have picked up a tail in about thirty seconds.

Had Doctor Black snitched? I doubted it, and I was confident that neither Thomas nor Ras Daniel had said anything. Whatever the explanation, there was opposition in the field, opposition large and flexible enough to run a surveillance team and mount an instant operation.

All I wanted to do was talk to Carol. Why would Cudjoe be worried about that? As I rinsed off the soap I had a salacious thought: Carol was beautiful by any man's standard; perhaps she was so good in the sack that Cudjoe would do anything to keep her. Men often do crazy things because of women.


At the front desk I arranged envelopes for Molasses and Trevor. Fifty bucks should buy the kid the world's best spear-fishing outfit.

Vicki was having breakfast on the terrace. She was wearing shorts, a tank top, huge sunglasses, and a tentative smile.

"Feeling better?"

"Much, thank you."

"Where's Linda?" I took a chair.

"Dead to the world." She removed her glasses and peered at me, calculation in her eyes. "I think she came in very late."

I shrugged. If Linda wanted to exchange confidences with her friend I had no objection; but I've never been one to kiss and tell. A waiter shuffled up with a coffee pot. I asked for melon, dolphin (not the kind that delight children at Marineland, but a local fish that is delicious smoked), and scrambled eggs.

"You eat a lot," said Vicki, "but you're not fat."

"I burn it off."

"I'm sure you do." Another speculative look.

She drank a cup of coffee while I ate. Vicki said she and Linda planned to spend their final day at Negril buying souvenirs. I said I was going to Ocho Rios and wouldn't be back before they left. She nodded absently, apparently inured to the fleeting nature of holiday friendships.

Daniel walked up, carrying a small British Airways flight bag.

"You're early," I said. "Have you had breakfast?"

"Yes. I thought we might as well get away as soon as possible."

It was eight-thirty – time to get moving. I told Vicki I'd leave Linda a note at the front desk and we said goodbye. I had to pack.

"You've slept on it," I said to Daniel, when we reached the suite. "Are you sure you want to come?"

"Of course."

"The situation has changed."

I told him why.

Daniel was more amused than alarmed. "Do you mean you had a fight on horseback? I wish I'd seen it, especially when you turned around and charged. It sounds like something out of *Camelot*."


At the desk, I made arrangements to hold my suite indefinitely. I retrieved my cash, asked the clerk to book for two at Sans Souci for the night, and requested a piece of paper and a manila envelope. I wrote:

Dear Linda,

Daniel and I are on the road to Ocho Rios. I won't be back until after your flight. Vicki says you're going souvenir hunting today. This coral carving can start your collection — and remind you of our night among the Lions. When you get home, please call my office (416-961-2000) and leave your phone numbers with my secretary. I'll call when I get back. Maybe we can go to a Bruins game one night. Meantime, a safe journey and may all your rides be musical.

Shuter.

I put the note and Dr. Black's carving into the envelope. Would Linda call? Sometimes people undergo personality changes on vacation, then revert when they get home. In Boston, Linda might be as shy as the old maid who blundered into a nudist camp — but I doubted it.

# CHAPTER TEN

# *Day Two (Saturday) – 9:20 A.M.*

For the first twenty miles, I checked the rear-view mirror, and twice I pulled off the road and waited. Nothing. If anyone was following us, he had to be a duppy driving a phantom vehicle.

The run from Negril to Ocho Rios is 114 miles, a major journey in Jamaica, where the best roads are only fair. Occasionally, we were slowed by trucks hauling bananas but at least there were no cane carriers on the move; they wouldn't start cutting on the sugar plantations for another month.

We rolled through the tiny communities of Green Island, Lucea, and Sandy Bay, listening to news reports and music from the Jamaica Broadcasting Company studios in Kingston. The music was more interesting than the news, most of which seemed to be about the latest achievements of government ministers.

Jamaicans use their highways as social centres, gathering in small groups to gossip, talk business, or speculate about the occupants of passing cars. They also use them as commercial centres. All along the route, roadside optimists were offering everything from ackees and breadfruit to aluminum pots and pans. Almost every small-holding had a hand-printed sign out, trying to sell something: puppies, kittens, eggs, goats, fish, handiwork, bananas, occasionally the small-holding itself.

"Sometimes," I said to Daniel, "I think the entire island is for sale."

"Poor places always are."

"The philosopher speaks."

"It's not very original, but it's true, especially here in Babylon. Only the rich can afford to own things."

"I've seen the signs: 'The poor can't stand no more.' Right?"

"Right." He grinned. "That is the title of my new song. We are going to introduce it to Kingston Monday night."

"Speaking of rich people," I said, pointing to an imposing set of gates, "you'll find a few down there."

We were passing Round Hill, an exclusive and super-secure resort on the outskirts of Montego Bay. Jackie Onassis stays there and it may be a measure of Round Hill's clientele that the other guests hardly give her a second look.

"Not many Jamaicans," said Daniel, "and certainly no Rastamen."

"Tell me something, Daniel. With your background, you ought to be well on your way to becoming a leader in this country. There can't be many young Jamaican guys with your advantages. But here you are, singing for tourists and promoting the Rastas."

He leaned forward and switched off the radio. "You sound like my father. He doesn't understand either, although he is less upset about my religion than about my music. He wants me to study law."

"What do you tell him?"

"That I'm a musician. He says, 'If you want to be a musician, be a good one. Go to New York and study at Juilliard.' But I am a Jamaican and I want to play the music of Jamaica. It would be pointless for me to perform the music of a Mozart or even a McCartney. What do they know of Jamaica? And what do Jamaicans care about springtime in Europe or young lust in Liverpool?"

"So you play reggae? 'The melodies of Europe set to the rhythms of Africa?'"

"That's right. Reggae is the people's music. It speaks to them and for them. Reggae is the music of love and hope and, sometimes, anger. The people understand it. If you had ever been to a Bob Marley concert, so would you."

"Understand what?"

"Bob can *move* the people. No politician, no industrialist can ever hope to have as much impact. Not here, anyway. And our leaders are beginning to realize the power of reggae, to see that music can be a tremendous force for good."

I wondered. Most politicians I know are leery of parallel powers and delight in cutting their figureheads down to size. The memory of the War Measures Act, imposed on Canada in the fall of 1970, when a bunch of loonies kidnapped a British diplomat and murdered a Quebec cabinet minister, was all too fresh. I recalled with a shudder the way some of my fellow-officers in Quebec had reacted to their wildly enhanced authority: kicking in doors at four-forty in the morning, hauling folk singers, poets, penniless writers, any-one they thought odd or out of step, off to the jails with the explicit approval of the politicians. In the end, of course, the RCMP had caught the kidnappers and killers by routine police methods; no special powers were needed. But the politicians didn't seem to care. In fact, their popularity zoomed among the very people whose rights they'd abro-gated. Would Jamaica's leaders and police be any different in a crisis, real or apprehended? Or would a Bob Marley hear the crunch of a policeman's boot in the middle of the night, the way a Pauline Julien had, one brisk October morning in 1970?

"Do you really think," I asked, "that the authorities would ever take a back seat to a musician?"

Daniel nodded. "Marley once forced the Prime Minister and the leader of the opposition to shake hands. The two men were bitter enemies, hadn't exchanged a civil word for months. But such is the power of reggae that they didn't dare refuse. It was a concert in Kingston. I was there. Thousands of Rastamen cheered, because we understood what Bob was doing, what he was saying. To borrow from one of your distinguished countrymen, Professor McLuhan, the message and the medium were identical: love. That is what the Rastas play and preach—love."

"If the Rastas are into love in such a big way they choose unusual methods of expressing it—looting and burning, flouting the law, and waging bloody warfare against the cops."

Daniel made no reply. Instead, he leaned forward and turned on the radio again.

The roadblock was set up on the outskirts of Falmouth, a market town. Police on either side of the highway were stopping and searching all vehicles.

"What do you suppose they're looking for?"

"Excitement, probably," Daniel sighed. "They're mostly blue-stripers."

"What?"

"Blue-stripers. The police with red stripes on their trousers are regular officers. The ones with blue stripes are the auxiliary, sort of part-time constables. They're even more officious than the regulars."

When we reached the head of the line, I produced my passport and driver's licence, handing them to the red-striper in charge. He smiled pleasantly at me, then began frowning at Daniel.

"Out," he said, with a jerk of the head.

The cop frisked Daniel, then studied his ID. Apparently satisfied he hadn't captured a Rasta terrorist, he told Daniel to get back into the car.

"What's the problem?" I asked.

"Open the boot, please."

He looked into the trunk but made no effort to inspect our bags, which meant they were looking for a person, not contraband.

When we were under way again, Daniel seemed unsettled, as though the roadblock had unnerved him.

"Don't let 'em get you down, Daniel. They're just doing a job."

"They've been doing their job with far too much enthusiasm," he said hotly. "Many people have become angry in the past few days. There has been a great deal of police activity. Many Rastamen have been detained. Some of the militants in Kingston are threatening reprisals. That's why we're giving the concert Monday. To try to calm everyone down. No one wants any more trouble."

We zipped through Discovery Bay, where Columbus made his landfall in 1494, the first of three occasions on which he discovered Jamaica. When poor old Chris dropped anchor, his ship was attacked by Arawak Indians. But their spears and canoes were no match for even a single cannon, just as the Arawak people themselves were no match for European greed and germs. The Arawaks fell quickly into extinction, like the Beothuks of Newfoundland. But at least no one had ever hunted Arawaks for sport, the way the whites had reportedly hunted the gentle Beothuks.

At Dunn's River Falls, probably Jamaica's most photographed beauty spot, I slowed the car. The river cascades more than a hundred feet down an escarpment, dropping in gradual steps. For a dollar, tourists can join a guided party and clamber up the falls. Janet and I had done it once, loving the cool water around our ankles as it rushed over mossy boulders. As usual there were dozens of cars and buses parked along the road today, and the hawkers and carvers were out in force with their tacky souvenirs. Unless some controls are imposed, the beauty of Dunn's River Falls will soon be destroyed. Right now, it's one more prop for Daniel's thesis that poor places are always for sale.

We passed the Reynolds bauxite facility and continued

into Ocho Rios—the name comes from the Spanish for "eight rivers"—with its hotels, boutiques, and busy market. The Sans Souci was on the far side of town.

"Hungry?" I asked, switching off the engine.

Daniel nodded.

"Me too. Let's check in and get some lunch. Then we'll go find your pal."

"Sweetness?"

"And light."

For the first time since the roadblock, Daniel smiled.


The girl at the reception desk had a warm greeting for me and a flicker of doubt for Daniel. "Your suite is ready, Mr. Shuter. We've given you a two-bedroom penthouse." She shuffled some papers. "There is also an urgent message for you. From Toronto. You are asked to call a Mr. McGregor immediately."

"Thank you," I said. "Could you arrange for some sandwiches and a half-dozen cold Heinekens to be brought up to our room?"

"Certainly, sah. What kind of sandwiches?"

I looked at Daniel. "Cold roast beef be okay? I know you Rastas have some dietary restrictions."

Daniel nodded. "Basically, we stick to a vegetarian regimen. But the only meat that is totally prohibited is pork. And, of course, shellfish, snails, and the like. Cold roast beef will be fine."

The girl smiled at him uncertainly. "I'll see to the sandwiches right away."

We followed a bellhop through the lobby, across the pool terrace, and along a garden path. There is only one word for the Sans Souci: opulent. It is built into the side of a cliff, has magnificent gardens and romantic pathways, two pools (one at sea-level, the other on the terrace fifty feet above), and even an elevator to deliver guests to and from the beach. The hotel has been partially converted into condominium apartments, many of which are owned by Americans, Canadians, and Britons who make them available as hotel accommodation. The Sans Souci has a superb dining room and one of the Caribbean's most ambitious wine cellars. Of course, it charges breathtaking prices.

Our suite was on the ocean side of a four-storey building, one of several scattered through the grounds. It was arranged on two floors. The lower level consisted of a large living room and kitchen, plus a covered balcony set up as an open-air dining room; upstairs were two large bedrooms, each with its own bath, as well as a vast terrace.

"This place must cost a fortune," Daniel muttered.

I shrugged. "Expense-account living. Take your choice of bedrooms. I've got to call the man who's paying our bills."

"Be nice to him," he laughed. "His generosity has enabled me to establish a first."

"What's that?"

"Unquestionably, I am the first Rasta ever to stay at the Sans Souci."

"No burning," I grinned. "And no looting. We're both to be on our best behaviour."

"Not even a towel," he promised.


McGregor answered on the second ring. He sounded testy. "Where have you been?"

"On the road."

"I've been trying to reach you all morning."

"What's the problem?"

"The Toronto papers are full of Jamaica."

"Anything about Carol?"

"No. The *Star* has a big story about ganja on the front page, entitled 'The Jamaican Connection: What It Means to Metro', but even a ten-year-old can tell there isn't a fact in it. It's just fluff and conjecture, with a limp follow-up on Llewellyn's murder."

"That's okay."

144

"And the *Globe and Mail* has a story in its entertainment section saying a group of reggae stars are planning a concert in an attempt to quell mounting unrest in Kingston's slums."

I chuckled. "I know all about that. In fact, one of the performers, Ras Daniel, is with me right now."

"A Rasta? In the Sans Souci?"

"He's a bit surprised too."

"I want a progress report. How close are we getting? What am I going to tell Alan today? And what are you doing in Ocho Rios?"

Who did he think I was? Superman? Sherlock Holmes? It's always the same: the guy in the field busts his ass while his control sits home in the bunker, bitching.

"Tell Malone whatever you like. I'm in Ocho Rios because this is where Cudjoe hangs out. I know his real name now, and what he does. And I've only been in the country twenty-four hours."

"Do you expect to wrap it up soon?"

"I hope so."

"So do I," he said flatly.

"Yeah. Listen, Douglas. How come you answered the phone? Where's Sam?"

He snorted. "Out spending his *mah-jongg* winnings."

"Got you again, huh?"

"Worse, he left me to prepare my own lunch. He's hosting a luncheon at the Faculty Club in honour of Northrop Frye. Poor Frye. Sam has decided the good professor is finally beginning to understand the Tragedies."

"You're joking."

"If only."


Our sandwiches and beer had arrived while I was on the phone, and Daniel had politely waited until I was free before even opening a beer. Now he poured one for each of us, and regarded me with concern. "Bad news?"

"Not really. Just a grouchy boss."

The beer was ice cold, and the sandwiches deserved a spread in *Gourmet*. While we ate, we discussed how we'd proceed. Daniel felt he'd do better on his own, prowling around. "No offence, Mike, but if it's a question of local colour, you're the wrong shade."

"Okay. I'll see the cops. They're sure to know Cudjoe, if everybody in Negril knows he's a trader. But first, I want to take a shower and change my shirt."

I showed Daniel how I rigged the burglar alarm, telling him that if he came back to the room on his own he was to remove the Do Not Disturb sign. That way, I'd know who'd been in and save myself a lot of sweat.

"Very cloak-and-dagger," he said, as we got into the car.

"An ounce of prevention. Now keep your wits about you. Don't do anything silly."

I dropped him outside a cozy-looking pub on the main drag. It was called Polly's, had a green parrot sign hanging over the door, and claimed to be air-conditioned. We agreed to meet there in ninety minutes.


It was a slow day at the Ocho Rios cop shop, a sturdy building reeking of disinfectant and needing paint. The desk constable was dozing in his swivel chair, half-listening to the radio and waiting for his shift to end. A long-forgotten mug of tea sat cold on the blotter. Overhead, a big fan rotated lethargically, inadequate to its task. Somewhere in the back of the building, a phone rang unheeded.

Two heavy-set women, wearing home-sewn cotton dresses and matching bandanas, were slumped on a wooden bench. They looked stunned and weary, and might have been sitting in any police station or emergency ward on earth. Locations may change and personal tragedies vary, but once matters are in the hands of the cops or the medics everyone runs to form. Whatever crises had brought them here – missing husbands, jailed sons, ravaged daughters,

146

stolen property – the two women had nothing left to do now but wait and worry.

"Good afternoon, constable."

He opened one eye to see who had dared disturb his rest. Satisfied I was merely a member of the public, he closed it again, yawned and stretched.

"I said, good afternoon."

"Yes, sah?" There was resentment in his tone, and boredom.

"Is the inspector here?"

"It Satiddy." Exasperation now; everyone knew the brass didn't work weekends.

"Well, who's the senior officer on duty?"

"De sergeant." Reluctantly, he sat up straight, in case I proved to be important after all.

I took a business card from my wallet. He looked at it for a while, as if suspecting forgery.

"I'd like to see the sergeant."

"What about?" He'd been trained to head off as many problems as possible.

"I'll explain that to him."

I offered him no further enlightenment, but simply stood there, arms folded, waiting him out. With a sigh he got to his feet and walked slowly back to a door, carrying my card like a miniature search warrant. He knocked, then disappeared into an office. Thirty seconds later he emerged and motioned me forward.

The sergeant, a big man, seemed delighted to see me; perhaps the shift was moving slowly for him too. He greeted me with a firm handshake. In his short-sleeved white shirt and fawn-coloured slacks, he looked cool and competent.

"Mr. Shuter?"

"That's right."

"Patrick O'Toole."

"Talk about your black Irish!" I laughed. "With your name and build, you couldn't be anything *but* a sergeant of police."

He smiled uncertainly. "An excellent joke. Sit down and tell me how the Jamaica police can help you."

He moved around his desk and began to sink into his chair, then straightened again. "Would you like a cup of tea?"

"Very nice." I hate tea, but it seemed important to him.

O'Toole went across to the door and ordered two mugs from the constable. Then he returned to his desk and regarded me with what appeared to be polite curiosity.

There was no point in trying to be cute. "I'm looking for a guy named Sweetness Jefferson. They call him Cudjoe."

Clouds gathered at the edges of O'Toole's sunny face. "Yes?"

"From what I gather, your office would know the guy. He's the type they had in mind when they coined the phrase 'known to the police.'"

O'Toole smiled, but some of the previous warmth was missing. "That is a British expression, I believe. Scotland Yard. I once visited London on a forensic course. It was a wonderful experience for a Jamaican policeman. London is very interesting."

"Cudjoe," I said flatly. "Where is he?"

He seemed hurt that I'd interrupted his reminiscing; doubtless he'd been warming up to lead me, street by street and pub by pub, through darkest Mayfair.

"Cudjoe," he repeated. "I'm slightly confused. You are with a Toronto airline, you say?"

I nodded.

"I see."

There was a knock, and the constable came in, awkwardly carrying two steaming mugs. O'Toole greeted him as though he were a Saint Bernard and we'd been trapped on an alp.

"Ahhh, tea!" O'Toole beamed at me. "Wonderfully refreshing."

Any moment now, he'd launch into a lengthy disquisition on the history, etiquette, and various strains of the damned stuff. I put my tea, untasted, on his desk and looked at him levelly: "I was asking about Cudjoe."

"Yes. Well, you see, Mr. Shuter, I am not certain what it is you want."

I told him about Carol. I'd told the story so often now it had begun to take on the patina of a well-worn nightclub act.

"Now I see," O'Toole said, pleased with himself.

"Fine. All I want to know is where to find Cudjoe."

He gazed at me sadly. "I'm afraid I cannot help you."

"Can't? Or won't?"

"Can't. I'm not sure I like the implication in your other suggestion."

At least he was sharp. Was he on the pad? Cudjoe wouldn't be the first dope dealer to bend a cop. When I said nothing, he continued: "It is true that Cudjoe is known to police, as you say. And it is true that he often spends time in Ocho Rios. But he is not here now."

"Where, then?"

"I don't know."

"How do you know you don't know? Do you normally keep tabs on him?"

O'Toole organized his face into a poker mask. "I'm sorry, Mr. Shuter."

"Sergeant, I don't believe you."

He sighed and gazed up at the ceiling. "Perhaps the situation will change. Where are you staying in Ocho Rios?"

"The Sans Souci. Why?"

"A fine hotel."

"Thanks for the tea," I said bitterly.

"You haven't touched it." He sounded hurt again.

"I hate tea. It stains the teeth."


Sitting in the cool gloom of Polly's, waiting for Daniel, I tried to figure out O'Toole's game. He was smooth, maybe even a good cop; but I have little patience with people who waltz me around. Finally, I decided that for reasons of his own O'Toole hadn't wanted me spooking Cudjoe. Maybe the local cops were planning a bust. Well, I had news for them; Cudjoe was already spooked.

I was ordering another beer when Daniel burst in.

"Better make it two," I said to the bartender.

"I found him!" Daniel said in a harsh whisper. "He rents a house on the shore."

I clapped him on the shoulder. "Good work."

"There's more," he beamed. "Cudjoe is part-owner of a nightclub here in Ocho Rios. The Tallyman. I am told he spends most of his evenings there."

"You *have* been busy."

"And," he said grinning, "Cudjoe has a brother in the area, a man named Thomas Jefferson. You'll never guess what *he* does for a living."

"White slavery?"

"He is a clergyman!" Daniel said. "He is minister of a church near Walkers Wood."

What next? Now my gigantic villain had a pious brother, saving souls in the boonies. Cudjoe would probably turn out to have a cousin somewhere who'd won the Nobel Prize in chemistry and a sister who chaired the Michigan United Appeal.


"There it is!" Daniel pointed to a driveway on the left. The gates were open, and there was a small sign announcing the name of the house – The Breezeway – to passing traffic. On the right, a sedan was parked by the side of the road, two heads low in the front seat. Without reducing speed, I drove past.

"You missed it!"

"There's a stakeout. It looks official."

"A stakeout?"

"Watching the house."

Daniel looked at me, puzzled, as we continued down the highway. "I don't understand."

I told him about my visit to headquarters and Sergeant O'Toole's refusal to co-operate. "The thing is, if the local cops are running an operation, we don't want to screw it up. Cops tend to get angry when civilians screw up their operations."

"Are you sure they're police?"

"Pretty sure. Did you get a look at the house?"

"It appeared to be empty. I couldn't see any cars."

"It probably *is* empty," I said wearily. "Nothing ever comes easy on these jobs."

The most sensible approach would be to wait for nightfall, but McGregor had the heat on. In the meantime, there was the little matter of the sedan. Would the cops roust anyone who showed an interest in the place? The last thing I wanted was to spend the night answering questions, but I'd have to risk it.

I found a place to turn, and headed back toward The Breezeway. As we came up on the property, I could see the two men slumping lower in the sedan.

I swung into the driveway, stopped at the gates, and cut the engine. "Okay, Daniel, you stay here."

Out of the car, I stretched, yawned, and said loudly: "It looks perfect!"

With that, I started slowly up the drive, looking hard for any sign of life. It was a middle-sized house, built on one floor and overlooking the sea. There wasn't a breath of wind, and I could feel the sweat trickling down my back. The crunch of my shoes on the gravel seemed extra loud. Twenty yards now. No curtains moved, no doors inched open, no dogs barked. I wondered what the men in the sedan were doing, but fought the temptation to look back.

I knocked on the front door, but there was no reply. Unless he was hiding under the bed, which I doubted, Mr. Sweetness Jefferson of Detroit, Michigan, was not in residence. Neither was Miss Carol Malone of Toronto, Ontario.

I strolled around the property. The lawns were brown, baked hard by the long summer. On the ocean side, there was a large terrace, strewn with patio furniture. There was also a brick barbecue with a rusty grill. Wooden steps led down the cliff to a small beach.

Curtains frustrated most of my efforts to see inside, although one window offered a glimpse of the living room. It looked comfortable, and neat—as though someone had made a point of tidying up before locking the doors.

Walking briskly back to the car, I moved to Daniel's side and muttered: "You were right. Nobody's home."

"What now?"

"Wait."

I went to the front of the Mercedes, stood with my arms folded, and gazed at the house for a while. Then, in a loud voice, I said: "The kids'll love it!"

I started to get into the car, then pretended to notice the sedan for the first time. I crossed the highway and peered inside the front window. "Excuse me."

The man behind the wheel gave me a murderous look, then stared straight ahead, hoping I'd disappear. He was wearing slacks, a T-shirt, tennis shoes, and a .38.

"Excuse me!" I repeated, rapping sharply on the glass.

The cop glared at me again, muttered something to his partner, and slowly rolled down the window.

"What do you want?" He almost choked on the question.

"I want to rent that house. It's on a list I got from the agency, but it's Saturday and they're closed. I thought you might know the owners."

"The house is not for rent. Move along."

"Well, I must say, that's not very friendly."

Another murderous glare; then the window began to close. Enough. I'd made my point.

# CHAPTER ELEVEN

## *Night Two (Saturday) – 9:35 P.M.*

The limbo dancer/fire-eater was just finishing his act when we arrived at The Tallyman, a stucco building with a large parking lot on the eastern fringe of town. The place was doing a lively Saturday night trade.

"A table for two, gen'min?" The waitress was a slight, coffee-coloured girl with a flashy smile; Dorothy Dandridge dressed up as Chiquita Banana.

"Please."

"Will you be eatin' suppah?"

"No, thanks."

We followed her swaying rear end through the club. The Tallyman was some Jamaican's idea of the tourists' idea of what a Jamaican nightclub ought to be: plastic Rasta, with an overlay of Holiday Inn. The motif was early banana boat. There was a large, poorly done mural of a ship taking on fruit which was being delivered to a tallyman by an endless line of happy-looking bearers. Bunches of imitation fruit hung green and yellow beside wicked-looking banana hooks on the other walls, which some decorator must have decided would look absolutely *gorgeous* there. There were a few outsized wood carvings of lions and "dready" heads and several reproductions of old United Fruit Company signs. Inevitably, the special house cocktail was a king-sized banana daiquiri.

Indirect lighting kept the place in a speak-easy gloom. Two stewards were working the long bar, opening Red Stripes and pouring pre-mixed cocktails. Opposite the bar there was a small, elevated stage which fronted on a dance floor. A four-piece band was just going off for a spliff break, replaced by a scratchy tape of Belafonte and Broadway show tunes.

"If this place is a front," I said, when our waitress went off in search of a Red Stripe for Daniel and a vodka for me, "our friend is nobody's fool. It looks like it's making a fortune."

Frankly, I had little hope The Tallyman would yield much. The fact that Cudjoe had apparently abandoned his house suggested he and Carol were long gone. They could be anywhere in the world by now. Dope dealers always have plenty of ready cash, and one of the principal joys of wealth is personal mobility.

The waitress arrived with our drinks and seemed miffed when Daniel paid with Jamaican dollars; evidently she'd been hoping I would pay in American, so she could make a little extra on the exchange.

Many Jamaicans, especially those working in tourism-related jobs, routinely defy the law by trading in the currency black market, where U.S. dollars fetch up to a third more than the official rate. As Jamaica's economic woes have mounted, the government has been forced to take ever harsher measures to sustain its own dollar and save foreign reserves. Imports are savagely restricted, and hotel bills can no longer be paid in local currency. Tourists are supposed to exchange their dollars, pounds, marks, or francs at the bank. Penalties for currency infractions are severe – almost always involving a jail term – and the currency police, a relatively new branch of the constabulary, are probably the most feared cops in the country.

But Main St., Anywhere always knows value, and the street people in Jamaica know the official exchange rate is silly; so a black market thrives while the Jamaican dollar drifts and the country borrows to pay its bills.

"This place," muttered Daniel, who'd been inspecting The Tallyman with a critical eye, "is about as Jamaican as Times Square."

"You sound like my pal Bishop at the JamJam."

When I described the Toronto club, Daniel said: "Black Panther posters? Don't they have Breast is Best signs, too?"

"Just the condoms," I laughed. But Daniel had a point. Billboards urging mothers to breast-feed their babies are a common sight in Jamaica, often appearing side-by-side with family-planning exhortations.

"Well, the JamJam sounds more authentic than The Tallyman."

"But maybe not as profitable," I said, indicating the busy bar.

"Places like this constitute a clear case of cultural imperialism," he said indignantly. "I believe it to be even more evil than its economic cousin."

"It's a two-way street. Otherwise, how do you explain the JamJam?"

He shook his head. "It may be true that, among some elements of North American society, the Third World is considered chic. But there is no serious threat to North American cultural values, such as they are. In Jamaica, however, our values are in constant danger of being overwhelmed by yours."

"It might surprise you to know," I grinned, "that you have just summed up the arguments of some Canadian nationalists who constantly bite their nails because we live next door to the big, bad United States."

The idea that a fairly wealthy country like Canada could feel menaced left him incredulous. "Don't make me laugh, Mike. You Canadians are notorious imperialists throughout the Caribbean. If anything, you're worse than the Americans."

"That's not fair. Don't confuse the Canadian banks with the Canadian people or the Canadian government. I'll grant you the banks may have been aggressive down here, but they're like that everywhere. And anyway, Jamaica has managed to bring them to heel by legislation."

"It's not just the banks," he said. "Your company is guilty, too. In fact, all the big tourism operators are imperialists."

"Don't be silly. Tourism is the Caribbean's biggest money-spinner. Every government down here is pushing it. We're partners in the industry, not exploiters."

"I don't agree," he said. "While it may be true that the sunshine and the beaches are a kind of renewable resource, the mass-marketing of them is almost an act of aggression against the Jamaican culture."

"That's just Third World sloganeering. I expected better of you."

Daniel sighed, and stared at his beer for a few moments. Then he surprised me again. "Do you know the architect, Arthur Erickson?"

"Only by reputation. Why?"

"He is a distinguished Canadian."

"I'm sure he is. So what?"

"Mr. Erickson understands exactly what I'm saying. He has called tourism an industry gone wild, has described package tours as a plague of locusts that wreak mindless havoc on their destinations, and has denounced the desecration of many beautiful parts of the world by sleazy developments and shoddy hotels."

"He has?" It was the first I'd heard of it.

Daniel nodded. "When you get home you must acquire a copy of the speech he made to his fellow-architects in Mexico City in the fall of 1978. It was very perceptive, especially in its comments about the imposition of North American tastes and values on the rest of the world. The Tallyman is a perfect example of that."

"Look," I said, suddenly weary of all this erudition, "so far today you've thrown me Marshall McLuhan and Arthur Erickson, and maybe even a little Karl Marx. Give me a break."

We gave it an hour, sitting through a standard floor show, the most exciting part of which came when a table of tipsy tourists tried to do the limbo. The fire-eater made a mouthful of gasoline and a kitchen match go a long way—about six feet in fact; the man had good lungs.

When our waitress sullenly deposited a third round of drinks, I told her I wanted to speak to the manager. She nodded indifferently and returned to the bar. A few moments later, a small, neat-looking Jamaican in a dark suit approached, smiling non-committally. He looked like an accountant, cautious and astute.

"You wished to see me, sah?" He had a thin voice.

"Yes, if you're the manager. Pull up a chair."

He sat down carefully. "Is there somet'ing wrong? A complaint?"

"Not really."

His eyes flickered toward Daniel, took note of the dreadlocks, and then returned to me, puzzled. "Well?"

"I understand a man named Cudjoe has an interest in this place. I want to talk to him."

The manager shrugged. "He is not here."

"We can see that," Daniel growled.

Ignoring Daniel, the manager looked at me and said politely: "May I ask why you're wishin' to speak with Cudjoe?"

"I'm looking for his girlfriend."

Recognition washed across his sharp little face. "Oh, mon! I doan believe it! You're Shuter!"

I was surprised. "That's right."

"Oh, mon!" he said again. "You're hot! What did you have to come here for?"

"What do you mean 'hot'?"

"I doan wan' any trouble."

"Neither do we," Daniel snapped. "Where can we find your boss?"

The manager shook his head. "I doan know."

"Is he with a Canadian girl?" I asked. "Have you seen him with a girl named Carol?"

Something shifted in his eyes. "Mr. Shuter," he said, barely whispering, "I try to run a good business here. I doan wan' trouble."

"Then tell me where to find Cudjoe."

He smiled wretchedly. "You lookin' for him, and everyone in his organization lookin' for you. But Cudjoe doan tell me about his other business, and I doan ask. I can't help you."

I was getting sick of that line.

"I wish you would leave," he continued, getting to his feet. "There are men here..." He looked at us imploringly, then turned and skittered away.

"I get the distinct impression," said Daniel, with a tight smile, "that we are not welcome."

"You scared him with your Rasta stare," I grinned. "Very dready."

"Oh, oh," said Daniel. "The bar."

Across the room, I could see our waitress talking to a thug. They were looking at our table. There was no sign of the manager; he was probably locked in his office, hiding behind the accounts receivable.

The thug nodded to the waitress and patted her rump as she turned to move back to her station. Then he called a huddle, which five other men joined. They were a rough-looking team. One by one, they peered at us, as if to confirm their good luck.

"Do you think they'll try something?" Daniel asked.

"Definitely."

The tape machine was cranking out "Send in the Clowns," which seemed appropriate, and a few of the failed limbo dancers were shuffling around the floor, more comfortable with a slower tempo. The huddle at the bar was taking on the characteristics of a lynch party, screwing up its collective courage.

"Just this once," Daniel said softly, "I wish the police would arrive. Even the blue-stripers."

They were ready, psyched up and eager. As they began moving toward us in a loose phalanx, I could hear Daniel taking deep breaths, pumping up his oxygen intake. I kept my eye firmly on the leader, who halted a yard from our table while his friends fanned out in a semi-circle.

"Outside," the leader said in a flat tone. He kept his shoulders hunched, as though ready to charge. His eyes were badly bloodshot and he was missing two fingers on his left hand. His face was peppered with pock-marks and he stank of rum. A lovely chap.

I leaned back in my chair, holding my vodka. I hooked my right ankle over my left knee under the table, then smiled. "We prefer it in here. It's closer to the bar."

"Outside." The man had a limited line of chat.

"Daniel," I said tightly, "this gentleman wants us to move."

I threw my glass at the leader's head, kicked our table over hard and went straight after them. It's the only way. There's no point in pussy-footing around in a saloon brawl; you might as well get on with it. The sooner you suffer the bruises, the sooner they start to heal.

My glass missed Three-Fingers' head, but bounced off his shoulder before smashing on the dance floor. Women began screaming and patrons scrambled out of our way.

From the corner of my eye, I could see Daniel wielding a chair like Frank Buck, holding off two of them. This wasn't exactly rugby, but I felt Daniel would manage.

I put two of mine out of commission with a groin kick and an elbow smash, and was wheeling around to deal with Three-Fingers when pain exploded in the back of my head, and I went down.

Someone had smacked me with a rum bottle. It must have been a glancing blow, because I was still breathing. In fact, I was gagging on the fumes; I've never liked rum. Someone was putting in the boot as I sagged on all fours. The boot hurt. It swung again and this time I grabbed it and tugged.

A man came down in front of me, kicking at my head with his free leg. I let go of him and rolled sideways. Another table went over in a clatter of glasses and I regained my feet.

Daniel had lost his chair and was grappling with his two, who were trying without much success to land a decisive blow. Three-Fingers and Mr. Boots were crouched side-by-side, watching me and catching their breath. One of the men I'd hit first was spitting bloody teeth and moaning softly; the other was doubled up on the floor, clutching his testicles and retching.

So far, the staff was hanging back and none of the other patrons had pitched in. I could hardly blame them; this was a major-league rhubarb. My head was aching savagely, and my shoulder, which had caught the brunt of the rum bottle, was turning numb.

Three-Fingers cursed and spat. There was a loud crash behind him, as Daniel went down in a tangle of arms and legs, still holding onto his partners. Three-Fingers wheeled and dashed to the wall, snatching up two banana hooks.

Three-Fingers handed a hook to Mr. Boots and they separated slightly, like serious knife-fighters. The hooks were fearsome-looking weapons – sharp and deadly; they could pluck out an eye or rip out a throat in a single swipe.

Sensibly enough, I began to retreat. My heart was pounding, my body was sweating, and my mouth was dry; if I wasn't terrified, at least I was showing most of the symptoms.

They were in no hurry. I became dimly aware that the screaming had stopped; everyone was quiet now, watching this macabre floor show. Belafonte began keening about some brown-skinned girl he had known rather too well. Daniel seemed to be holding his own, rolling around on the floor.

As I backed away, Three-Fingers lunged forward with a vicious swing. His hook missed my belly by less than a foot, but he wasn't going to miss forever.

160

My heel hit the leading edge of the stage. Carefully, I stepped up and risked a glance around. I'd have given a fortune for a sturdy guitar to swing with, but the musicians had taken their instruments with them when they'd gone on their break. However, the limbo dancer/fire-eater had left his equipment. It would do.

The bamboo pole was about eight feet long. Holding it like an army recruit doing bayonet drill, I made one or two feints at Mr. Boots, then jabbed sharply at Three-Fingers' head. I caught him on the cheek, tearing it, and he fell back with a shriek. His partner looked hesitant.

When you've got the advantage, seize it. I snatched up the gasoline bottle and, holding the pole in one hand, began dousing them with the other. Before they could gather their wits, I hurled the empty bottle at them and grabbed the matches.

There was an enormous *whoosh* and people started screaming, including my two assailants. Their clothes went up like a pine forest in August.

I dashed off the stage and headed for Daniel, who had managed to knock one of his opponents unconscious and who was now sitting on the other, happily bashing the man's head on the floor.

"Are you nearly finished?" I asked.

Daniel looked up and grinned. His nose was bleeding and his shirt was in shreds, but he had apparently survived the scrum without major damage. He gave his friend's head one more whack, then rolled to his feet.

Around us, there was chaos. Patrons, some of them shrieking, and a few laughing, were scrambling for the doors. Mr. Boots and Three-Fingers were rolling around on the floor, trying to smother flames.

I walked deliberately to the bar, picked up a soda siphon, and returned to the dance floor where I played fireman for a few moments. Neither thug seemed particularly grateful for his Saturday-night bath. But neither seemed disposed to continue our debate.

The Tallyman's employees were trying to restore order and tidy the place when Daniel and I walked out to the car. No one tried to follow.

Room service agreed to bring a bottle of Remy on the double. "Strictly medicinal," I told Daniel, who was still breathing hard. "We both need it."

"That was fantastic!" he said. "When they were going at you with those hooks I thought we'd had it."

"Your college must have had a helluva rugby club."

"We weren't bad," he grinned. "But anyone will fight when he's frightened and trapped. I don't mind admitting I was very scared."

"Okay, professor. Let's check the damage." His nose had stopped bleeding and didn't seem to be broken, but his knuckles were scraped raw; like most amateurs, Daniel punched with a closed fist. As for me, there was a large bump on the side of my head but the skin was intact. If I still wore an RCMP haircut, I'd be bleeding to death. My shoulder was already turning an ugly yellowish purple but nothing felt broken.

"We'll survive," I decided as room service knocked. I poured two giant measures of brandy and we sank gratefully into comfortable chairs.

"Strong medicine," Daniel said, after tasting his Remy.

"The only kind."

"What a day!"

"And it's not over yet." I stifled a yawn.

"What are you going to do? Finish the bottle?"

"No. A little nightwork, which is something I've never enjoyed."

"Nightwork?"

"I'm going to break into a house. Despite all the fun you had tonight, we didn't accomplish much, and I'm running out of leads. There may be something in The Breezeway."

"There's still the Reverend Thomas Jefferson."

"I thought you Rastas were suspicious of the Christian clergy?"

"We till the same fields," he grinned, "promising a better tomorrow."

Daniel wanted to be a housebreaker too but I needed him at base camp. "If I'm not back in two hours, something's wrong. In that case, I want you to swallow your Rasta prejudice and call the cops. Phone O'Toole and tell him where I've gone."

Daniel, who was developing a taste for adventure, accepted the assignment reluctantly. "I don't think you ought to go there alone."

"I've been going places alone all my life. Don't worry about me. Worry about you. I don't want you falling asleep until I'm back."

I went upstairs to shower away the rum and change into standard cat-burglar kit: dark slacks, black sweater, tennis shoes. Then I rummaged in the kitchen until I found a screwdriver and a flashlight. "Okay. It's twelve-thirty. If I'm not back by two-thirty sharp, you know what to do."

Once again he surprised me—this time by getting to his feet, walking me to the door and shaking hands rather formally. "Take care."

"Don't drink all the Remy," I said gruffly. I was growing quite fond of Ras Daniel, philosopher and rising reggae star. One day, I'd have to teach him how to hit a man without skinning his knuckles.

The police were still watching The Breezeway, although the shift had changed and now there was a panel truck where the sedan had been parked. I felt sorry for the cops; stakeout duty is usually as boring as a strange town on a Sunday night. As I drove past the gates I managed a quick glimpse of the house; it was bathed in pale moonlight and looked lonely.

A quarter of a mile along the road, safely out of the cops' line of vision, I pulled onto the shoulder and cut the engine. I was directly opposite the entrance to another beach-front house. A rusty chain sagged across its gravel driveway and a small, weathered sign warned PRIVATE PROPERTY – NO TRES-PASSING – BEWARE OF DOGS. I locked the car and started up the drive, carrying the flashlight. The private property was deserted; no dogs came snarling out of the dark. So much for truth in advertising.

Twenty minutes later I was standing at the bottom of The Breezeway's beach steps. I climbed to the top and stood in the friendly shadows of the brick barbecue, watching and listening for any sign of life. Nothing.

The door on the ocean side was solid-looking, so I moved to a window, using the screwdriver to pry off the screen. If the house was equipped with a security system, I'd soon know; the police were only a minute away.

The window catch was no problem. I slid the glass up and pushed aside the curtains. A fast pan with the flashlight revealed a large, comfortable-looking living room with overstuffed easy chairs and an enormous sofa.

I climbed in. The house smelled musty; it hadn't been aired for days. Cupping the flashlight to reduce the beam, I made sure the curtains on the road side were tightly drawn. I didn't want the cops noticing a light.

Satisfied, I began a methodical search. I had no idea what I was looking for, but there's almost always something.

A small writing desk in the living room was no help. Neither was a large wall unit which held two shelves of books, mainly cheap editions of English novels, a black-and-white television set, a new-looking Sony stereo system and a pet's cage, empty now.

There were a few magazines on the coffee table, but they were all more than a year out of date. I checked the titles – *Vogue*, *House Beautiful*, *Cosmopolitan*, *Forbes*, *The Economist* – and decided they weren't Cudjoe's. He probably didn't stray too far from *Penthouse*. Obviously, he'd rented The Breeze-way furnished.

At the west end there were two small bedrooms which shared a bath. In one, the dresser and closet were bare; in the other, there were a few worn-out shirts and two pairs of trousers. A servant's room, from the look of it.

The kitchen had the usual staples and utensils, but some-one had emptied the refrigerator. There was a wall phone, but I didn't check to see whether it was in service; if the cops had a wire on, they'd know someone was in the house.

Curiously, there were no papers of any kind: no receipts, cancelled cheques, shopping lists, notes, or letters. Most people's lives are littered with paper, but not Cudjoe's. Maybe he couldn't read.

My flashlight was losing power, but I was nearly finished.

The master bedroom was more interesting. It contained a king-sized bed – which made sense, because Cudjoe was the size of a Tutsi warrior – and a closetful of clothes, neat on wooden hangers. Among the clothes were several expen-sive-looking suits bearing the label of a Detroit tailor. The dresser was filled with shirts, socks, shorts, and sweaters. My flashlight was growing steadily dimmer; probably the batteries were ancient.

I moved to the night-table beside the bed and opened its shallow drawer. Something red caught my eye – a book of matches from the Three Small Rooms, the restaurant in Toronto's Windsor Arms Hotel. It wasn't much of a clue, but it indicated Carol had been here. I stood for a while, con-sidering the implications; Carol and Cudjoe, entwined on the bed, smoking spliffs, making love, and drifting through the dark hours. The image left me depressed, unsettled. Nightwork chips away at the soul.


Man has been softened by thousands of years of civilization but he remains the product of millions of years of evolution;

the senses may have dulled but the instincts have stayed machete-sharp. Alarm bells began jangling along my central nervous system. Danger. The adrenal glands started to pump, the heart accelerated, the muscles tensed: involuntary preparations for battle or flight, instinctive responses as old as the species.

I was looking for it before I knew it was there, before I heard the strange, dry clicking, before I saw it. Extreme danger. The lungs expanded, the respiratory system went into overdrive, the lower abdominal muscles went bow-string taut. I swung around, aiming the faint beam of the flashlight.

A snake lay coiled across itself in the bedroom doorway, eyes glittering malevolently. In the dim light, I could see its diamond markings and twitching, upright tail.

A rattlesnake, for chrissake! What the hell was it doing in Cudjoe's boudoir? Then I remembered the empty cage in the living room.

Having identified and assessed the danger, my body shifted down from red alert to condition yellow, and the senses took over again.

The rattler was perhaps five feet long, thick and angry-looking. The thought that we had both been moving around in the dark shadows left me weak at the knees.

I tried to remember what I knew about rattlesnakes. Not much. But I knew one thing: they don't live in Jamaica. The island is virtually snake-free.

The rattler rearranged itself and shook its tail. It must have heard me and come slithering along to see whether I'd be good to eat. I was too big for it to eat; therefore I was danger-ous. It wouldn't turn its back on an enemy, so we had a standoff.

My flashlight was growing alarmingly faint. I had to do something fast or take a chance on turning on the lights. I didn't want to do that because of the stakeout, but I had no intention of fighting a rattlesnake in the dark.

166

As usual, I needed a weapon. The screwdriver was useless, and this time there was no bamboo pole left behind by an obliging entertainer. If I could just get past the damn thing, I'd find something in the kitchen; but I was in the bedroom and the snake was in the way.

I shifted my weight slightly, and it responded by recoiling itself and rattling furiously. Its head stayed low and slightly pulled back, ready to strike.

The flashlight dimmed some more. Okay, Shuter; move it. I edged toward the closet and stripped one of Cudjoe's silk-and-mohair numbers off its wooden hanger. The hanger was unwieldy but fairly heavy. A start. I moved back to the bed, and propped the flashlight on the night-table, aiming its now-pathetic beam at the snake. Then I picked up a pillow.

The snake followed my every move, stupidity and death in its stare.

With the big pillow clenched in my fist and the hanger in my right, I was as ready for battle as I was going to be: a marshmallow knight with a floppy shield and a wooden sword.

I shoved the pillow toward it and felt rather than saw it strike. The damned thing hit the pillow like Ali thumping the heavy bag. Its fangs were still embedded in linen and feathers when I smashed it across the back of the head. It was a solid blow, and the snake's body thrashed with the shock. It didn't seem to like the hanger so I whacked it again. Then again. And again. And finally, again.

Was it dead? Or only stunned? I wasn't sure. I sprinted to the kitchen and opened the refrigerator door to make a little light. Within seconds I found a heavy butcher's knife and a broom.

Cautiously, I returned to the bedroom. The snake was twitching but the fight had gone out of it. I prodded it with the broom and it twitched some more. Aiming just behind its head, I swung the big knife hard, and it was over.

What kind of creepy mind would leave a rattlesnake in an

unoccupied house? Or even have one in the first place? Cudjoe wasn't just a thug; he was a psychopath.

For the first time since McGregor had turned me loose on the Malone case, I felt personally involved. The scrap in The Tallyman, even the caper with Molasses had been all in a day's work; but the snake somehow made it personal.

# CHAPTER TWELVE

## *Day Three (Sunday) — 9:00 A.M.*

"Nobody," said Richard Bishop hotly, "manhandles my reporters. And nobody tells me how to do my job. I'm breaking the Malone story tonight and the hell with Holidair."

I hadn't slept well and I was hung over on Remy, which can be as bad as snake bite. Daniel had organized a pot of coffee and I was drinking some of it with a shaky hand, listening to Bishop sputter.

"Shuter, I've been sitting on this thing for three nights. In my business, that's an eternity."

"We had a deal."

"We did not. We had an agreement — that the Malone story didn't rate the national news. Now it does."

"What happened?"

"We've had Suzie Q digging into the Llewellyn murder. She tried a couple of reports, but I killed them because they were too speculative. Well, Quill's a good reporter, and determined, so last night she went back to the JamJam."

"And?"

"And on her way out she was accosted. I don't know, they may have been the same punks you beat up."

"What did they do?"

"Tried to scare her off. Told her to forget about Lucky. Being Susan, she told them to go screw themselves. Then they shoved her around. Pinched her boobs, I gather, and grabbed her ass."

I laughed. "Can't say I blame them."

"It's not funny, Shuter. She didn't think so, and neither do I."

"Okay, okay. Then what?"

"They let her go and she phoned me at home – raging."

"So?" I held out my cup and Daniel filled it.

"So I told her to pack. She's on her way down there now, with a crew."

Terrific. "Goddamnit, Bishop, I don't think..."

"I don't care what you think. I'm cranking up the Ottawa bureau. We've got pictures of Carol. Her old man will talk to us. We'll interview Patsy Baird, get the usual 'no comment' from McGregor. I can report that the girl is missing, that her father's in a dither, that Holidair is upset enough to send you looking for her, that there appears to be a connection between her disappearance and a drug-related murder that has the Toronto cops buffaloed, that the Jamaican authorities are worried about the case's impact on their tourist trade and that the Canadian government's upset, too. It's a helluva yarn."

"Have you spoken to McGregor?"

"No. I got your number from Helen."

"He's going to be upset."

"Shuter, I work for the National Television Network, not Holidair. I don't *care* if McGregor's upset."

"Where's Quill staying?"

"Kingston. The Sheraton."

"Why Kingston? Carol went missing from Negril."

"Because," Bishop said, "her first piece will be a situational to flesh out stuff we'll package at this end. The capital's the logical place for her to do it. We can always cut in stock footage of the resort areas. Also, there's a ground station in Kingston so she can feed from there."

There was nothing I could do about it now. "You're not making my life any easier."

"Are you getting anywhere?"

"You've got the big team of investigators. Ask them."

"Don't get sore, Shuter. What else could I do?"

"You could have bought Quill a girdle," I said wearily. "Maybe even a bra."


It was another glorious morning, the sky flawless and the mercury headed for the mid-eighties. Daniel and I were driving through the lush terrain of Fern Gully, a steep canyon which knifes inland from Ocho Rios.

I had a sour stomach and a nagging sense of foreboding. I seemed to be winning battles without coming any closer to winning the war. Carol remained as elusive as ever, although maybe Cudjoe's brother would help.

Bishop had me in a bind. McGregor was going to blame me for NTN's impending scoop—with reason. If I'd gone to the JamJam alone, Susan Quill would be snug in bed with her Siamese cats this morning instead of on an Air Jamaica flight to Manley International. Bladon wasn't going to be happy either. Unless he'd won a lottery in the past couple of days, his mood was going to be as black as Cudjoe's heart.

Daniel had been quiet all morning. My account of the fight with the snake had eroded some of his gung-ho spirit and now he was brooding.

"What's the problem, Daniel?"

"Cudjoe's the problem. He's an evil man. I could cheerfully kill him."

"Hardly a thought for a churchgoer on a Sunday morning."

"You forget, I'm a Rastafarian." He turned and stared at me. "Do you know the Bible?"

"Not really. Sunday school stuff."

"Well, this is Sunday. Consider Isaiah, chapter thirty-four, verse eight: 'It is the day of the Lord's vengeance, and the year of recompenses.'"

"Why vengeance?"

"I don't know," he said quietly. "The fight, I guess. The snake. All Cudjoe's insults to the brethren."

"So you'd leave Cudjoe to God, as Isaiah suggests?"

"No. I'd be guided by Deuteronomy, chapter thirty-two, verses forty-one and forty-two."

"Which says?"

"'I will render vengeance to mine enemies, and will reward them that hate me. I will make mine arrows drunk with blood, and my sword shall devour flesh.'"

"Okay, I'm impressed. You know your Bible. And I think you could be a strong enemy. But I always thought Isaiah was right, that vengeance was the Lord's, and that you Rastas preached unity and love."

"It is," he said flatly, "and we do. But in Cudjoe's case I think Jah would accept us as his agents."

The Rastafarian faith had always struck me as being silly and deliberately anti-intellectual, more calculated to shock non-adherents than to comfort converts.

"I'll be damned," I said, probably prophetically, "if I can figure out why you're into the Rastas. Surely you don't believe all that guff?"

He slouched and closed his eyes. "What do you know about the Rastas?"

"A bit." I told him that I knew the Rastafarians were a relatively new cult, dating from mid-nineteen-thirties. They had emerged from the "Africa for Africans—at home and abroad" preachings of the late Marcus Garvey, a Jamaican national hero who'd gone to the United States to found the United Negro Improvement Association and become an inspiration to blacks all over the world. Garvey was supposed to have prophesied the coming of a black Messiah in the guise of a king crowned in Africa. When, in nineteen-thirty, Ras Tafari, crown prince of Ethiopia, had his coronation in Addis Ababa and took the title of Haile Selassie I, king of kings, lord of lords, elect of God, conquering lion of the tribe of Judah, a handful of Jamaicans decided Garvey's prophecy had been fulfilled and that Selassie was God, or Jah, an elision of Jehovah. The original Rastas were drawn from the slums of Kingston, where they'd been disgruntled members either of Orthodox Christian congregations or the Afro-Christian sects which had evolved during the previous century. The new cult was black-supremacist, condemned Jamaica as hell (or Babylon), and looked to Ethiopia as heaven. The whites were the oppressors, the police and army their agents. Ganja was a gift of Jah, a kind of manna. It enabled Rastas to achieve a higher spirituality which they described as "sonship" with Ras Tafari himself. Early ridicule and a succession of police and military operations against the cult had failed to stop its growth, especially among the uneducated and the poor. Now, the Rastas were beginning to build strength in the rural areas, too.

"Why do you dismiss our teaching as guff?"

"Come on, Daniel. Haile Selassie as God? He died in nineteen seventy-five. Back to Africa? I can assure you, you wouldn't like it there. Eternal life for all true Rastas? Ask Lucky."

"Lucky is not dead, any more than Jah is dead. His spirit has simply moved to another place. Like Jah, he has decided to absent himself from the temporal world for a while, but he lives. It is all in the Bible."

"You people are too selective in your reading."

"Not at all," he bristled. "True, we find most of our inspiration in the Old Testament — Leviticus, Numbers, Deuteronomy, Ezekiel, Psalms, and, if I say so myself, the Book of Daniel. But we read all the Bible, and pay special attention to the final book, Revelation."

I slowed the car and asked him to explain his conversion.

It began, he said, with music but was given a powerful shove by his awareness that Jamaican's socio-economic system was failing the people. The Rastas were in a position today similar to that of the early Christians — chafing under the rule of others, getting a raw economic deal, longing for a future free of drudgery. "People develop religions to suit their needs. There is no point in talking to me about logic. In spiritual matters, logic always yields to emotion. Even as a boy in Sunday school, I was able to challenge the logic of the Christian church, although I understood that it worked for many people. But it doesn't work for me." He paused. "Anyway, the Christian churches are in cahoots with the oppressors. They perpetuate Babylon."

During the first two centuries of slavery in Jamaica, Daniel said, the blacks had been deliberately ignored by the Christian church, because the oppressors feared that the concepts of brotherly love and equality before God would unleash a revolt against the slave system. Into the vacuum, inevitably, had come the old tribal religions, brought from the African homelands but adapted to Jamaican conditions. Finally, in the early nineteenth century, the Christian churches – mainly the Methodists and Baptists – began missionary work in Jamaica and enjoyed considerable success in converting the blacks. For the next hundred years, while the people read their Bibles and toiled under the sun, political conditions changed (slavery was abolished, Britain took over direct administration of the island from a corrupt and inept local legislature), but economic circumstances did not. The white man's God seemed to have forgotten all about his black children. Most people had simply carried on in penury, hoping the next world would be as good as the Christian clergy promised. But a few began to doubt the churches' word. After Garvey's speeches and Haile Selassie's coronation, given the economic and social wasteland that Babylon had become, Jamaica was more than ready for the concept of a black God and a black heaven. Indeed, the Bible seemed to promise both. Rastafarianism was a faith suited to the times and conditions, as logical as any other and just as comforting.

"Comfort?" I said. "Burning and looting, warring with the police, the whole concept of dread? Where's the comfort?"

"In the pride we instil, in the heaven we look to."

"As far as I'm concerned, heaven and hell are here and now. It's up to each of us to decide which one we want to spend our days in."

He snorted. "And if there is no choice? What if the people have only hell? Then do you not suppose it is reasonable of them to hope for a heaven elsewhere? Isn't that what the Christians preach, and for the same reasons?"

"Okay. Maybe people do need a heaven. But in Ethiopia? Come on."

"Why not? Why shouldn't heaven for a black man be in Africa? Where man began? Psalm sixty-eight, verse thirty-one: 'Princes shall come out of Egypt and Ethiopia shall stretch forth her hands unto God.'"

When I didn't reply, he continued: "You know, the Book of Revelation shows beyond any doubt that God is black. It speaks of his woolly hair and his complexion of burning brass."

"I'm sorry to have to tell you, Daniel, but Ethiopia is an impoverished Marxist-Leninist dictatorship, sapped by war, mismanaged by the military, and threatened by separatism. Jah's empire is gone forever, and the Rastas' heaven along with it."

"Actually," he said easily, "most of us now believe repatriation to Africa is less important than the liberation of Jamaica and the destruction of Babylon."

"So the movement is political, then?"

"All religions are political to some degree."

"And the concept of dread? Is that political too?"

He shook his head. "Some wear locks as a means of protest against the oppressors' social values. Others are simply trying to emulate African warriors. But the true sons of Ras Tafari wear locks because Jah has commanded it."

"He has?"

"In Leviticus, chapter twenty-one, verse five: 'They shall not make baldness upon their head, neither shall they shave off the corner of their beard, nor make any cuttings in their flesh.'"

Instead of replying, I stepped on the gas.


The churchyard, dusty and cluttered, looked like a failing used-car lot. The Mercedes was as out of place among the bicycles, half-tons, and battered sedans outside the Church of the Pan-African Redeemer (non-denominational) as my white skin and Daniel's Rasta locks were inside it. We took a pew, ignored quizzical stares from others in the congregation, and waited for the service to begin. The Reverend Thomas Jefferson had a packed house.

"You'll notice," Daniel whispered, "that there are almost no young men here. Girls and older couples, yes, but no young men."

"Why is that?"

"Because a Christian church offers them less than a Rasta yard."

"You mean because there's no ganja here."

The musicians—two guitarists, a drummer, and a trumpet player—took their places at the front of the church, a small choir formed up at the rear door and the congregation got to its feet. The processional was "Shall We Gather at the River," up-tempo, and everyone sang along with the choir. Even Daniel joined in, grinning.

Jefferson was a big man—at least six-three, and broad—with close-cropped hair going grey at the temples. He had a powerful voice and a speaking style that would have been the envy of most television evangelists. Turned loose on the Bible Belt, he would have been a sensation.

For the next hour we were treated to a display of participatory worship at its best: rollicking revivalist hymns, a succession of passionate prayers, a rip-snorting sermon, all punctuated with congregational ejaculations of "Praise the Lord!," "Yeah, brother!," and "Ahh-*men*!"

As the text for his sermon, Jefferson had chosen a verse

176

from the second epistle of Paul to the Corinthians: "Every man according as he purposeth in his heart, so let him give; not grudgingly or of necessity: for God loveth a cheerful giver." The sermon itself was a shameless pitch for funds, but it was delivered with such eloquence that no one seemed to mind.

When the collection plate was passed, I noticed in amazement that there were far more bills than coins, and I surprised myself by contributing twenty bucks. Guilt. It had been years since I'd attended a regular Sunday service.

Daniel simply passed the plate without adding a penny.

"Nothing for Babylon?" I whispered.

"The man's a charlatan."

"Daniel, he's a man of the cloth, not to mention a terrific speaker."

"He's a glib vulture, preying on the natural generosity of the poor."

After the service, we waited for Jefferson to finish shaking hands with the faithful. He had a word of encouragement or reassurance for everyone, and he smiled a lot when he wasn't looking deeply sincere: a man at peace with himself and his world, I decided, a Martin Luther King of the bush.

The sun was hammering down, and flies buzzed halfheartedly around the yard, trying to scratch out a living. Children, careful of their Sunday dresses and flannels, played a noisy game of tag while they waited for their parents and the journey home.

I finally walked up to Cudjoe's brother while Daniel hung back. "Mr. Jefferson?"

Clear brown eyes measured me; close up they reflected shrewdness rather than compassion but his smile was warm enough. "Good morning." There was the barest hint of a question in his greeting.

"My friend and I enjoyed the service."

Jefferson's eyes flickered toward Daniel. "Everyone is welcome in the Lord's house."

"My name is Shuter. My friend is Ras Daniel."

Jefferson regarded me with polite curiosity, but didn't offer to shake hands. "We don't often get white folks – or disciples of Ras Tafari – at our services. What can I do for you, Mr. Shuter?"

"I wanted to talk to you about your brother."

"Sweetness?" Something changed in his expression.

I nodded.

"Come to my office."

We followed Jefferson along a pathway to a neat frame house, white with green trim. A new-looking Volkswagen was parked in the yard and a flagpole flew the gold-green-and-black cross of Jamaica. Jefferson led us to a side door. The walls of his office were bare except, incongruously, for an old *Playboy* centrefold featuring a stunning Jamaican girl: Miss Rosanne Katon, Playmate-of-the-Month, September 1978.

Jefferson took off his suit jacket and invited us to sit down. "It's a warm day. Would you like a beer?"

My kind of clergyman. "Please."

"No thanks," said Daniel.

Our host opened a door leading into the main part of the house and hollered: "Charlene! Andrea! Bring some cold beer!"

"Who are Charlene and Andrea?" I asked.

"My wards. From Kingston. I'm trying to save them from a life of wickedness and sin."

"Oh," I said, looking around. "Nice house."

"The Church of the Pan-African Redeemer kindly makes it available. Those who do God's work need shelter, and a place to reflect."

"I never heard of the Church of the Pan-African Redeemer – before today."

He smiled easily. "We're a small church, trying to minister to the needs of the people here. It's challenging work, but rewarding."

"I'm sure it is." This was going to be a cinch.

The door opened and a foxy girl in her middle teens flounced in, carrying a bottle of Red Stripe and a single glass. She stopped and stared in confusion at Daniel and me. She was wearing a thin, champagne-coloured nightgown that revealed pendulous breasts and a dark pubic patch. She also sported lip gloss and a lot of dark-green eye-shadow.

"Oops!"

"Andrea!" Jefferson snapped. "Cover yourself, child! We have guests."

Andrea shrugged, and put down the beer. "You shoulda warned me, Tommy."

"Get out, Jezebel! Tell Charlene to bring another beer, and make sure she's modest."

Andrea sashayed out the door, slamming it. Jefferson grinned slyly and shrugged. "Saving souls is never easy." He poured the Red Stripe and passed it to me.

There was a soft knock on the door. If anything, Charlene was even foxier than Andrea; she was wearing short shorts, a "Legalize-It" T-shirt and only slightly less makeup. She put another bottle of beer and a glass on the desk, turned, and wiggled out of the room without a word.

"A lovely child," Jefferson murmured, at which point Daniel snickered.

"Mr. Jefferson," I said, "about your brother..."

"Are you a business associate of his?"

"No."

"Friends?"

"We've never met."

He sipped his beer. "What, then?"

"I'm looking for him. He's with a girl."

Jefferson laughed. "That's Sweets! Always with a girl."

"Can you tell me where he is?"

He gave me a stony stare. "Yeah, Shuter, I can tell you. But I won't." Wayne County had crept into his accent, pushing the corn pone aside.

"It's important."

"So, who gives a shit?"

"I beg your pardon?" A half-hour ago he'd been praising the Lord.

"Listen, honky, Sweets is my kid brother. He ain't too bright, but he's my brother all the same."

"And cut from the same cloth!" Daniel snapped. "You're a disgrace!"

Jefferson frowned at him. "Shut your mouth, boy! I don't need sass from no dumb island nigger."

Daniel started up from his chair, but I waved him back. "Let it go."

"Listen to the man, boy, or I'll take down your pants and give you a whuppin'."

"Be careful, Uncle Tom," I said softly, "or I'll be doing the whuppin'."

Jefferson laughed, and drank some more beer. "You look like fuzz, Shuter. That why you lookin' for Sweets?"

I shook my head. "It's private."

"Well, you better hope you don't find him. Sweets ain't full of Christian charity like me." He grinned. "You ever been to Dee-troit?"

"Once or twice."

"Know it?"

"A bit. Lindell's. Joe Muir's."

"That's downtown. You know the Six-Mile? Out by Woodward?"

"No."

"Used to be my turf. Shoved smack there for years. But I took a fall, grabbed five to ten in Atlanta. Ever been in the joint?"

"Just as a visitor."

He nodded. "Well you wouldn't like it. That's what I keep tellin' Sweets. A man does a little time, he gets thinkin'. He misses things. Charlene and Andrea, f'rinstance. I decided I didn't want to go back. There's easier ways to grind out a buck. Now I push Jesus, 'stead of junk. It don't pay quite as good, but it ain't half bad."

180

Jefferson reached into his pocket and took out a thick wad of bills, dropping them on his desk. "Not a bad morning's work. One thing about these island niggers, Shuter: you put on a show, they put up the dough."

I put down my beer and got to my feet. "Come on, Daniel."

Jefferson grinned. "You find Sweets, you say hello for me, okay? But say it quick, Shuter, before he tears off your head."

I moved across to the desk and pawed through the pile of money. He growled in surprise. "Hey! Leave that!"

I found my $20-bill and waved it under his nose. "I made a mistake during collection."

"You mother!"

"Remember; 'the Lord loveth a cheerful giver.'"

Daniel had the grace not to say he'd told me so as we drove back to Ocho Rios.

# CHAPTER THIRTEEN

# Day Three (Sunday) – 12:50 P.M.

The bottom thread was missing. The chambermaids had tidied our suite before we'd left for the church, so we'd had unauthorized visitors. The question was whether we still had them.

Holding a finger to my lips, I cautioned Daniel to stand still. I put an ear to the door and listened hard. Not a sound. If anyone was inside, he wasn't moving around. I backed away slowly and motioned Daniel to follow me down the stairwell. Outside, I whispered: "I'm not sure. Maybe, maybe not."

"Who could it be?"

"It's not Charlene and Andrea, come for an afternoon of salvation."

He didn't smile. "What are you going to do?"

"Probably make a fool of myself. You stay here."

If there was no one in the suite, I was going to feel silly. But better red in the face than dead on the floor. I moved to the end of the building, and looked up the four storeys to our terrace. I could see the iron grillwork and railing thirty feet above. It wouldn't be easy, but there appeared to be just enough window ledges and handholds.

I kicked off my loafers, cursing their leather soles. I'd have to make the climb shoeless, without knowing what I'd find at the top. I hate being shoeless in a fight; it's worse than being without your pants.

The sun seemed to take on a heightened brilliance. Three or four people were splashing in the lower pool. Up by the main building waiters were bustling about, serving lunch. No one was paying any attention to me, which was fine.

Taking a deep breath, I hauled myself up to the first window and began to climb. Twice I was almost stymied, able to manage only the most tenuous of fingerholds. The concrete path looked harder with every foot I rose. My shoulders and arms started to ache, my fingers were numb and I was beginning to feel like an out-of-shape Edmund Hillary.

After what seemed an eternity, I managed to hook an arm around the balcony grillwork. I'd made it – if not exactly for Elizabeth, England, and St. George, then for McGregor, Holidair, and Carol Malone.

Pausing to catch my breath, I glanced down and saw Daniel watching me, still looking worried. I placed a second hand on the grillwork, pulled and found myself staring into the sights of a .45-calibre revolver. The barrel looked almost as big as a piece of sewer pipe.

"Shuter, you somethin' else!"

Cudjoe, grinning.

"What happened, man? You lose your key?"

He was relaxing on a deck chair, his shirt open to the waist, a jolly black giant taking the sun. But his eyes were anthracite and the .45 was as steady as the price of gold used to be.

"Come on, brother. Get over the railing before you hurt yourself."

I swung onto the terrace and stood before him, puffing. My shirt was plastered to my back and sweat was rolling down my face like condensation on a summer beer glass.

Cudjoe wasn't alone. A second man, also carrying a handgun, was watching from the shade under the trellis. He was about a foot shorter than Cudjoe and wiry, but he looked mean enough. His Beretta wouldn't make as big a mess as Cudjoe's .45, but it would get the job done.

"There was a second thread, huh?" Unlike his brother's,

Cudjoe's voice was strangely thin, almost squeaky. Coming from such an enormous diaphragm, it sounded like a mistake, as though a recording engineer had slipped up somewhere. But there was nothing thin or squeaky about the rest of him. He looked huge, unmanageable.

"I said there was a second thread, right?"

I nodded.

"Careless of my men. You surprised to see me?"

"Not really." Unconsciously, I'd dropped my voice almost an octave from its normal range. Childish. Next, I'd be challenging him to arm-wrestle.

"We saw you through the window," he said. "You an interestin' dude."

I shrugged. Cudjoe looked briefly at the man in the shade, but kept the .45 pointed at my chest; from this distance he couldn't miss. "Jimmy, bring up the singer."

"Leave him out of it," I said, as Jimmy moved off the terrace. "He's just a kid, along for the ride."

Cudjoe's eyes stayed hard and cold. "Yeah, Shuter, you an interestin' dude. But right now you a fly on my cheek. Why you buggin' me, my man?"

"I think you know."

"She okay, Shuter. She as happy as a Motown hooker on GM payday, and gettin' almost as much action. Don't you worry none about her."

"She's important, Sweets. Her father's a big shot. You're playing out of your league, way over your head."

"I don't know 'bout that. I ain't exactly short."

"Big doesn't impress me."

He glowered briefly, then shook his head, his long locks sweeping back and forth across his face, almost obscuring his vision. "It don't matter to me if you impressed. What matters is, you butt out."

"As soon as I talk to the girl."

"Shuter, I could waste you like a roach" – he snapped his fingers – "and never give it a second thought. But you just not worth the bother. Now don't press it. I got business to do. Important business."

"Sweets, I don't care if you move enough grass to turn on the world. All I want is to make sure the girl's all right."

"It's this way, brother. I don't . . ."

He was interrupted by the return of Jimmy, leading Daniel onto the terrace. Behind Daniel were two more men. One of them carried a Kalashnikov, a very serious toy. Where the hell would Cudjoe get an AK-47? Almost anywhere, of course; when it comes to shipping arms to the Third World, the Russians are virtually in the mail-order business.

"Mike, I . . ." Daniel looked miserable.

"Shut up, Rastaman!" Cudjoe snapped. "I'm talkin'."

Jimmy pushed Daniel across the terrace, indicating we were to stand side by side. The guy with the Kalashnikov looked on grimly. The fourth man seemed to be stoned.

"Like I was sayin'," Cudjoe went on, "I got work to do. I ain't got time to mess around with you turkeys."

"But here you are," I said, "messing around anyway."

"Right, because you don't seem to take a hint. Three different times now you busted up some of my men, so I thought to myself, I thought: 'Cudjoe, go see the man. Talk to him nice. And maybe he stop buggin' you.' Know what I mean, Shuter?"

"You know what I want."

"You wanna talk to Carol, right?"

I nodded.

"Impossible. She not here, but I arranged the next best thing." He waved to his lieutenant. "Jimmy, bring that out here."

Now what? And what had Cudjoe meant by three run-ins with his men?

Cudjoe looked surprised when I asked him. "Man, you so busy you can't remember all your scraps? The Tallyman, the beach at Negril, Toronto. That's three, ain't it?"

"Toronto? You mean those kids work for you?"
He shrugged.
"Did you order them to kill Lucky?"
"Lucky was snitchin'," he said coldly.
Daniel stirred beside me. "You're riffraff!"
"Riffraff," Cudjoe repeated, rolling his eyes. "Now, would you listen to that? Let me tell you somethin', Rastaman. Me and Shuter here understand each other. We're pros. But you, you nothin'. So watch your mouth."
"You don't frighten me," said Daniel, in a voice that suggested he wasn't quite telling the truth.
"I should," said Cudjoe, reasonably enough.
"I said to leave him out of it, Sweets. It's not his beef."
"Then tell him to be nice." He leaned back and yawned, but the .45 didn't waver. It was becoming uncomfortable in the sun.
Jimmy returned, carrying what looked like a portable radio in a leather case. He handed it to Cudjoe.
"Now," Cudjoe grinned. "I figured you'd probably want to hear from Carol, so I brought this." He swung the case around. It held an inexpensive Panasonic cassette recorder.

"Mr. Shuter [it said in a calm voice that sounded good, even filtered through the machine's mini-speakers], this is Carol Malone. I know you've been looking for me. Probably the airline sent you because of Daddy. Well, I just wish everyone would leave me be. I'm fine, and I'm sorry if people have been worried, but I hoped Patsy would keep everyone calm. I guess she hasn't. Anyway, tell Daddy I'll phone soon and to expect me home well before Christmas. Tell Mom and my sister that I love them very much, that I'm okay. Please, Mr. Shuter, make them understand that I am happy and enjoying my holiday."

The tape whirred on for a moment, then Cudjoe pressed the Stop button and looked up at me with a salesman's smile. "See? She just fine, man. Nothin' to get excited about. Here." He pressed the Eject button and tossed the cassette to me. "Take that to her daddy."

"It's not enough," I said quietly. "There's too much steam on this one. A tape won't do."

For the first time, Cudjoe showed anger, a glimpse of what he'd be like if crossed. He slammed a big fist on the arm of his chair, and waved the gun at me like an admonishing finger.

"Shuter, I'm gettin' tired of this. Now let me lay it on you, one more time: I'm busy with somethin' right now. I ain't got time to screw around over no white pussy. You can see the bitch when I'm tired of her. But if you don't keep your nose outta my business I'll chop it off."

I decided to push. "You're the pussy, Jefferson. You shuffle around down here playing tough guy, scaring the rubes. You wouldn't have a prayer against me."

Raw hate blazed out of Cudjoe. "You dreamin', honky. I could shove this piece right up your white ass and haul it outta your throat."

"Meow," I said, watching him struggle to regain his self-control. He did—barely.

We were silent for a few moments. The meeting was over, but I couldn't see how we were going to end it. It was as though we were all riders on a runaway Ferris wheel.

Finally, Cudjoe stood. "We gonna go now and you gonna stay exactly where you are. You not gonna move a muscle."

"Says who?"

He glowered again. "Look there." Cudjoe pointed across the grounds to the elevator tower. There was a man in the top window, a man with a rifle. "And there." Cudjoe pointed at the roof of the main building. Another one.

"They're a long way off."

"They both ace shots," he said. "You don't think so, you can always try them. But I was you, Shuter, I'd make sure I stayed exactly where I was till they gone."

We were ducks on the pond; the nearest cover was a dozen feet away, or about thirty shots from two M-16s. "Maybe you've got a point."

"Yeah," he said, "maybe I do."

"By the way," I said, "how are you getting around? The cops are looking for you."

He uttered a derisive snort. "The fuzz down here couldn't find their ass with a mirror. I come and go as I like."

"They've got roadblocks up."

"Yeah, but I got me a Red Stripe truck. Jimmy been drivin' it. That truck piled high with beer cases. I just made a little space under them. No roadblock gonna shift a hundred cases of beer."

I'd noticed the truck in the Sans Souci driveway when we'd come back from the church and assumed it was making a delivery.

"Don't get all excited, Shuter. I won't be usin' it after today." He yawned and stretched, then waved at the two riflemen. They waved back and settled down over their weapons again, barely visible.

"Okay," he said to his men, "let's split. Be smart, Shuter. Go home and tell Carol's daddy she okay. You be happier in Canada. And healthier."

He stuck the .45 in his belt and started to stroll off, as cool as I was hot. Would nothing shake him up?

"Sweets," I said, as he reached the terrace door, "your rattlesnake had an accident."

He froze, then turned slowly with something close to grief on his face. "You kill it?"

I bowed formally. "A pleasure. Last time I saw it, it was in pieces."

He nodded his huge head three or four times, as if in pain, then focussed a hard stare on my face. "Next time, you gonna be the one in pieces."

For almost five minutes, Daniel and I remained motionless, helpless. If I'd been on my own I'd probably have risked a lunge for cover. But the fact there were two of us complicated things: we made a bigger target and it is always hard to synchronize a move.

So I stood there, seething. Left on their own, Cudjoe's men might be nitwits but the man himself knew how to put together an operation. He'd handled me like a two-year-old.

I kept my eye on the guy covering us from the main roof. Several times, he sneaked backward glances to see whether Cudjoe had reached the truck. Then, abruptly, the rifleman was gone—or at least out of sight. Slowly, I turned my head and tried to catch a glimpse of the one in the elevator tower. There was no sign of him.

"Daniel, I think they've gone."

"I can't see anyone," he whispered. "What now?"

"When I count to three, dive to your right. I'll be moving to the left. When you're on the floor, keep rolling. Don't stop until you're inside, on the stairs."

"Why the stairs?"

"Because those rifles can knock down walls."

"Okay," he said, sounding shaky.

I counted it off.

There were no shots.

I ordered Daniel to stay in the suite, and dashed down the stairs, again cursing my lack of shoes as I sprinted through the Sans Souci gardens.

There was no sign of the beer truck when I reached the Mercedes. Even if I caught Cudjoe, I wouldn't be able to do much. Trail him, perhaps. I was unarmed and he was packing enough firepower to give the Van Doos pause for thought.

I rammed the Mercedes through a bootlegger's turn and roared out of the parking area into the driveway, skidding around the first bend.

Somehow, I managed to stop in time; I'd have totalled the Bricklin.

A huge palm tree lay across the drive, blocking it. Tricky

bastard! Score: Cudjoe 21, Shuter 0, and the clock was running.

"I don't know," Daniel said, as we sat drinking Heineken and recovering, "but from what you've told me your mission seems to have been accomplished."

"What makes you think so?"

"The cassette should satisfy Mr. Malone. True, Carol has chosen a rotten companion, but she sounds happy enough."

I shook my head. "Carol made that tape under duress."

"She sounded fine to me."

"She sounded terrific," I sighed, "but Carol is an only child."

"I don't understand."

"She asked me to give her love to a sister she doesn't have. Why? Unless she was trying to tell me not to believe the rest of it."

Daniel looked worried again. "That was clever of her."

If anything, the tape made matters worse. About the only patch of blue I could see was the fact that she was alive—or had been in the past day or so.

Daniel had been thinking. "But why would he bother to hold her against her will? Cudjoe changes women fairly often. If he's bored with her, why doesn't he just send her packing?"

"Maybe she knows something he wants kept secret. Maybe he can't rely on her."

"What?"

"It could be anything. Details of a big ganja shipment. Who his contacts are. Even where he's spending his time. Remember, the local cops are looking for him."

"Why risk coming here?"

I took another beer from the fridge. "He's cocky. And anyway, he didn't risk much. That was a well-planned sortie. I think he was hoping to talk us off. After The Tallyman, he probably decided we weren't going to be scared off."

190

"I've just had a horrible thought," said Daniel. "If Carol is such a nuisance, Cudjoe is perfectly capable of getting rid of her. Permanently."


Sam Chung sounded depressed, as though the Robarts Library had suspended his privileges or he'd learned there was irrefutable proof that the Bard's plays had been written by a team of Elizabethan hacks.

"What's the matter, Sam? Was your luncheon for Professor Frye a failure?"

"Oh, hello, Michael. No, it was quite a success. There was a good deal of stimulating discussion, although I must say much of it was ill-informed. There's a strange inability on the part of some Canadian academics to understand the character of Polonius. They insist on regarding him as a sort of Scandinavian Falstaff."

"Including the good professor?"

"No. I'm happy to say young Frye is developing into a promising Shakespearean."

Young Frye? My God! "Then why are your noodles in a knot?"

"I'm afraid Mr. McGregor is responsible for my unhappiness. He is in a foul mood. A reporter has been calling."

"Put him on."

I briefly considered withholding some of the more disturbing elements. But it had been drummed into me, over the years: a field man must keep his control fully informed. And anyway, McGregor had total confidence in me, didn't he?

"Michael!" Or did he? He sounded far from confident.

"There have been some developments," I said tentatively.

"There certainly have! Your friend Bishop has been phoning."

"I know. He called me this morning."

"I gather he intends to make an issue of this on tonight's news."

"So he says."

McGregor didn't reply, and I sat listening to the faint echo of other conversations along the international line. Finally, I said: "Perhaps I'd better bring you up to date."

"Machine-guns?" he said, when I'd finished. "Molotov cocktails? Crooked clergymen? Rattlesnakes? What in the name of God are we caught up in?"

"A mess," I said, unnecessarily.

"Are you certain Carol made the recording unwillingly?"

"Yes."

He grunted into the phone. "What am I supposed to tell her father?"

"I suggest you tell him as little as possible."

He considered it briefly. Then: "Our PR people suggest we make no public comment. What do you think?"

"You know what I think about them, Douglas. They always suggest we make no comment, and they're always wrong. The only thing they know about PR is wining and dining travel editors and arranging freebies for reporters. Frankly, I don't know why you maintain the department."

"Don't start on that again," he said. "What do you advise?"

"Limited candour."

"There's no such thing."

"It's better than no comment. That always makes people sound like they're hiding something."

"Be specific."

"Phone Bishop, tell him you'll meet one of his staff and be as helpful as you can. Do the interview in your office. It's more business-like. You can say, quite honestly, that Holidair is concerned enough about one of its passengers that you've sent someone to Jamaica to look for her. Make the point that we'd do it for anyone who went missing."

"But we don't."

"Douglas, we don't very often have one missing this long."

"That's true, I suppose."

"As for drugs or any Toronto connection that NTN tries to establish, we don't know a thing."

"Very well. I guess you're right." He cleared his throat. "This Cudjoe. You make him sound like some sort of master criminal."

"Not quite. But he's big and tough and cagey."

"Can you handle him?" McGregor sounded almost worried about me.

"That depends on where and how. But yes, probably."

# CHAPTER FOURTEEN

## *Day Three (Sunday) – 3:05 P.M.*

"May we come in?" said Sergeant Patrick O'Toole, not really asking permission. He was with another man, all cop: a no-nonsense type with a crisp moustache and a well-tailored grey suit.

"Why not?" I swung the door wide. "Everybody else does."

"This is Chief Superintendent Crandall," O'Toole said, sounding proud about it. "From Kingston."

"The brass," I said, offering a hand. Unlike many Jamaicans I'd met, Crandall had a firm grip. He looked at me bleakly, a senior policeman working a Sunday afternoon and unhappy about it.

"How do you do?" Crandall's voice was deep but hoarse; he either shouted a lot or smoked too much. His eyes swept the room, stopping at Daniel. "Who's this?"

"A friend." I was getting tired of people growling at me, and Crandall sounded like a growler. "What do you guys want?"

Crandall stepped past me and marched up to Daniel, who was sprawled in a chair. "What's your name?"

"Daniel." He didn't rise or offer to shake hands. Instead, he leaned back and scowled, a classic study in Rasta hostility toward cops.

"Where did you find him, Shuter?" There was a weariness

194

in Crandall's tone. Coupled with the taut way he held his body, it suggested a man under heavy pressure.

"Ras Daniel's okay. He's Jamaica's next Marley."

"Of course." Crandall's frown softened. "You're Danny Harris. I haven't seen you for years, not since you joined the brethren."

"Do you know Daniel?"

"I know his father, Mr. Justice Harris."

So it was Daniel Harris. I'd been with the kid a day and a half and never thought to ask his surname.

"Then you know," I said, "that Daniel's okay. He's been helping me. Or maybe it's the other way around. Either way I think you guys missed a bet."

Crandall gave me a puzzled look.

"Ras Daniel would have made a helluva cop."

"The Jamaican Constabulary Force is not yet recruiting from among the Rastafarians."

"Maybe it should," I grinned. "In San Francisco they've got a quota for gays."

He smiled coldly. "While I agree that, in principle, a police force should reflect the community it serves, I'm afraid our political masters are not ready for policemen in dreadlocks." He paused. "Or dresses."

Even Daniel had to smile.

Crandall walked slowly to the sofa and sat down, producing a packet of Dunhill cigarettes and a disposable lighter. O'Toole hesitated, then followed and sat beside his chief, a faithful Labrador wishing he had a tail to wag.

I kicked the door closed and stood in the middle of the room, wondering what they wanted. Crandall was punishing his cigarette, inhaling deeply and blowing thin smoke through his nostrils. He was a solid-looking man, about my height and perhaps ten pounds heavier. His skin was very dark and there were flecks of grey at his temples. I put his age at about forty-five hard-lived years. O'Toole had arranged his face into what he obviously hoped was an alert expression and was sitting up very straight, ready to dash after any stick Crandall chose to throw. Daniel, meanwhile, continued to loll in his chair.

"Well, Crandall, what's it to be? Bridge? Doubles tennis? Tag-team wrestling?"

"No jokes, Shuter. I'm not in the mood." He leaned forward and flicked ash in the big tray on the coffee table. "You have been in Jamaica for only forty-eight hours, but you have managed to make a thorough nuisance of yourself. Frightening people on our beaches, setting fires in our nightclubs, interfering with our police. We are always pleased to welcome visitors, but I'm afraid we expect them to behave."

Another lecture. I was beginning to feel like a recruit, back in Regina. "Save it for the Chamber of Commerce."

He stubbed out his cigarette and waved an impatient hand. "I said I wasn't in the mood."

We glared at each other. Aside from Daniel, I wasn't making many friends on this trip.

Crandall sighed. "Sergeant O'Toole has given me a report on your conversation yesterday, and there are one or two questions I wish to ask. Why, really, are you crashing around Jamaica looking for the ganja trader, Jefferson? And what are you going to do if you find him?"

Daniel snorted. "You're a bit late, superintendent."

"Why?" Crandall was still glowering at me.

"Barely an hour ago," Daniel said, "we had a fascinating meeting with Cudjoe, right here on our terrace."

"Jefferson was *here*? When? Where did he go? Was he alone?" He rattled off questions like a back-fence gossip in small-town Canada. "How did he get here? How did he leave?"

"He came in a Red Stripe truck," I said. "He left the same way."

"A Red Stripe truck?" Crandall was incredulous. "You mean he's motoring around Jamaica in a beer wagon?"

"Maybe he gets thirsty."

O'Toole couldn't keep out of it any longer. "And you just let him go?"

I shrugged and walked across to a chair. "He didn't come alone, sergeant. He brought along some automatic rifles and a Kalashnikov."

O'Toole started to say something else but Crandall waved him into silence. "Shuter, I insist on an explanation."

It was an order, and Crandall had the air of a man who was used to his orders being obeyed. Besides, what harm could it do? I was still describing our session with Cudjoe when O'Toole went to the phone and began barking instructions. An APB was to be flashed immediately, although from what I knew of the Jamaican sense of urgency "immediately" probably meant some time Tuesday afternoon; all beer trucks were to be stopped and searched. I doubted the police would catch Cudjoe, but headquarters would probably catch hell from the Desnoes & Geddes people.

Crandall listened without interrupting while I told my story. I gave it to him straight, the way I'd have made a verbal report in the RCMP—no embellishment, no conjecture. When I'd finished, he asked: "Were you ever a policeman?"

I nodded. "RCMP. Fifteen years."

"What rank?"

"Staff-sergeant, when I quit."

He frowned. "Are you all the way out?"

So that was it. "My paycheques have stopped."

"That's not always the same thing."

"Where I come from, it is." It isn't; more than one Mountie has "resigned" and gone temporarily into the private sector—on direct orders. What did Crandall think? That the force was poaching on his turf? Probably. The RCMP occasionally runs operations outside Canada without informing the local authorities. Other countries do it too, of course, and it used to make us very unhappy when we caught one of them at it. The Jamaicans would be no different.

Crandall lit another cigarette. "Ottawa is aware of the situation here. Perhaps you are too?"

"What situation?" It was time someone told me what was going on.

"You are going to extraordinary lengths to find a missing passenger, even if she is the daughter of a federal politician."

"What situation?"

"I'm afraid it's classified."

I laughed bitterly. "Don't be ridiculous, Crandall. What earth-shattering secrets does Jamaica possess? Have you invented a death ray? Acquired the Kremlin's plans to invade Bimini? Come across Margaret Trudeau's address book?"

He wasn't amused. "It's a matter of national security. Most delicate."

"National security," I mimicked. "Most delicate. All very hush-hush. You're as bad as Bladon, talking in riddles."

"Bladon. Inspector Stuart Bladon?"

"One day to be Deputy Commissioner Bladon," I muttered, "unless they find out about his gambling habit."

Crandall let that pass. "I've met Bladon several times. At conferences."

The old-boy network among senior policemen around the world is rivalled only by that of the Liberal Party in Canada.

We fenced for a while, and eventually I told him I had consulted Bladon before coming to Jamaica. Crandall wanted all the details but refused to say why.

"Look," I said, exasperated, "I know you've got some kind of problem, and obviously it involves ganja and Cudjoe. But I assure you, Bladon told me nothing about it."

A little warmth crept into Crandall's expression. "You don't trust me, Shuter, and I have doubts about you. But it seems we both trust Inspector Bladon. Perhaps he might reassure each of us, about the other."

I considered it. I should talk to Bladon anyway. "Okay, we'll call him." I attempted a hospitable smile. "Anyone for a cold beer?"

O'Toole shook his head, but Crandall said he'd like one, so naturally the sergeant changed his mind.


Bladon was in the den of his semi-detached house in Scarborough, watching the National Football League and moaning because the Minnesota Vikings were clobbering the supposedly stronger San Diego Chargers. The Vikings were also clobbering the $25 he had bet with one of his constables.

"I'm telling you, Shuter, I couldn't get a break on a ski hill. I laid the eight and a half points, and those assholes from Minnesota are playing like the Pittsburgh goddamn Steelers."

"Just be glad," I said, "that you don't work the gambling detail for some Mickey Mouse municipal outfit. You'd have to bust yourself at least once a week."

"I bust myself once a week now," he said glumly. "How's it going down there? You found her yet?"

He listened, occasionally swearing at something that happened on his TV screen, while I brought him up to date. "This Cudjoe is everything I thought, and less. A bad-ass dealer. And he's got a gang approximately the size of the Canadian civil service."

"He looked like a dandy," he said vaguely. "All that hair."

I told Bladon about Cudjoe fingering the JamJam Rastas, and he said he'd inform Bill McNicholl. The Toronto police seemed to be dragging their feet on the Llewellyn murder.

Then I said I was with a Jamaican cop who claimed to be an acquaintance. Bladon promptly described Chief Superintendent Peter Crandall as a first-rate policeman.

"You should get on okay with him, Shuter. He's a pro, playing for a bush-league club. They mean well enough down there but, hell, you know how it is: they're sort of the Quebec Provincial Police in black-face. Crandall hasn't got much back-up."

"I'm going to put him on."

Crandall took the phone and, after the briefest exchange of pleasantries, moved straight to the point: was I to be trusted? Whatever Bladon's reply, it was lengthy. Crandall held the phone for several minutes, sipping his beer and grunting from time to time. At last, he said: "I see . . . I think you may be right. I'm running out of time . . . Of course I should clear it first, but that could take forever . . . Yes, they're all alike . . . No, I assure you, ours are worse . . . Very well, leave it with me."

He seemed friendlier after he'd broken the connection. "Well, Shuter, you certainly get good marks from Inspector Bladon. Top of the form. One day I'll have to ask you why you packed it in." He dug out another cigarette. "I wonder, would you care to take a stroll? I'd like a word in private."

"There's nobody here but your sergeant and my pal." I owed Daniel that much.

"I'd prefer a stroll."

I turned to Daniel and shrugged an apology: "We shouldn't be too long. I guess you'll be able to keep Sergeant O'Toole entertained."

"Don't worry," he said with a wan smile. "I'll give him my 'Legalize-It' speech."

"I've heard that one," growled O'Toole, disappointed at being left behind. "Sing me a song instead."


By the Sans Souci's lower swimming pool, in the shade of the elevator tower, there is a small bridge over a fenced-in natural inlet. The sea washes in and out of a shallow cave inhabited by a big turtle named Charlie and three jackfish. Crandall and I had stopped on the bridge and were looking down, watching Charlie and his sleek cell-mates move back and forth in their small, shuttered world. The shadows were lengthening and the on-shore breeze had freshened. I found myself thinking about my own fish and wondering whether Maria was feeding them enough.

"One way or another," Crandall said quietly, "we are all in a cage, trying to get out." Gesturing vaguely toward the turtle, he flicked his cigarette butt into the water. The three jackfish made an immediate pass at it, in case it was edible. "We are all reaching for straws. Right now, I'm no better off than those foolish fish."

Another philosopher. Jamaica seemed to be full of them. "Okay, Crandall, what's it all about?"

A waiter shuffled by with tea for a couple lounging by the swimming pool. Two overweight men, scarlet from the sun, were playing gin rummy while their wives splashed noisily in the water. "Let's go out there," said Crandall, pointing to a small gazebo built on a rocky point. "It's more secure."

We walked along a rough pathway to the gazebo, a weather-beaten structure that offered a stunning view of the sea. There were benches inside and we sat facing one another. Crandall seemed to be having trouble organizing his thoughts, so I decided to declare myself. "Before you start, you'd better understand I may feel compelled to brief my boss. You'll have to take my word that he's reliable, discreet. But I'm in Jamaica on his account."

Crandall studied my face as though it held the key to whatever door he was trying to unlock. "I must say, Shuter, you play fair."

"Sometimes," I grinned. "But I usually fight dirty."

"Good. You're mixed up in a dirty fight." He lit another Dunhill. "I flew up here today for two reasons. One, I am keenly interested in Jefferson right now, and therefore in anyone else who shows an unusual interest in him. And two, I'm becoming a little desperate. Clutching at straws, if you will. After Sergeant O'Toole spoke to me yesterday, I became curious. Were you playing some undisclosed game or were you really looking for a missing airline passenger? A check on your activities in Jamaica made me suspicious, so I thought I'd have a look. But Bladon assures me that you are, in fact, what you claim to be. He also says you used to be a good policeman."

"San Diego must have scored three touchdowns while you were on the phone."

Crandall frowned uncertainly, then decided it didn't matter. "Bladon added that you were often impossible to manage, a rogue officer who delighted in bucking the system and ridiculing the orders of superiors."

"That sounds more like him."

"However, he suggested I take you into my confidence. To be frank, Shuter, Jamaica is in trouble. Big trouble."

"And Cudjoe's involved?"

"He's more than involved. He's entirely responsible. The man has declared war on this country, and so far he's winning."

"Individuals don't make war on nation-states, Crandall. It doesn't work that way."

"Doesn't it?" He ran a hand through his hair. "It's amazing how vulnerable governments are to a challenge by ruthless men. It doesn't require very many men, either."

"Cudjoe didn't strike me as a revolutionary," I said sceptically. "He struck me as a racketeer, probably a good one."

"You're right, in the sense that he doesn't give a damn about politics. But take my word for it, he's a subversive of the most dangerous type."

I nodded absently and stared past him at the sea. It was empty and silver, stretching north toward Cuba; no yachts, no freighters, not even a fishing boat. Crandall was getting ready to take me into his confidence, to tell me something an old colleague like Bladon had held back. Why?

"I'm a little ashamed to admit," he said, as though he'd read my mind, "that you've enjoyed more success against Jefferson in two days than the entire Jamaica Constabulary Force has in a week. That's one reason I'm going to breach security. The other..."

"Some success," I said bitterly.

"The other reason is that I'm stuck. I've been put in charge of a task force assigned to deal with this. But too many ministries are involved, too many bureaucrats. Frankly, Shuter, I need someone to talk to, someone who won't be analyzing my every phrase, looking for imaginary slights or political advantage. Also, once I've outlined the situation we face, I think you'll agree our interests coincide."

Sweetness Jefferson, Crandall began, had moved to Jamaica three years earlier. As the son of a Jamaican woman he'd had no problem immigrating, and he'd settled initially in Kingston. Within weeks, he'd come to the attention of the police. It was obvious he was a thug, but he was clever. After a few months, he took the name Cudjoe, let his hair grow, and began dealing dope. He quickly became a powerful figure in the shadowy world of the ganja trade, exporting the stuff as well as distributing it domestically. And, like all the big boys in that business, he wrapped himself in a lot of insulation.

"We tried a dozen times to catch him out," Crandall said, "but all we ever managed was to arrest a few of his underlings. Before long, he was openly laughing at us."

A year and a half ago, Cudjoe moved to the North Shore where he invested in a handful of enterprises, including The Tallyman. These gave him a legitimate source of income and made him even more difficult to prosecute. Meantime, he continued to expand his share of the ganja business, buying out competitors or scaring them off. He steadily enlarged the army of criminals in his employ and they were a murderous lot.

"He maintains loyalty and discipline by the usual underworld means," said Crandall sourly. "Cash, and his own superior viciousness. I'll give one illustration, which we heard from an informer. Apparently Jefferson caught one of his lieutenants short-changing him, so he made an example of the man."

"How?"

"He crucified him. Quite literally. Nailed the poor devil to a cross and let him bleed to death in the sun."

Today, Crandall went on, Cudjoe controlled most production as well as internal distribution and foreign sales. He had allied himself with gangsters in Miami, New York, and Toronto – three cities with large Jamaican communities. The North American appetite for marijuana was insatiable, but Cudjoe was doing his best to satisfy it. Jamaica had provided a perfect base.

"Until," Crandall said, "we had a run of good luck. We intercepted two shipments in a single week. A total of eleven tons."

I was impressed. Maybe the Jamaicans were serious about controlling the trade, after all. "What happened then?"

"He went into a rage. Right round the bend."

"When was this?"

"Ten days ago, after we seized the second shipment."

So Carol would have been with Cudjoe when he got the news and blew his top. Obviously, he had gone to ground and taken her along, either for company or because she knew too much. "You said he'd declared war?"

"In effect. The man's arrogance is staggering. He telephoned the Prime Minister personally and issued an ultimatum: either the police stopped harassing his operation or he'd bankrupt the country."

"You're kidding."

"Unfortunately, no. He was quite specific and I assure you, we take the threat seriously."

"How could one man bankrupt a country?"

Crandall looked at me levelly. "He told the Prime Minister he'd shut down the tourist industry."

"How?" But I already knew the answer. Sonuvabitch!

"A terrorist campaign against visitors."

Business would dry up overnight. I thought about McGregor's observations on the frailty of public confidence. Then I thought about the 20,000 seats we'd sold. No wonder Crandall said our interests coincided.

"Could he bring it off?"

"Perhaps. He's already given us a sample of what he can do."

"Don't tell me," I said tightly. "The parasailer at Negril, the plane explosion at Boscobel, the swimmer at Port Antonio."

Crandall was surprised. "Yes, but how did you know? We were able to make them look like accidents."

"I had a feeling. The timing, the locations."

He shrugged helplessly. "He said he'd show us he meant business. Well, he showed us. But next time we may not be able to cover up. He told us some of the things he had in mind. Random killings, mass poisonings, arson. And, you'll love this, Shuter: he said he'd begin by shooting down an airliner."

I stared at Crandall. "He's crazy!"

"Maybe. But such things are possible, and it wouldn't take very many of them. It's no secret that Jamaica must have the two hundred million tourism generates every year. We are already living on handouts from the World Bank." He paused. "I'm sorry to say there is at least some sympathy in Kingston for making a deal. The rationale seems to be that a lot of voters use ganja, and it *is* an industry of sorts, a cash crop. But the Prime Minister wants Jefferson stopped."

"And he's put you in charge?"

Crandall nodded. "He's also playing a direct role. He has spoken to your Prime Minister, to the President in Washington, to the British Prime Minister. All three governments offered assistance."

I looked at him sharply. "Troops?"

"The British offered a few troops. A token, really. But Jamaica can't accept outside help. For political reasons, the government can't admit it's incapable of protecting the country. Anyway, it would take too many soldiers to guard every beach, every hotel, every public building, and no one wants to take a holiday in an armed camp. So it's up to the police and the JDF."

"I suppose there's a deadline?"

"He gave us two weeks. Till midnight Saturday. But we really don't have that long. We expect statements later this week from London, Washington, and Ottawa cautioning their citizens against coming here—and urging those already in Jamaica to leave."

"That would do it," I said. "But it wouldn't help Cudjoe move his grass. Once the balloon goes, it's up. If he wrecks the tourist trade, you'll be able to track him down at your leisure."

"I know. He's not being very logical, is he? But Jamaica would still be the loser."

"How many men does he have?"

"We're not sure. Not counting the small-fry, at least fifty. We know they're well-armed."

"Yeah. I've seen some of their stuff."

"That's not the problem. The army and the police can handle Jefferson's men, if we can find them. The problem is, we haven't a clue where he's set up his base."

"Jamaica's not a very big country."

"No, but the interior is sparsely settled. There are countless hiding places."

"What do you want from me?"

"I'd like to show you our operation, explain what we're doing. I think I've allowed for every contingency, but you might notice something I've overlooked."

"Who else is in on this?"

"What do you mean?"

"Well, Bladon claims the RCMP guys here haven't been briefed, but you can bet the CIA and the Brits are prowling around."

He shook his head. "If they are, they're being quiet about it. The CIA's presence in Jamaica would be even more embarrassing than a division of British troops."

That wouldn't bother Langley, but there was no point in telling Crandall: he'd know it too. "What about the DEA?"

"They've cut back a lot, since Nixon. The Drug Enforcement Agency is aware of Jefferson, certainly. But they haven't taken a hand. Frankly, I think everyone overestimates our ability to cope. I expect most people outside Jamaica would find the situation incredible."

Not Langley. Nothing's too far-fetched for Langley. But if they hadn't been in touch with Crandall, they weren't going to bother me—unless I somehow got in their way. "Okay, what's our next move?"

"Are you in?"

"All the way."

"Good." He smiled faintly, and got to his feet. "Our next move is Kingston. I've got a police plane waiting."

At least I'd learned the score, even if it wasn't very encouraging. And speaking of scores, I had one to settle with Bladon: he'd known, and sent me after Cudjoe blind. No more twenty-five-year-old whisky for him; he was going straight back to beer and pickled eggs.


Daniel agreed to drive the car to Negril. He'd been planning to fly back in the evening anyway, via Trans-Jamaican Airlines.

"Be careful," I said, "and don't get all upset if you're stopped at a roadblock. The police have enough problems now."

"Where will you stay in Kingston?"

"The Pegasus, I guess."

"I'll call tomorrow, when the Lions and I arrive. You'll want tickets, I suppose?"

"For sure."

"Tickets for what?" said Crandall, who'd been waiting impatiently.

"For the reggae concert," I said. "Daniel and his Rasta pals are trying to save your neck. It's kind of a police benefit show."

Crandall made a sour face. "It'll take more than a few songs to save my neck. Come on, Shuter, let's go."

I packed hurriedly, shook hands with Daniel, and gave him the car keys. "Leave it with Gilly Byles. I'll be back at the Coconut Cove at some point."

Crandall was looking curiously at the box of Tide. "Planning on doing your laundry?"

"No jokes, Crandall. I'm not in the mood."

# CHAPTER FIFTEEN

## *Night Three (Sunday) – 6:00 P.M.*

The police pilot put the twin Commander down tidily at Tinson Pen Aerodrome thirty-five minutes after we'd lifted off from Boscobel. We made our final approach from the west, coming in low over a shantytown that lay squalid and embarrassed in the haze. Row upon row of pathetic shacks leaned up against one another as if they were too decrepit, too dismayed to stand on their own. From the air it was a depressing scene: rusty roofs and limp clotheslines, packing-crate walls and littered alleyways. From the ground it would be worse. The slums of Kingston are notorious, the hellholes of Babylon; the smoke rising from the evening cook fires might have been evidence of burning sulphur. The only green I could see was the grass overrunning a long-abandoned housing project. With its half-poured concrete walls and geometric layout, it looked like a Mayan ruin lost in an urban jungle.

Ahead of us, the city sprawled unhappily between the harbour and the Blue Mountains, grey now in the gloaming. There was a cluster of modern-looking buildings along the waterfront and, off to the left, the hotels and office blocks of New Kingston lorded it over their older, shorter neighbours. No cruise ships lay at anchor and no yachts moved across the harbour. Kingston, a once-gay colonial capital gone shockingly to seed, is no longer a fun town.

During the flight, Crandall and I had compared notes. I told him about my meeting with Cudjoe's brother and suggested that the Reverend Thomas Jefferson be put under surveillance. But Crandall knew all about the brother and the Church of the Pan-African Redeemer. As far as the police knew, Thomas Jefferson had behaved himself in Jamaica, aside from his church hustle. And if the cops busted every religious charlatan, Jamaica would have to launch a crash program of jail construction.

Crandall agreed that Carol was a victim of time and circumstance, and that Cudjoe was probably holding her as a security measure. But, in truth, Crandall showed only perfunctory interest in her; she was a minor player on a very big stage.

Then I remembered Suzie Q and Bishop.

Crandall was upset to learn Carol was about to become a major player, at least in the public's mind. Ever since Cudjoe had issued his challenge to the government, the authorities had been successful in keeping the story out of the media. Of course, managing the news is easier in Jamaica than it is in most democracies: the government controls the television system, one of the two daily newspapers (the other, the Kingston *Daily Gleaner*, is a gutsy independent journal, irreverent and harshly critical of nonsense, from whatever quarter) and one of the two radio operations. Moreover, government officials haven't been shy about helping editors with their story selections and editorial policies. But once foreign reporters began arriving, the lid would come off.

Crandall was like Bladon and, indeed, cops everywhere – unduly concerned about the press. The police are like actors, politicians, athletes, everyone the press covers: they think rave reviews are appropriate, criticism irresponsible. I suggested the NTN story might be a disguised blessing; Crandall could use a highly publicized search for the missing girl as cover for his anti-Cudjoe operations. He gave me an odd look and didn't reply.

We taxied to the small terminal building and the pilot cut the engines. Tinson Pen is Kingston's second airport – a one-runway affair used mainly by private aircraft and Trans-Jamaican Airlines, which connects the capital with Port Antonio, Ocho Rios, MoBay, Mandeville, and Negril. The big stuff lands at Manley International, built on a spit of land jabbing into the harbour.

Crandall was going to his office to see whether there'd been any developments. Like me, he doubted the beer-truck alert would yield anything; Cudjoe had too big a head start. Then, he said, he was going home for dinner in the faint hope his family still remembered who he was. I was welcome to join him.

"Thanks, but I want to get settled in at the hotel and talk to my boss. He's not going to be happy."

"Will you come to a briefing in the morning? I'll have someone call for you. Eight-thirty."

Crandall had a car and driver waiting, and offered to drop me at the Pegasus. But I wanted my own transport, so we shook hands, thanked our pilot, and I lugged my stuff into the building to see about a car. Which is how I met Vivian Beckford and the celebrated Becky.

Tinson Pen is Mr. Beckford's turf; when he's not under hire, he's there polishing what is unquestionably the world's most extraordinary taxi. Becky is a 1931 McLaughlin Buick, a classic touring car with a high-back seat and a canvas roof the size of a store awning. There is more steel in one of Becky's black fenders than there is in two Honda Civics – and a thousand times as much character. Mr. Beckford bought Becky used in 1934 and the car had been in the taxi business ever since. After almost three-quarters of a million miles, it was still going strong, powered by a straight-eight engine that was probably the toughest General Motors ever produced. Becky was built in Oshawa, a suburb of Toronto, by Colonel Sam McLaughlin, a legendary auto pioneer who lived to be 102 and who was a great Canadian philanthropist. Colonel Sam had been a passenger in Becky on several occasions, the last when he was in his early nineties. According to Mr. Beckford, McLaughlin had been very proud of the car—and well he might have been. Show me another taxi, rising fifty.

Beckford, a spare, nut-brown man in his late seventies, was something of a celebrity in Kingston. So was his car, which had been written up in *Time* and was used in one of the early James Bond movies. He kept it on the road by round-the-clock maintenance and with the help of visitors upon whom he relied to mail him spare parts from Canada or the States. To a collector, Becky would be worth as much as $35,000. But to Mr. Beckford, the car was worth more than money; it was at once his livelihood and his life-long friend.

We came to a quick agreement: Becky would be at my disposal for a daily rate. I promised not to add too many miles provided one, I could sit in the front seat, and two, he would tell me all about the car and the people who'd been in it.

Mr. Beckford put my luggage in the back, cautioned me not to slam the door, and pressed the starter button. The engine rumbled into life. It was a ten-minute drive to the Jamaica Pegasus, a 350-room, seventeen-storey hotel on Knutsford Boulevard in New Kingston, supposedly a more secure area than downtown. Mr. Beckford asked whether I intended to dine at the Pegasus; otherwise, he recommended the restaurant at Devon House, the national art gallery. But I wanted to visit the Blue Mountain Inn, provided Becky could manage the trip. No problem, he said solemnly; the inn was a splendid place.

While I checked into the hotel, which is standard-modern and owned by the Trust Houses Forte group in conjunction with British Airways, Mr. Beckford organized my dinner reservation. Then he went out to the car to wait while I went up to my suite. I wanted to shower, change, and phone McGregor.

"At all costs," said McGregor crisply, when I'd brought him up to date, "you're to stop him."

"Well, maybe not at *all* costs."

"Be careful, of course. That goes without saying. But we can't have people shooting down aircraft, can we?" Typically he was more offended by Cudjoe's general threat against aviation than worried about all the money we could lose in cancelled bookings.

"No, I guess not."

McGregor grunted something unintelligible, then asked me what I was going to do.

"I don't know. See what Crandall's people have, I suppose. He seems to think I might be useful."

"What can I do at this end? Is there any point in me trying to get Ottawa to help?"

I explained that Ottawa, Washington, and London had all offered to assist the Jamaicans, but that the government hadn't felt able to accept. "Have you done your interview yet?"

"Yes. I did it here, in my den. I feel more comfortable in my den."

"How did it go?"

"He asked a lot of damn-fool questions."

"Well, don't worry. It'll work out."

"It had better work out. There's a lot at stake." He muttered goodbye and hung up.

I looked up the Sheraton's number and placed a call to Susan Quill's room. She answered on the third ring.

"The foreign correspondent," I said. "It's Mike Shuter."

"Well, hello again."

"How are you?"

"Wet. You got me out of the shower."

"Does that mean you haven't got any clothes on?"

"Just a towel."

"Don't move," I said. "I'll be right over."

She laughed. "Where are you?"

"Next door. The Pegasus. Have you done your story?"

"Yes. It was a bit of a scramble."

"I thought you might tell me about it over dinner. I've got a table at the Blue Mountain Inn and a car you've got to see to believe. It's called Becky."

"My hair's wet." She thought a moment. "Can Becky wait forty-five minutes?"

"Becky," I said, "has been waiting for more than forty-five years. I'll see you in the lobby."


Susan was charmed by Mr. Beckford and knocked out by the old Buick. I was knocked out by Susan. She was wearing a tailored white shirt, a khaki cotton skirt, and just a hint of eye-shadow. Her hair shone and a faint but exotic scent drifted about her shoulders. We sat beside one another in the high-back seat while Mr. Beckford coaxed Becky toward the Mona campus of the University of the West Indies. It wasn't quite dark, but the street lamps had come on.

"I feel like the Queen or someone," said Susan, waving at a group of youngsters who'd shouted hello as we chugged past.

"I don't think *she's* ever been in this car," I said, "but almost everyone else has. Winston Churchill, Sir Stafford Cripps, Augustus John."

"Really?"

Mr. Beckford had told me about driving Churchill in a parade through Kingston in 1947. Cripps' daughter had been married in Jamaica, and Becky had been the wedding limo. Augustus John had used Becky on his Kingston pub crawls, some of which were nearly as celebrated as the great painter himself.

Mona Campus, where Ras Daniel had minored in philosophy and majored in reggae, looked like a pleasant place to study. One of its features was a seventeenth-century aqueduct, fashioned in stone and reminiscent of something you'd see in Provence. It used to bring water from the Hope River down to the port area.

Emerging on the far side of campus, we swung left and made our way through the goats, dogs, and people who cluttered the ramshackle market district of Papine. Then we turned right and Becky began the tortuous climb up a winding road. The mountains, which rise more than 7,000 feet in places, thrust up around us, ancient and patient as Job. Behind, the lights of the city twinkled in the gloom. Ahead was country as wild and impenetrable as it had been when the original Cudjoe and his Maroon followers held an earlier Jamaican administration at gunpoint – and won.

The Blue Mountain Inn, like the aqueduct below, dates from the seventeenth century. It is nestled beside the highway, on the edge of the Hope River, a wild stream, swollen now with the November rains. The inn has a large courtyard, a few out-buildings and a dining room/lounge opening onto a lovely terrace with tables, chairs, and an old grape arbour. A path winds through a tropical garden stretching a hundred yards upstream. The dining room might have been lifted from an English coaching inn: mahogany and horse brasses, heavy plate, and red-velvet plush. On two sides, it is open to the elements and a view of the river, although shutters can be lowered in bad weather. There is a huge fireplace in the bar area and a hand-painted sign over the terrace door, a quote from Thomas Moore: "Let thy sorrow sleep awhile. Let thy joy alone be remembered."

"What a lovely thought," said Susan. "It's perfect for this place. Sorrow doesn't belong here."

"Don't tell me, Suzie Q, that under your Brenda Starr trenchcoat there beats the heart of a romantic."

She gave me a wry smile. "Old-fashioned, isn't it?"

We sat on the terrace, sipping vodka martinis and watching the last light leave the sky. I ordered pepperpot soup, salad, and curried lobster. The wine list was extensive, but the waiter said ruefully that almost everything was out of stock. There were a few bottles of Chablis left, and I asked him to chill one.

Eventually, we were called to the dining room. While we ate our soup, I asked Susan what had brought her winging down.

"Didn't Richard tell you?"

"He said you'd been molested or something."

"Molested is too strong a word. Pawed is closer."

"And you got mad?"

"Let's say I wasn't too happy. But Richard got mad."

"What did you say in your story tonight?"

She took a sip of wine. "Are we here for business? Or pleasure?"

"Pleasure, I hope. I was just curious."

"I don't mind. Maybe we can help each other."

"Maybe." I doubted whether she could help me much, and anyway I didn't want to get into an exchange of confidences. I've never met a reporter who wouldn't shaft you for a good story.

"My piece was just a situational. We didn't have time to set up any interviews."

"Who would you interview?"

"The police, politicians. The usual."

Not if Crandall could help it. "So, what situation did you report?"

"A routine piece. Trouble in paradise, city on the brink, that sort of thing." She brightened. "I did my standup outside the gates of the Prime Minister's residence. It made a nice contrast to the slums we shot."

"Who's with you?"

"A cameraman and a field producer. They wanted to get wrecked on Red Stripe and I wanted to wash my hair." She smiled. "I'm glad I did. Otherwise, I'd have missed Becky – and this place."

While we worked our way through the lobster, we talked about Jamaica and the sorry state of Kingston. Eventually,

Susan asked whether I'd made any progress. I was non-committal.

"You know," Susan said, looking serious, "I understand Carol Malone. At least, I understand part of her. I did a lot of digging last week, found out quite a bit about her. She's extraordinarily beautiful."

"I know."

"And she's clever, a good illustrator. But she's frustrated. She wants to be a painter, and she doesn't have the talent."

"That's a bit harsh."

"It's the truth. I can sympathize with her."

"Why?"

"I want to be a writer. That's why I got into journalism. But I'm not good enough, so I slid into television and do you know what? Really, I get by on my appearance."

I shook my head. "That's not what Bishop says."

"Oh, I'm not a bad reporter. And I work hard. But that's how I got my first break—the fact that I'm a reasonably attractive woman."

"And you think that's Carol's story, too?"

"I know it is. Her boyfriend told me."

"Boyfriend?" It was the first I'd heard of any boyfriend.

"A nice guy, but boring. He's a lawyer."

"I know some interesting lawyers."

She grinned. "Name two. You've got an hour."

"Well, I..."

"'The first thing we do, let's kill all the lawyers.' *Henry the Fourth*, part two."

I laughed. "What've you got against lawyers?"

"I used to go out with one."

She didn't elaborate, and I didn't pursue it. Instead, I said: "So Carol's lawyer friend thinks she's frustrated?"

"Yes. And he's probably right. God can be pretty cruel sometimes, mismatching ambition and ability. Anyway, Carol wants to be a painter and can't do it. So she works as an illustrator, and sells most of her stuff because advertising's a man's world—like television—and she's beautiful. There are plenty of good men illustrators who can't keep the rent paid, you know."

"Tell me more about the lawyer."

She dug a cigarette out of her bag. "A nice guy, as I said. He loves her, I guess, but she's forever running off in search of something else. Down here, for instance. Anyway, he seems resigned to her skittishness, but, of course, he's older."

"An old man in his thirties, eh?"

Susan laughed. "You remembered. No, he's in his forties. Ancient."

Our coffee arrived, and we both ordered Remy. We didn't say anything for a while, and I reflected upon the vulnerability of the species: me, to innocent cracks about my age; Susan, to false doubts about her talent; Carol, to her God-given beauty. What vulnerabilities did Cudjoe have? Over-confidence, perhaps. And greed.

We took our cognac onto the terrace and stood in the moonlight, listening to the river tumble over the rocks. We were 400 miles south of the Tropic of Cancer, but there was a definite chill in the air. No wonder the inn had a fire-place.

"I should have brought a sweater," said Susan, shivering.

"Here." I took off my jacket and draped it across her shoulders. She looked lost in it.

"That was a terrific dinner," she sighed, "and this is such a beautiful place." She put a friendly arm around my waist and snuggled closer. "Be warm."

"Did you know," I said, acutely aware of her closeness, "that Lord Nelson used to come to this inn for R and R?"

"Did he bring Lady Hamilton?"

"I don't think the admiral's lady ever got to Jamaica."

Susan chuckled. "Then he came here with Hardy."

"Maybe," I laughed. "The English navy, you know."

She looked up at me, grey eyes suddenly serious. "Kiss

me, Hardy." She lifted her mouth and waited patiently while I put down my brandy and turned toward her. I took her face in my hands and kissed her softly on the lips, then on the forehead. She put her other arm around my waist and pulled me closer. My jacket slipped off her shoulders and fell in a heap at our feet. "Again, please."

I found myself trembling slightly as I moved my lips down to her mouth. Her tongue teased mine and we held the kiss a long time. I slid a hand down to her firm rump and she ground her pelvis into my upper thigh. Her breathing pattern quickened. If we didn't slow down, Suzie Q and I were going to commit an indiscretion of Nelsonian dimensions, right on the terrace. Releasing her, I stepped back slightly. She looked up and grinned. "Thank you, Hardy."

"The name's Shuter." I bent down and retrieved the jacket.

"Shuter," she said, experimentally, as though trying the word for the first time. "I don't know. 'Kiss me, Shuter' doesn't have quite the same dramatic ring."

"Well, they're not your last words."

"No," she laughed. "At least, I hope not."


When Becky rolled to a stop outside the Sheraton, Susan shifted slightly in my arms and put her lips to my ear. "It's my bedtime. Would you like to come up and tuck me in?"

"Are you sure?" We'd been cuddling like a couple of teenagers during the drive down from the mountains.

"Sure about what?"

"That you want me to tuck you in?" I was sure Susan Quill didn't offer her favours lightly. But she was a long way from home, we'd had quite a bit to drink, and I didn't want to take advantage.

"Completely sure. Do you think I'm brazen?"

"The answer is yes—to both questions."

I told Mr. Beckford I wouldn't need him until mid-morning. Hand-in-hand, Susan and I walked into the hotel. It was almost midnight and, except for a security guard and the night desk clerk, the lobby was empty.

Her room was a standard double: two big beds, two uncomfortable-looking chairs, a desk/dresser, where she'd been doing some typing, heavy drapes, a dressing and make-up area off the bath. I'd been in a hundred like it over the years.

"I'm sorry I can't offer you a drink," said Susan. "I didn't get any duty free. But maybe room service could send up something."

"I've had enough."

She smiled gaily; was she nervous? "Well! Here we are!"

Yes, she was nervous. "Here we are," I said softly, holding out my arms. She came to me, tense. I kissed her and she relaxed a bit, leaning into me. I nuzzled her neck, inhaling her scent. "What's that called?"

"My perfume? Opium."

"I'm addicted already." I gave her a gentle squeeze. "Look, I'll go, if you want."

"No. I want you to stay. Please."

Slowly she began unbuttoning my shirt, running a hand over my chest while I awkwardly opened her blouse. Her breasts were surprisingly full, almost too heavy for her frame, but firm. I cupped one, lifting it slightly; it was soft and smooth and warm.

"You're very beautiful." Another of my deathless lines.

"So are you."

I removed my hand. "You're not supposed to say that to a man."

"Why not?" Abruptly, she stepped back and began undoing her various buttons, snaps and zippers. Within seconds she had shrugged off her blouse, stepped out of her skirt and peeled off a pair of impossibly tiny white pants. "Let's get in bed."

While I got out of my clothes, she swept the covers back.

"You *are* beautiful, even with the bruises." She was looking up at me, inspecting my body with a frank curiosity that I found oddly appealing.

I stood at the end of the bed and admired her slim legs, her flat belly, her breasts and the hollow in her throat. She was leaning back against the double pillows, legs slightly apart, one knee raised. Her pubic hair was dark blonde and thick, and her pudenda glistened, pink and swollen among the curls. Susan was a masterpiece of erotic engineering, and she was horny. So was I. As I stood looking down at her I felt myself become tumescent.

I lay down and gathered her into my arms, running my hands up and down her body, loving the silky feel of her skin, enjoying the tentative caresses she offered in return. When I reached down between her legs, she gasped, then moaned.

I don't know.

Cudjoe, Carol, Crandall and all the rest of it should have been worlds away. But suddenly, unaccountably, they were right in Susan's room with me. So were McGregor and Ras Lucky, Bladon and Bishop. Hell, I suppose Janet's duppy was there, too. A bloody convention. My erection wilted like the Maple Leafs in the Stanley Cup playoffs.

It's happened before, but only when I've been very drunk and with someone very boring. This time I wasn't drunk and Susan was anything but boring. Her breath was ragged in my ear, her tongue electric. But then she sensed something was wrong, became aware that I wasn't responding. After a moment or two she reached down and found me flaccid.

"What's the matter?" She sounded hurt.

"I don't know. Tired, I guess. Too much on my mind." I stroked her smooth back.

"But a minute ago ... Don't I ... ?"

"It's not you, Susan. I want you very much. But tonight I'm just ..."

"Shh." She cut me off with a kiss, ran her nails lightly

across my abdomen and thighs, then moved down in the bed. Her tongue was soft, her mouth hot, her fingers deft, and I felt myself responding. But for some reason, I didn't want her to continue. It seemed artificial, unfair. I reached down and drew her up alongside me, holding her close.

"Let's not force it."

"I don't mind doing that."

"There'll be other nights." There'd better be.

Strangely, I didn't feel humiliated or even embarrassed. I was too exhausted, too preoccupied. I held Susan in my arms for a long while. She was an understanding woman, wise beyond her years. Eventually, she began to snore lightly. I doubted she'd fake that, so I got up and dressed quietly. I don't think she heard me leave.

# CHAPTER SIXTEEN

## *Day Four (Monday) – 9:10 A.M.*

Committees are notoriously slow and invariably divided. Not only do they design horses that look like camels, but they usually call in consultants to help with the drawings. That way, they have someone to blame when their performance is criticized. Governments, however, love committees and establish them at the first sign of trouble. It's a reflex action, based on the twin commandments of modern political administration: delegate all difficulties and supervise all successes. Committees have another attraction to governments; quite often, by the time they get around to reporting on a problem, the problem has disappeared of its own volition.

But Cudjoe wasn't going to disappear on his own and the committee set up to deal with him knew it. The meeting, in a large windowless room deep within police headquarters, had been convened at eight A.M. I'd joined it fifty minutes later, and been introduced by Crandall to a roomful of worried men. Two or three of them appeared hostile, and I couldn't blame them. I was a foreigner, and worse, a civilian.

We sat at a long oak table, which was cluttered with a water jug and glasses, coffee pot and scratch pads, listening while Crandall delivered a crisp summary of the situation. The situation wasn't good: Cudjoe had gone to ground again; there had been a lot of panicky overnight Telex traffic between Ottawa and Kingston because of Bishop's newscast; a half-dozen pre-dawn raids in West Kingston had yielded nothing; and the deadline was one day closer.

While Crandall talked, I studied the other members of the task force. There were three other cops present, representing the Flying Squad (which did the raiding), Narcotics (which provided intelligence) and Records (which kept track of it all). There was also a full colonel from the JDF, the only uniform in the room. He sat very still and his sharp eyes missed nothing. The bureaucrats seemed to be standard issue — cautious men in well-cut suits, white shirts and silk ties doubtlessly acquired on government-paid junkets to New York, London, wherever. They represented the Prime Minister's Office, the Foreign Affairs Department, the ministries of Correctional Services, and National Security (a very hard-looking character who wouldn't have been out of place in Langley or Dzerzhinski Square), and the Jamaica Tourist Board.

When Crandall finished his report, he asked whether there were any comments. There were, mostly relating to the Canadian news report and the additional problems it would cause. Already there had been inquiries from local reporters, who'd been alerted by wire-service scalps of the NTN piece. Most of the bureaucrats wanted to stonewall the press about Carol.

To my mild surprise, Crandall disagreed. He repeated my suggestion, crediting me, that the government go high-profile over Carol's disappearance and use it to mask the larger problem. He wanted her picture all over the papers and television, statements of concern from the tourist authorities and Foreign Affairs Department, a police request for public assistance, the works. The man from National Security, whose name was Morgan, objected strongly, but the PMO's representative sided with Crandall. The debate went round and round, ending inconclusively with the bureaucrats deciding to buck the question up to their ministers. I began to appreciate Crandall's frustration.

Then Morgan made a little speech, occasionally pounding the table for emphasis.

"I don't have to tell you all," he said, looking directly at Crandall, "that we at the Ministry of National Security are dissatisfied with the way the police are handling this situation. It has been ten days now, and what's happened? I'll tell you what's happened. Nothing's happened. Jefferson remains at large and Jamaica remains in trouble.

"Now let me tell you what's going to happen, if the police don't make some progress in the next forty-eight hours. I'm going to see the Prime Minister and demand that he turn this investigation over to my ministry. Our agents will not be as gentle with these terrorists as the police seem to have been."

While Morgan was talking, I tried to estimate the support he had among the committee members. Most of them maintained poker faces, but two or three seemed sympathetic. Crandall listened politely, but it was obvious he was in a rage.

"There is no point," he said tightly when Morgan finished, "in squabbling among ourselves. I welcome, as always, constructive suggestions, from whatever source. But I reject categorically that the police are doing anything less than their utmost to find Jefferson and smash this threat to the nation. No one is more aware than I of the gravity of the situation. I remind you, gentlemen, that the responsibility for failure is mine. Now, let us have done with obstructionism and get on with the job."

Crandall paused and looked around the room, as if daring anyone else to criticize his efforts. When no one spoke, he nodded curtly, then glanced toward me.

"Gentlemen, as I told you earlier, Mr. Shuter saw Jefferson yesterday. I thought it might be useful if he reported to the committee in person. He is, as I said, a former officer in the

Royal Canadian Mounted Police and he comes with their highest recommendation."

I stood, and quickly described my job. I gave them a brief recap of my various encounters with Cudjoe's men and then a detailed report on yesterday's events at the Sans Souci. The army colonel questioned me closely, and seemed worried about the M-16s and Kalashnikov. The cop from Narcotics said my description of Cudjoe's lieutenant, Jimmy, fitted a local hood named Jimmy Reid, who had dropped out of sight recently. Morgan asked me several questions which seemed more intended to embarrass the police than to elicit information. And the Tourist Board representative wanted to know whether I thought McGregor would keep his Jumbos flying into Sangster, come what might.

After my number, the meeting prepared to adjourn. The politicians would decide at their noon cabinet session how to handle the press, and the PMO would pass the decision along to Crandall. In the meantime, the committee was grateful for my interest.

Crandall asked me to accompany him to his office and we trekked along a series of murky corridors, then up a flight of stairs. He had a cramped corner suite overlooking Old Hope Road, busy now with mid-morning traffic. He sat behind his desk and lit a Dunhill. "They weren't pleased, you know. They weren't pleased at all."

"Guys like that are always suspicious of outsiders."

He took a deep drag, exhaling with a sigh. "Morgan's after my head. He's a cunning little swine."

"There's always one."

"I'll deal with him—after I catch Jefferson." Crandall yawned. "Right. I thought I'd show you what we've done, what we're doing. You might have an idea or two."

For the next half-hour, aided by maps, files, and computer printouts, Crandall outlined his operation. It was impressive. Even Bladon would have conceded that much. The entire police force, including the auxiliary, had been mobilized. Everyone who'd ever been connected with Cudjoe, however remotely, had been questioned at least once—except, of course, for those who couldn't be found. Roadblocks were up throughout the island. Every mile of road was being patrolled regularly by police and army vehicles. The country had been gridded off and was being systematically searched from the air with police planes and army helicopters looking from sunup to dark for Cudjoe's stronghold. JDF gunboats and police cutters were patrolling the coastline, halting all suspicious-looking vessels. The army was on full alert and guarding airports, many public buildings and a few senior officials. There was a plan for troops to secure the major hotels and beaches forty-eight hours before the Saturday deadline, if Cudjoe remained at large. Army communications specialists were monitoring radio frequencies at random, hoping to pick up a signal; it was assumed that Cudjoe was in radio touch with the outside world from his base.

"Well?" said Crandall.

"You've done a helluva job," I said truthfully. "It's almost as though the country's on a war footing."

"We *are* on a war footing."

I had one suggestion: that Crandall make arrangements with the Jamaica Telephone Company to record all international calls; Cudjoe obviously had been talking to Toronto at some point, since he knew about Lucky's death and my run-in with his men outside the JamJam Club.

"I *knew* you'd spot something," said Crandall, pleased. "Anything else?"

"Not that I can think of. I must say, I feel a lot better, seeing your arrangements. The sonuvabitch has bitten off too much."

"Maybe," Crandall mused, "and maybe not. All of this may look impressive, but we still don't know where he is. Somehow, we've got to find his hideout." He lit another cigarette. "I meant to say, that was a good idea you had for dealing with the press. We can't stop them now, so we might as well use them." He took a deep drag. "I suppose I'd better go and rally the chaps. Will you be available later?"

"You can either reach me at the hotel or leave a message there. Right now, I've got an errand to do."


Most police work is a grind and most cases are solved by the grinders, plodders who follow the book. Crandall's elaborate operation against Cudjoe reminded me once again that the sheer weight of numbers works against the criminal. So does forensics, a dispassionate science which answers more tricky questions every day than Ann Landers, Abigail Van Buren, the "Playboy Adviser," and the Oracle at Delphi have in their combined histories. But every once in a while the plodders and the lab wizards are by-passed and a case is resolved by pure fluke or by an outside element wholly unrelated to the central investigation. A box of Tide, for example. Or a thoughtless act.

Mr. Beckford pulled into the curb in front of the Reggae World and switched off Becky's engine, prepared to wait. I put the detergent under my arm and opened the car door.

The Reggae World was one of those hybrid musical emporiums peculiar to Jamaica – part-store, part-studio. It offered a thin selection of imported records and tapes and a vast array of locally produced material. Almost every teenager in the country seemed to have made a record or two, but then music to the youth of Jamaica is like basketball to kids in Harlem and hockey to young men from Chicoutimi: a way out.

The shop also carried an assortment of odd-lot components – speakers, turntables, tape decks, receivers – and a few television sets and radios. But most of the Reggae World's cash flow came from making unauthorized dubs of foreign albums brought in by customers or scrounged by the proprietors. It was a business that owed its existence to the country's severe restrictions on imports and the futility of pursuing infringement-of-copyright suits against marginal Jamaican entrepreneurs. You'd have a better chance of going into a Moscow court and collecting a judgment against the Politburo.

The walls were covered with posters promoting the latest Marley, Toots and Tosh releases and the place was throbbing with the uneven sounds of Zap! Pow! Except for a staff of two, and a half-dozen kids, who were hanging out at the rear, the store was empty. I was glad I wasn't lugging the rent.

A girl was standing hopefully by a cash register near the door, doing her nails and humming along with Zap! Pow! She smiled mechanically when I approached. "May I help you, sah?"

"Winston Llewellyn around?"

She nodded and pointed to the kids. "Winston! A gen'min here for you!"

"Thanks," I said, but she'd already gone back to her nails, disappointed that I wasn't a cash customer.

Winston was in his early twenties, thin, and not as tall as Lucky had been. He was neat in scrubbed jeans, white T-shirt, phosphorescent running shoes, and a small toque fashioned out of navy-blue wool. His demeanour was serious. He looked almost bookish behind his glasses.

"You askin' for me?" His voice was soft but flat, virtually atonal.

I held out my hand. "I'm Mike Shuter. From Toronto."

"T'ron'o," he repeated, taking my hand briefly and gazing impassively into my eyes.

"I knew your brother." I'd been wondering all morning how to handle this. I'm no stranger to bereavement, but I felt a bit awkward meeting Ras Lucky's brother; I felt partly responsible for the man's death.

Winston nodded and bit his lip. "We all pray for him yes-tiddy, at de Baptist church." An edge crept into his voice, a hint of anger or maybe heartache. "He only twenty-nine, mon."

"It was a lousy way to go."

Winston nodded again and looked down at his shoes. "Dey cremate him in Canada. We didn't...We couldn't..."

"It's a long trip."

"We send up flowers," he said, almost defiantly. "Dey cost forty dollar."

"We? Your family?"

"Dere just me and Ruth. An' her two kids."

Ruth would be the sister. "Lucky asked me to bring you this, for Ruth." I handed him the Tide, conscious of how inappropriate it seemed. "He said it was hard to get this stuff down here, and I..."

"She be t'rilled," said Winston, sounding sincere. He held the package across his stomach and tried to smile.

Thrilled? It didn't seem like much of a legacy. Janet's bequest popped into my head. Christ! "Look, Winston, I owed your brother some money. I guess you and your sister ought to have it."

His smile faded. "Money? David never had no money. Not to lend."

"This was a business thing." How much was a return ticket, economy class, Toronto-Kingston? Maybe $300? "I owed him three-hundred dollars. I want you and your sister to have it."

"Business," he said bitterly. "Ruth an' I doan take no ganja money."

"It's got nothing to do with ganja, Winston." I took a card and three U.S. $100-bills from my wallet. "Your brother helped me with something."

He studied the card for a while, then passed it back. But he kept the money. "No problem, Mist' Shutah. It good o' you."

I was curious about Winston: he wasn't a Rasta, had no

use for the ganja trade, and was supposed to know everyone in town. "Winston, are you working or anything today?"

He shook his head. "Dey no job in Kingston, mon."

"Then you're free for a little while. How about coming somewhere for a beer? Or a coffee? I'd like to talk to you a bit more about your brother."


Winston had often seen Becky around town and now he was sitting tall in the back seat, wishing the top was down in case we passed one of his friends.

Mr. Beckford seemed determined that I pay a visit to Devon House at some point, so we decided to go there. It's a lovely colonial mansion, at the corner of Hope and Waterloo Roads. The Prime Minister's residence and the governor general's mansions are just up the street – in Kingston's high-rent, low-crime district. Devon House is the repository for the country's modest collection of paintings and sculpture. To the rear, in what used to be the slave quarters and stables, there are several boutiques and handicraft shops. On the south side, there is a bar-restaurant where the food is good. Winston and I took an outside table and sat in the shade of a huge mahogany tree planted during Spanish times. We both ordered coffee and Winston let me talk him into having a toasted chicken sandwich.

We chatted for a while about Kingston, the problems of finding a job, the pleasures of music, and the difficulties of being the only man around a small house shared with an unmarried sister and two young children. While he ate his sandwich, I told him about meeting his brother. Next I told him about Carol and explained why I was trying to find her. Then I took a chance: Carol, I said, was being held at a secret hideout by a ganja trader named Cudjoe, and I had to find the hideout.

"Cudjoe a bad person to mess wit'," he said. "Dey say he killed some people."

I looked at him steadily. "You're going to find out sooner or later, so you might as well know now: Cudjoe's men murdered your brother."

He put his cup down hard, spilling a little coffee on the tablecloth. "How you know dat?"

"The man told me himself."

"Cudjoe told you? When?"

"Yesterday. In Ocho Rios."

"Why dey kill him?" Winston seemed close to tears.

"Your brother was mixed up with some bad people."

He blinked hard and swallowed. "I know, mon. David often tol' me it not easy for a Jamaican to get along in T'ron'o, to get de money."

"The ganjamen seem to get the money, Winston. Lots of it."

"Not David." He frowned. "De T'ron'o police. Do dey know 'bout de men dat kill him?"

"I told them. Don't worry, they'll arrest the people responsible."

"But not Cudjoe," he said bitterly. "Dey never catch him."

"I'll get him. Or the Jamaican police will. Eventually."

Winston pushed his sandwich plate into the centre of the table. He looked at me morosely and was silent for a while, thinking. "Maybe we go ask Sarah. She should know."

"Who's Sarah?"

"Used to be Cudjoe's woman. He still see her sometimes."

"Where is she?"

"Near to Ruth an' me. In Trench Town."


It was high noon when we left the car at the edge of Trench Town, a teeming slum where outsiders almost never venture. Even the police are reluctant to patrol there, except in heavily armed platoons. There are a lot of gangs in Trench Town – and a lot of guns. There are also thousands of people steeped in despair, people to whom violence is as normal as breathing and hope as alien as Mars. It is a place of narrow streets, tumble-down shacks, stinking sewers, naked kids, empty bellies, hollow lives. Trench Town is not just the shame of a nation; like hard-core slums the world over, it is the shame of the species.

Winston led me through a maze of alleys and laneways, clutching the box of Tide, and occasionally nodding hello to an acquaintance. There were few answering smiles. People watched our progress sullenly, their hostility almost tangible. Women, old in their thirties, peered at us from behind dark doorways. Several groups of young men, most of them in dreadlocks, and some of them smoking midday spliffs, glared and muttered as we crossed their turf. Every few yards, a scrawny dog, miserable in the humidity, would manage to snarl and cower at the same time.

"Tough neighbourhood," I said, after we had passed yet another knot of street thugs.

"You be okay wit' me," said Winston. "But you alone, dey prob'ly kill you for you watch."

We kept up a steady pace. A line from a dimly remembered gunfighter movie drifted into my head, a sign at the entrance to a lawless prairie town: "When you ride into Purgatory, say goodbye to God." Walking through Trench Town, it was easy to see why the Christian churches were failing in Kingston, why the Rastas were gathering strength; God didn't come here any more.

No wonder Winston spent his days at a record shop. And no wonder Ras Lucky had dealt his way to Toronto. I'd gnaw a leg off to get out of a trap like this.

"Our place down dere," said Winston, pointing along a pathway to the left. "Sarah just up ahead."

On the way from Devon House, Winston had told me about Sarah. Cudjoe had met her shortly after he'd arrived in Kingston and they'd stayed together for a year and a half. Eventually, Cudjoe had become tired of her, bored with her lack of sophistication. He was moving up in the world.

When he moved to Ocho Rios, he left Sarah behind. She was bitter, particularly about the white women Cudjoe now preferred. Abandoned and broke, but still carrying Cudjoe's brand, which put her off-limits to other men, Sarah had moved back in with her family in Trench Town. Now she sat around waiting for Cudjoe's intermittent summonses. She was frightened of Cudjoe, and hated him; but she was submissive, at least partly because he sometimes gave her a little money.

We found Sarah sitting on the front steps of a cinderblock house in better repair than most in the neighbourhood. She was gorgeous – copper-skinned, wide-eyed, lean and tall, stunning in a full Afro. A teenage superstar, but that was no surprise: Cudjoe would hardly have spent a year and a half with a turkey.

"Hello, Sarah," said Winston respectfully. "We come to see you."

She looked at me curiously, saying nothing.

"Dis Mist' Shutah, from T'ron'o," Winston explained. "He a friend to David."

Sarah nodded solemnly. I guess she meant hello.

"Mist' Shutah anxious to meet wit' Cudjoe."

She shifted her gaze to Winston, keeping her face expressionless. "Why?"

"He tryin' to find a girl. An important girl. From Canada. She wit' Cudjoe now." Winston sounded embarrassed about it.

Sarah rearranged her flawless features into a faint sneer. Then she shrugged. "That *her* problem."

I caught a flash of movement beyond the doorway, but no one emerged from the house to see what I wanted. Along the street, several people stood watching us, keeping their distance; a white man talking to Cudjoe's woman was probably bad news, and the people of Trench Town didn't need any more bad news.

"No," I said, smiling, "that's *my* problem. I've been to the house in Ocho Rios, but they're not there. I gather Cudjoe has another place, somewhere in the country. I hoped you might tell me where it is."

She held my eye, then looked away. "I doan know any-t'ing about it."

"It's urgent, Sarah."

She ignored me, turning to Winston for support. "All at once, everybody tryin' to find Sweetness. De police askin', too."

"Never mind the police," I said. "This is business, between Cudjoe and me. He won't like it if he learns you wouldn't help me."

"If Sweetness want you, he find you," she said.

Sarah wasn't going to talk, but I was certain she knew where Cudjoe was. She got to her feet, looked at me blankly, and turned, walking slowly into the house: graceful, beauti-ful, vacant—a black Barbie doll. I felt like shaking her bones, but if I laid a glove on her I probably wouldn't get out of Trench Town alive.

"Come on, Winston. It's no use."

He nodded unhappily. "I see you back to de car."

We ran the hostility gauntlet again. No one got in our way. At the car I thanked Winston and asked whether he was going to the reggae concert.

"Hadn't planned to. De ticket t'ree dollar. But now..." He patted his pocket and grinned.

"Save your money. I'll get you a ticket. A friend of mine's playing."

"Who, mon?"

"Ras Daniel."

"De Lions. Yeah. Dey great!"

"You can meet them, if you want. I'm staying at the Pegasus. Come by about six and I'll fix you up."

"T'anks, Mist' Shutah. Maybe I better go see Ruth now, tell her 'bout de money."

I grinned at him. "You're a good man, Winston."

"Maybe I go see Sarah one more time. Ask her again. Maybe wit'out you dere, she..."

"She won't tell you anything. She's frightened of him."

"Yeah, mon, but she hate him, too."

"Be careful," I said. "He plays rough."

Just before Becky turned the corner, I looked back. Winston was standing in the street, the Tide under his left arm. His right arm was raised in a half-salute.

I'd had more phone calls than a Toronto bookie on an NFL Sunday. The concierge produced a sheaf of messages from my mail slot, and I sorted through them in the elevator. There'd been calls from Susan (two), McGregor, Bladon, Bishop, Daniel, the *Toronto Star*, the *Globe and Mail*, the CBC, and, most recently, from Crandall.

The threads were undisturbed. I phoned the matron and asked that my suite be made up. Then I called room service and ordered a sandwich and a couple of bottles of Heineken. I took a fast shower. I could wash Trench Town off my body but I wouldn't be able to wash it out of my mind.

The maid and room service arrived simultaneously. Wrapped in a towel, I let them in, opened a beer, and ate my sandwich. It looked like a long afternoon on the phone.

I started by throwing away the messages from the Toronto papers and the CBC. The hell with them. Then I crumpled Bishop's. The hell with him, too. There was no answer in Susan's room. She was probably out filming. But at least she'd called, which was a good sign. I left my name with the Sheraton switchboard.

McGregor was in a tizzy. Holidair's offices were under siege by the media; there were a dozen reporters, photographers and TV cameramen camped in the reception area. Our public relations geniuses were fumbling the ball on almost every play and McGregor was in a rage about it. Helen was trying to talk him into giving a full-dress press conference, while the PR department wanted to issue a written statement. They probably wouldn't get it written before Friday. I urged him to take Helen's advice; otherwise there'd be no peace. He could simply repeat for the others what he'd told NTN the day before. After a lot of grumbling, he agreed. Meantime, he reported, Alan Malone had released a vague statement in Ottawa, expressing confidence in his daughter's safety and good judgment. McGregor listened impatiently to a recap of my morning and then he told me to keep digging. I told him to keep cool.

Bladon was in his office, trying to figure out which way to bet on the Monday-night game between Houston and Cleveland. The Oilers were at home and three-point favourites, but Earl Campbell was on the limp. I told him to take the points and asked why he'd phoned. He said Metro homicide had rounded up two of the JamJam punks and would charge them with Lucky's murder later in the day; the other three were still at large. The RCMP had continued to avoid any public connection with the Llewellyn murder, so Bishop wasn't being totally irresponsible. Bladon also said he'd heard from Crandall and he gathered that I'd been useful. I told him "used" was a better word and that I'd figure out a way to get even before I got home. He just laughed, told me to get off my duff and hung up without saying goodbye.

Daniel was at his parents' home in Stony Hill, a residential district at the foot of the Blue Mountains. He'd arrived at mid-morning, via Trans-Jamaican. His drive from Ocho Rios to Negril had been without incident, unless I counted three roadblocks. The Mercedes was safe at the Coconut Cove. His parents wondered whether I'd like to join the family for an early dinner, but I begged off; perhaps I'd meet them after the concert. Daniel said he'd leave a half-dozen tickets at the Pegasus, as well as a pass admitting me backstage. I asked whether he could leave two backstage passes; Winston Llewellyn was a fan.

Which brought me to Crandall.

"The PM has decided to go public with Miss Malone's disappearance," he said. "There'll be announcements in time for the evening news."

"Are you planning a press conference?"

"We'll save that for tomorrow. The announcements will be enough for them today."

It wouldn't help Susan much; NTN had already reported Carol's vanishing act and the Jamaican government's concern. "Would you do something for me? The Canadian reporter I told you about yesterday, Susan Quill. Would you give her an interview?"

"Why?"

"She's already reported the stuff that'll be in your announcements, so she'll be looking for something fresh. It might be smarter to feed her a few tidbits than to leave her to dig around on her own. She's pretty sharp."

"Does she know about Jefferson?"

"No." I thought for a moment. "Well, she may know Cudjoe's name. She might have picked it up from the girl Carol was travelling with. But I'm sure she doesn't know any details."

"If she's got his name," he said glumly, "it won't take her very long to find out who he is and what he does."

"All the more reason to see her. You should be able to misdirect her a bit, if his name comes up." Part of me wanted Susan to stay ahead of her competition; but another part wanted her kept away from the real story.

"Very well. Tell her to call me." He paused. "Did you do your errand?"

"Yep. I also had a walking tour of Trench Town."

"Are you mad, Shuter? What were you doing in Trench Town?"

"Looking for Cudjoe." I told him about Winston and our meeting with Sarah. "She *knows*, Crandall. She knows where he is. I'm sure of it."

"Sarah. That rings a bell. Hold on a moment." I could hear papers rustling. "Yes, here it is. Sarah Brown. We interviewed her twice, but she was no help. Apparently she and Jefferson are no longer friendly."

"My information is that they still see each other occasionally."

"All right," he sighed. "If you think it's worth it, I'll have somebody bring her in. I'll talk to her myself, but I'll have to do it this evening. I've got the PM in twenty minutes. God knows how long that'll take."

"I'll have Susan Quill call your office."

The instant I replaced the receiver, the phone rang. It was Susan. "Your line's been busy for ages," she said. "I finally got the switchboard to leave me on hold."

"Hi. How are you?"

"Not very exciting, apparently."

"Now, Susan, I'd..."

"I was just joking. I'm fine. How are you?"

"Still tired. I had a busy morning."

"Me too, but I'm not getting very far. Richard's pleased, though. The story's getting a big play at home. They're going to take a late feed from me if I get anything worth while."

I cleared my throat. "Listen, Susan, do you want a fresh angle for tonight? I don't want to interfere in your work, but..."

"Are you kidding? I need all the help I can get."

"Call Chief Superintendent Peter Crandall at police headquarters. He's in charge of the search for Carol."

"A chief superintendent?" she said, surprised. "They must be taking it seriously."

"They are. Later today, the police and the government are going to ask the public for assistance."

"I've been trying to get the police to see me. But I've been getting the runaround."

"Crandall will see you. I arranged it."

"That's terrific." She paused. "Are you going to the concert tonight?"

"I guess so."

"We're going to shoot some of it. It's too late for tonight's show but we might salvage a bit for tomorrow. It should be good colour." She dropped her voice a bit. "Am I...will I see you? Maybe after the concert?"

"Absolutely." I chuckled into the phone. "Unfinished business."

"Not business," she laughed. "Pleasure."

"Whatever."

"If you're not too tired," she said, twisting the knife.

"I'm going to have a nap right now. Us old guys in our thirties need our rest."

I told the switchboard to hold my calls for three hours, drew the bedroom drapes, and climbed into the sack, exhausted.


The phone woke me just after five o'clock. I'd been in a deep, dreamless sleep and I was disoriented, uncertain where I was. The air-conditioning had been operating at full throttle and the bedroom was chilly. I fumbled in the dark for the bedside lamp switch and picked up the receiver.

"Something's just come in," said Crandall softly, "that you're not going to like."

"What?"

"Your young friend from Trench Town, Winston Llewellyn."

"No," I said, sick.

"I'm sorry," said Crandall. "He was found this afternoon."

Not Winston. We were going to the concert. I'd arranged a backstage pass for him. Not Winston, too. Why did I let him go back there? Why?

"Shuter? Did you hear what I said?"

Poor Winston, who wouldn't take dirty money, who loved music, who agreed to help me when all his instincts told him to back away. The memory of his waving as I left him alone on the fringe of that hellacious neighbourhood

240

burned behind my eyes, then dissolved into a kaleidoscopic pattern of crimson and black. How could I have been so stupid, so unthinking?

"Shuter...?" Crandall's voice came drifting into my head like a long-forgotten melody late at night.

"I'm here." Yeah. In bed, like the dumb sonuvabitch I am.

"Did you hear me?"

"How did he die?"

"He drowned. Or I should say, he *was* drowned. You really don't want to know the details."

"Yes I do."

There was a brief silence. Then Crandall sighed. "There's no doubt it was murder," he said quietly. "Your friend's hands were tied behind his back. He was found face-down in one of the open mains."

A sewer? A stinking sewer? They did that to him? "That's two," I said, more to myself than Crandall.

"I beg your pardon?"

"I said Cudjoe owes me two."

"You're probably right, but we have the usual problem— no witnesses, no suspects. I'm afraid we don't get much co-operation in that district, and..."

"Are you in your office?"

"Yes. This came in just after your reporter friend left. I wanted..."

"I'll be there in fifteen minutes. Wait for me."

"Well, yes. Of course. But what...?"

"I'm going to need one or two things."

"Shuter, the police will..."

"Screw the police!"

I banged down the phone and started getting into my clothes. Bobby Kennedy had it backwards: don't get even, get mad. Getting even isn't good enough.

The room wasn't chilly any more. It was stifling. And I was on fire, in the mood to raise hell. Raze it to the ground.

# CHAPTER SEVENTEEN

## *Night Four (Monday) – 5:40 P.M.*

"A flame-thrower?" Crandall was incredulous. "Are you sure you wouldn't like me to requisition a tactical nuke, while I'm at it?"

"Jamaica doesn't have any," I said tightly. "Come on, Crandall. Stop pussy-footing. I'll bring it back."

"You're not going there alone, and that's that!" He slammed a big fist on his desk. "And you're not going to burn Trench Town to the ground. At least not with government equipment. I've got enough problems now."

"I'm not into urban renewal," I said, "although *someone* ought to burn the place down. Try to think of this as theatre. *Son et lumière.*"

"*Son et lumière,*" he repeated sarcastically. "A machine-gun and a flame-thrower. Lovely."

"And the dogs. Don't forget the dogs."

He looked at me unhappily. "Shuter, I can't authorize this. In fact, I ought to lock you up."

"You want Cudjoe, don't you?"

"He is not in Trench Town." Crandall stubbed out his cigarette and immediately began fumbling for another one.

"The girl knows, Crandall. And she'll talk."

"Then we'll bring her in."

"No," I said. "You've had two sessions with Sarah, and what have you got? Zip."

He gave me a sour look. "So, we'll have a third session."

"She won't tell you anything. Why should she? She's not afraid of the police. But I promise you, she'll be afraid of me."

"What about police brutality?" he said bitterly. "Rubber hoses, little accidents in the stairwell, things like that?"

"That's bull and you know it. It's a matter of conditioning. People believe the police are their protectors."

Crandall got to his feet, walked across to the window and stared down at the street. It would be better if I had his co-operation, but I'd manage without it. Miss Sarah Brown and I were going to have a little chat and, short of locking me up, Crandall couldn't stop it.

"I suppose you have a preference," he said quietly, not turning around. "For a machine-gun, I mean."

"It's only a prop. Something mean-looking and noisy. An Ingram, perhaps."

"An Ingram," he sighed. "Splendid. I was afraid you were going to demand an Uzi."

"Have you got one?"

He turned, scowling. "No, Shuter, I don't have an Uzi. Or a Kalashnikov. Or a bazooka, for that matter. And I don't want to start the Third World War."

"But you do have an Ingram."

He nodded wearily. "Yes, I think we can find one of those. Mind you, it'll probably mean the end of a brilliant career. Not to mention my pension."

"Holidair can always use a man of your capabilities."

"I couldn't cope with the excitement." He managed a humourless smile. "I'll have to call Colonel Adams about the flame-thrower."

"Fine."

"Do we really need the dogs?"

"Visual effects, to quote Bladon." I looked at him doubtfully. "What do you mean, 'we'?"

"You didn't imagine I'd let you do this alone, did you? You'll need someone watching your back."

"Good of you."

"It has nothing to do with my generous nature," he said. "I'm going to have to sign for all this equipment, and I'm not letting it out of my sight."


By six-thirty we were ready, and for once I wasn't under-equipped. Crandall had signed out a machine-gun, and the army had sent round a flame-thrower with a nervous-looking lieutenant who showed us how it worked. The flame-thrower was a lightweight model developed by the Americans for the Viet Nam war, capable of squirting a tight stream of defoliant more than two hundred feet. It looked a bit like a scuba-tank, and was fitted with back-straps and a long nozzle containing a simple range-finder and firing mechanism. The lieutenant handled it gingerly and Crandall didn't argue much when I announced I would carry the thing. He could have the Ingram.

The dogs were Alsatians, fierce-looking and huge. We were introduced to them outside headquarters in a small courtyard shielded from the public gaze by a high stuccoed wall. Their handler, a police sergeant, assured us they were as playful as puppies, as long as they were with friends. Otherwise, they were lethal weapons. The dogs seemed eager to do their tricks for us while the sergeant delivered a short lecture on their handling. They'd been trained to react to a series of one-word commands and would attack, retreat, heel, or roll over instantly. They would also protect their handlers to the death. The dogs panted happily while I scratched their ears and patted their big heads.

"Are we set, then?" asked Crandall, after the sergeant had withdrawn, satisfied his charges wouldn't remove my hand or the chief superintendent's throat.

"Except for something I want to buy on the way."

He frowned. "What?"

"Another prop. A cheese-grater."

His frown deepened. "Shuter, I think we're overdoing this now."

"Trust me."

We put the gear and the dogs in the back seat of an unmarked police car and Crandall drove to a nearby hardware store, still open for the early-evening trade. It took the proprietor a while but finally he found a cheese-grater in his stockroom.

"I don't know what you're planning," said Crandall, when I got back into the car, "but I have a feeling I'm not going to like it."

"Just leave this to me."

"I may have been granted temporary special powers, but I'm still a policeman. I don't want innocent people hurt."

"Cudjoe is already responsible for at least seven deaths in this thing. How many more can you stomach?"

He didn't reply, but set his lips in a thin line. He put the car in gear and eventually we located the street where Winston had waved goodbye.

Crandall helped me put on the flame-thrower, adjusting the straps. He had an unlit cigarette in his mouth. "Here," I said, waving the nozzle at him. "A flick of my Bic."

"Be careful with that thing," he muttered. "It's not a toy."

While he locked the car, I affixed the cheese-grater to my belt and attached the dogs' leashes, wrapping them around my left hand. With the flame-thrower, two police dogs and the cheese-grater, I was ready for anything a 110-pound girl could throw at me: eyebrow tweezers, a nail file, bobbie pins, the works. If Cudjoe could see me, he'd probably die laughing. Fine. Any way would do.

Trench Town hadn't changed in the past six hours; it was still a hell-hole, stinking and crowded. As we trudged deeper into the slum, the dogs padded along at my side, sniffing the foul air and looking as mean as the devil himself. To the rear,

I could hear Crandall's measured stride, his big shoes slapping the ground with authority. He was whistling softly, almost tunelessly.

It was strange. Outwardly, I was calm enough to be cracking morbid little jokes. But inside, I was seething at my own stupidity, growing angrier with every step. Carol Malone, the airline, Jamaica's worries, seemed remote, almost beside the point. Winston's death reduced everything to a basic proposition: Shuter vs. Cudjoe, and let the bystanders beware. Sarah Brown, for example.

The street toughs were out in force, scowling and grumbling as we passed, their pack bravado checked by the dogs and the Ingram. I doubted any of them would recognize a flame-thrower but they'd damned well know I wasn't a scuba-diver, looking for a coral reef.

We came to an intersection and I stopped, momentarily uncertain which way to go. The dogs heeled obediently, waiting for me to make up my mind.

"What's the matter?" asked Crandall.

"I think it's to the right, but I'm not sure." I closed my eyes, trying to remember the route.

"Keep moving."

"Hold on," I said impatiently.

"I don't want to worry you," Crandall said in an almost jocular tone, "but we have company."

I looked around slowly. Company, hell. We were leading a parade. Fifty yards to the rear, a mob was staring at us, silent and full of menace. "They won't come any closer, Crandall. If they do, put a burst over their heads."

Before he could reply, something buzzed through the air. A millisecond later I heard the soft crack of a rifle. Sniper. Probably a .22 calibre. Left side. Growls from the dogs. My brain assimilated the data while I was on my way down to the filthy street, rolling as another shot came.

The Ingram made a fearsome noise. Cordite overwhelmed Trench Town's everyday stench. Crandall couldn't have been

246

aiming at anything more specific than the Blue Mountains, a half-dozen miles away, but the sniper took the hint. There were no more shots.

I had half-rolled, half-crawled to the right, stopping behind a shanty wall. The dogs had come reluctantly and now they were snarling, keen to get into the game. The street mob had scattered when the machine-gun opened up, and it seemed loath to form up again. Crandall, meanwhile, had calmly regained his feet. With the Ingram still pointed in the general direction of the sniper, he walked unhurriedly toward me.

"What do you make of it?" I asked.

"A kid, I should imagine. No one serious. Otherwise he would have kept firing. I'm sorry to say there are a lot of firearms in this part of the city, despite the gun laws." He grinned abruptly. "Don't worry. Word travels fast here. Everyone in West Kingston will know by now."

"Know what?"

He patted the Ingram. "Know we mean business. I doubt we'll be bothered again."

"Okay," I said, taking a reef in the dogs' leashes, "let's do it."

People were still watching from the shadows of their houses, but now they were more afraid than belligerent. Finally, I spied Sarah's house, dusty and hot-looking in its tiny yard.

"This one," I said to Crandall, stopping at the path and looking for signs of life.

"Somebody must be home," he said. "The door's open."

It was time for my number. I dislike guys who manhandle women; I think they're contemptible. But I didn't want Sarah to know that. Or Crandall. I wanted them to think I was Jack the Ripper, a real lady-killer. "Sarah!" I hollered. "Get out here!"

There was no reply.

"Sarah! Out here! Now!"

Again, no response. It didn't matter where we did this, but I wanted her to make the first concession; it would make the next one come easier.

"I don't think we need a search warrant to go in," said Crandall, who was becoming impatient.

"No. I want her out." I turned to the house again. "Sarah! Get your ass out here, or I'll fry it!" I felt a bit like the big bad wolf, huffing and puffing at one of the three little pigs.

"Now, Shuter..." Crandall protested, as I started to unlimber the flame-thrower.

"Shut up!" I snapped. "I know what I'm doing."

There was a big breadfruit tree a hundred feet or so along the street. It would do. There aren't many trees in Trench Town, and this one was old, at least sixty feet tall. It probably pre-dated most of the houses in the district, and I felt a twinge of guilt; but surely Jamaica would sacrifice one tree to save the national economy.

Holding the nozzle the way I had seen the lieutenant do it, I touched the trigger. There was a hiss, then a whoosh. My God! No wonder he'd handled it gingerly. The tree was enveloped in a ball of fire. Sheets of flame roared through its branches and black smoke billowed upward, mingling with the evening haze. Defoliation? That tree was being cremated, consumed. Ten-year-old images skittered through my mind. The dodgers. The agony of that girl at Kent State. The Moratorium. One-two-three-four, Tricky Dicky stop the war. The Dow Chemical people. Dylan. But the only thing blowin' in this wind was ashes. Ashes and the dogs' whimpers.

"Jesus, Mary, and Joseph!" Crandall gasped. "Don't ever do that again!"

I wheeled and aimed at the house. "Last chance, Sarah!"

Her hair appeared first, the top of her Afro showing cautiously at the edge of the doorway. Then her forehead and her huge, unblinking eyes. Sarah Brown was terrified.

"What you wan'?" Her whisper was barely audible over the crackling of the flames.

"Out here, you little bitch!"

She stayed in the doorway, cowering. "What you wan', sah?"

"Here!" I pointed to the ground at my feet.

Sarah began to cry.

"Hurry up!"

Sobbing, she started toward us, and I had my first concession. There was nothing graceful about her now. "Please, sah!"

"Where is he?"

"Who, sah?" She'd stopped about four feet from where I stood. The dogs were growling, but holding their position.

"Cudjoe."

"I tol' you, sah! I doan know!" She kept her eyes on the ground. She was frightened of me, certainly; but she was more frightened of Cudjoe. I only burned down trees; he killed people.

"Yes you do, Sarah. And you're going to tell me."

She shook her head, fat tears spilling down her lovely face. Beside me, Crandall was breathing heavily. "Please," she whispered.

Handing Crandall the leashes, I unbuckled my belt. What had Lombardi said, when he used to send Taylor, then Hornung, then Taylor again into the line? Or around the end, behind Kramer and Gregg? Attack their strength. Never mind their weaknesses. Go right after their strength, break it down, smash it, and the rest will fall apart. What was a pretty girl's strength? What set her apart, made her special?

"Right," I said. "It's time for your facial."

Sarah looked at me dumbly, the tears still rolling.

Abruptly, I reached out and seized the front of her cotton dress, twisting it in my left hand and jerking her toward me. The material was damp with perspiration and her small breasts were heaving. I held the cheese-grater up to her smooth cheek. "They can't fix it, you know," I said softly, touching her with the rough metal. "All the doctors in the world won't be able to fix it."

She moaned, still not sure what I was planning to do. I pressed a little harder and drew the grater downward a millimetre or so, not breaking the skin.

Sarah screamed then, a penetrating wail.

"Hamburger," I said, when the scream tailed off into a sob. "That's what you're going to look like." I pressed again, scratching her this time.

"Now just a damned minute!" sputtered Crandall, as Sarah shrieked again.

"Shut up!" I said, not looking at him. "It's up to her."

Sarah was hysterical. "Oh, God! Please!"

I pressed again. "The cheeks first. Then, I think, the nose. The soft parts."

"Black River!" she gasped. "Please! Stop!"

"Where?" I lifted the grater.

"Black River. I doan know exactly where." Her nose was running and her forehead was beaded.

"Thank you." I released her dress front and she sagged against me.

"He kill me now," she said miserably.

"No, he won't. I promise you. Where's Black River?"

"West end of the island," Crandall said tightly. "Tell me, miss. Is Jefferson's camp on the coast or inland?"

She looked at him, defeated. "It somewhere in de Cockpit. Look Behind."

I glanced at Crandall inquiringly. "She means the District of Look Behind, Shuter. It's on the rim of Cockpit Country."

"Where the original Cudjoe made camp?"

He nodded.

I gave him a sour smile. "There. You see? Nothing to it."

Crandall shook his head. Along the street, the breadfruit tree had been reduced to a smouldering stump. In the gloom of Sarah's house, I could dimly make out the shape of an older woman, watching us. Her mother?

"There's something else, Sarah," I said quietly. "Winston's sister, Ruth. Will you show us, please?"

She nodded, past all resistance.

"Now what?" Crandall sounded unhappy.

"Something I have to do. We'd better take Sarah into custody anyway. She'll need protection until we wrap this up."

He looked at me grimly. "Would you have done that? To her, I mean?"

I shrugged, unfairly disappointed in him. "What do you think?"

"I don't know. I just don't know."

I threw the grater to the ground. It had done its job.


Ruth Llewellyn wasn't home. A neighbour was looking after her two boys, aged four and two and a half, while Ruth was off seeing about funeral arrangements. The neighbour, a kindly soul, who was at least fifty pounds overweight, didn't know which undertaker Ruth had gone to see. I took out a business card, wrote on the back that I was a friend, and said I would like Ruth to call me at the Pegasus. The neighbour promised to give it to her.

Crandall, Sarah, and I returned to the car without incident. Even the street toughs had disappeared. No one wanted to mess with a crazy man who made trees explode.

Sarah stumbled along with us, resigned to a desperate fate. Her tiny world had collapsed, although if she had an ounce of brains she'd soon realize it was for the best. Sarah Brown had youth, beauty and a life to live, which isn't a bad combination.

Crandall hadn't said a word since we'd left Sarah's house. I wasn't sure whether he was outraged at what I'd done, offended by the way I'd spoken to him, or simply engrossed in planning the next move.

At the car, Sarah got in front with Crandall and I climbed in the back with the dogs and the equipment. If Sarah's information was correct, then Cudjoe's power play was going to develop a short-circuit fairly soon. But I felt no sense of achievement. Instead, I felt grubby. I wanted to go to the hotel and stand under the shower for about a week.

Back at headquarters, Crandall quickly arranged for the flame-thrower to be returned to Colonel Adams, the dogs to their handler, and the Ingram to the police armoury. A matron was summoned and Sarah was delivered into her care. Sarah was not to be locked up, Crandall ordered, but taken to the superintendent of women police who would have her billeted and kept under twenty-four-hour protection until further notice. Sarah went meekly with the matron, relieved to be gone from our company.

"Let's go along to my office, shall we?" Crandall said brusquely, and I followed him through the now-familiar corridors. He closed his office door and slumped behind his desk.

It was a full minute before he spoke. "You wouldn't have. I'm sure of it."

I looked at him, but said nothing.

"The reason I'm sure," he went on, "is Ruth Llewellyn. You're sincere there."

I shrugged. "Is it so important?"

"Yes. I'd hate to think I could misjudge a man as completely as that."

"Then you're right. I wouldn't have."

"I know," he said frowning. "I don't know quite what to say."

"You had to believe it, if she was going to believe it."

He nodded slowly, then smiled. "*Son et lumière*. An incredible show!" He paused. "I've been thinking about this, and I want to see for myself. It's almost dark now, so we'll have to do it in the morning."

"Aerial reconnaissance?"

He nodded again. "In the meantime, not a word. To anyone. And that includes your Mr. McGregor. I'm not even
going to tell the Prime Minister, until I'm sure."

"You're right. About tomorrow: maybe I'd better rent a
plane."

"Can you fly?"

"Faster than a speeding bullet. I learned when I was sta-
tioned in the Northwest Territories."

"You're a resourceful chap, Shuter."

"People keep telling me that." I got to my feet. "Tomorrow
morning, then."

"Let's say ten o'clock. Tinson Pen."

He stopped me as I reached the door. "A question, if you
don't mind."

"Shoot."

"The cheese-grater. Wherever did you get that idea?"

"I once heard a story about a Montreal pimp who used
one on a couple of girls who'd got out of line. They never
worked again, but he had no more trouble with the rest of
his stable."

Crandall shuddered, then looked down. "Lovely people in
this world, aren't there?"


That night Daniel and De Lions were launched as reggae
superstars. There were 50,000 music fanatics in Kingston's
National Stadium, which was built to seat 35,000 for the 1966
Commonwealth Games, and most of them were spliffed-out.
Cudjoe was definitely in a growth industry.

The concert was the musical event of the year, and it
attracted people from Jamaica's social spectrum, including
quite a few politicians. The whole thing was staged under the
watchful eye of the police, on hand to forestall rioting. They
needn't have worried; however upset the West Kingston *hoi
polloi* were with Crandall's raids, the music and the weed
kept most of the stadium crowd happy. Even the Rastas
thronging the infield were mellow.

Although I arrived late my seats were vacant; they were in a VIP section, jealously guarded by ushers. The stage area was cordoned off by a rope and a solid line of police, who kept their backs to the performers and stared implacably at the mob on the infield grass.

Mountains of speakers boomed the music to every corner of the stadium, and beyond. At least 5,000 people milled outside the walls, ticketless but still enjoying the show. In fact, aside from some inept lighting, the concert was a fairly slick production.

Each group was limited to two numbers, no matter how vociferously the crowd demanded encores. Some of the performers simply appeared on stage, waited out the roars of greeting, and then played and sang their pieces; others made short speeches, usually invoking Jah's name and urging everything from the legalization of ganja to universal love. Every time one of the stars mentioned the cops, there was a chorus of cat-calls, but most of the jeering seemed good-natured.

Shortly after I'd taken my seat, a man in the row behind tapped my shoulder and asked whether I was Mr. Shuter. It was Daniel's father, Mr. Justice Harris. The judge cut a handsome figure, tall, grey-haired, impeccably dressed in a dark suit and white shirt. Apparently Daniel had spent much of the day regaling his parents with our adventures in Ocho Rios. His father had been fascinated, his mother appalled. Being a lady, Mrs. Harris had declined to attend the concert.

I made the usual comments about what a fine son the judge had. While we chatted, I got the distinct impression that Daniel's father was rather proud of him, despite his son's espousal of Rastafarianism and his refusal to study law. The judge had heard the government and police announcements regarding Carol Malone and had seen her picture on the evening newscast. He asked whether I'd made further progress, but didn't press when I was vague in reply. I wondered whether he was aware of Cudjoe's ultimatum; senior jurists frequently are party to government secrets.

254

About two-thirds of the way through the program, it was Daniel's turn. He and the Lions received a restrained welcome–they were a regional group, after all–but they touched the crowd with their first number, a sweet lament about lost love. We were still applauding when Daniel took the microphone and asked for everyone's attention. He made a brief speech extolling the beauty of Jamaica and her people, the wisdom of Jah and the principle of brotherly love. Then, in more strident tones, he lambasted a social system that trafficked in oppression and distributed prosperity so unevenly. The crowd listened restlessly; it was a night for music, not political harangues. But the speech was a lead-in to the first public performance of his new song, "The Poor Can't Stand No More," destined to become a reggae standard. Later, I got him to write down the words:

*The poor*
*Can't stand no more.*
*I say the poor*
*Can't stand no more.*
*No more hunger, no more pain*
*No more darkness, no more rain*
   *It's time for sunshine from above*
   *Time for laughter, time for love.*

*The poor*
*Can't stand no more.*
*I say the poor*
*Can't stand no more.*
*No more beatings from the law*
*No more prisons. Hear I, Jah!*
   *It's time for justice everywhere*
   *In this rich land we all share.*

*Patience is supposed to be a virtue*
*According to the men of government*
*But, brethren, have you noticed how this virtue*
*Is preached by rich folk bloated with content?*

*What's the hurry? they all say*
*Not to worry, wait a day.*

*No more waiting, that's for sure*
*No more begging at their door*
*No more sweeping up their floor*
*No more patience from the poor.*

*The poor*
*Can't stand no more.*
*I say the poor*
*Can't stand no more.*
*No more sermons, no more lies,*
*No more waiting. Realize*
    *That the time's come for the poor*
    *To tell the rich: Enough! No more!*

It ignited the crowd. When Daniel finished the final, driving chorus there was a roar which built in a long crescendo. He had touched a nerve. I could see him, smiling as the sound washed over him and the chant went up: *"More! More! More!"* When it became apparent that the format would not be altered, that there'd be no encore by Daniel and De Lions, the crowd reluctantly let them go. The group made its exit, waving.

It was just after eleven o'clock when I spied Susan. She was standing off to one side of the stage, in an area reserved for the media. I shook hands again with Mr. Justice Harris and asked him to convey my congratulations to Daniel. The judge wished me luck.

The backstage pass got me past the police and security guards, and eventually I made my way to Susan's side. She was wearing tight white jeans and a T-shirt, and she looked delectable.

"Quite a show."

"Michael! Where did you come from?"

"The grandstand. Where's your crew?"

256

"They've packed it in. We've got miles of good stuff. We'll never use it all."

"Did you catch my friend Daniel's bit?"

Susan grinned. "I thought he was going to send everyone out lootin' and burnin'."

"Ras Daniel," I said, "doesn't approve of lootin' and burnin'. He's a law-abiding Rasta. How was your story tonight? Pleased with it?"

Susan nodded. "The interview with Crandall helped a lot. I led with the government's appeal, and the fact that they've finally acknowledged Carol's disappearance. Richard said he liked it."

"Good for you."

"The CBC's here." She sounded almost happy about it. "So's the *Toronto Star*. They're playing catch-up, and I just hope I can keep it that way."

"All business, aren't you?" They're so damned competitive, these reporters.

Her eyes took on an impish quality. "Not always."

Another group had come on stage, but I'd had enough. I put an arm around Susan's shoulders. "This is almost over. What do you say?"

She smiled up at me. "Our unfinished pleasure?"

I nodded solemnly, realizing how much I needed her. I wanted to be gentle, warm, tender; not simply because of the night before, but also because of my two visits to Trench Town. Immediate expiation, a personal apology to the female sex. And, after Winston's death, a reaffirmation of life.

# CHAPTER EIGHTEEN

## *Day Five (Tuesday) – 8:15 A.M.*

I opened my eyes slowly to find Susan watching me, amused about something. She was lying on her stomach, chin cupped in both hands, smiling, and wearing the shirt I'd had on the night before. It was cool in the room. The drapes were slightly open and the morning sun threw a brilliant rectangle on the far wall.

"Hi."

"G'morning. What's so funny?"

"You are. You snore." Susan's morning voice was very husky, almost breathless. Cigarettes, of course.

"So do you." I've never been very gallant in the morning.

"I do *not!*" She reached forward and jabbed me lightly in the ribs. "Don't be wicked."

I fumbled for my watch. "What time did you wake up?"

"I don't know. A while ago. I wanted to let you sleep." She grinned. "I like you better when you're not tired."

"Very funny." I closed my eyes again, content, remembering our love-making. It had gone on a long while.

"What *did* happen there, really?" Her fingers lightly traced the purple-and-yellow blotch on my shoulder, my souvenir from The Tallyman. "A love bite from some brazen hussy?"

"You're the only brazen hussy I know."

She jabbed me again. "No. Really. What happened?"

"That, snoopy, is the result of a powerful rum punch."

"I didn't know you could get bruises from a hangover."

"The guy forgot to take the rum out of the bottle."

"Poor Shuter." Susan leaned forward and kissed the bruise, then put her head on my shoulder and stretched out beside me. "I've brushed my teeth."

"I haven't." I rolled away and sat up. "How about ordering some juice and coffee?"

"Okay." She puffed up the pillows and leaned against them. "Do you know what I feel like?"

"Intimately." I'd reached sanctuary in the bathroom so the pillow missed, hitting the wall instead.

"I meant for breakfast."

"What?"

"Champagne. Champagne and orange juice. I feel deliciously decadent."

I stuck my head around the bathroom door. "It's called Buck's Fizz. And you're not supposed to be decadent, Quill. You're supposed to be a sensible young woman, a reporter."

"Most reporters are decadent," she said airily. "What's it called again? It sounded rude."

"Buck's Fizz."

"I'm going to order some." She picked up the phone.

Poor McGregor. The airline might survive Cudjoe but would it survive my expense account? "Not for me. Just order a half-bottle. I've got to fly a plane this morning."

Forty-five minutes later, she was sipping her second Buck's Fizz and smoking her first cigarette of the day, luxuriating. We'd made love again, without the urgency of the night before, and once again it had been exquisite. No ghosts intruded, and as I lay back with my coffee I decided that Susan Quill could become habit-forming. I'd better be careful; I wasn't ready for any entangling alliances.

She put down her champagne and snuggled close. "What did you mean about flying this morning?"

"I'm going sightseeing," I said vaguely. "I'll only be gone a couple of hours."

"Does it have anything to do with Carol?"

"Listen, Susan, I don't want to talk about it right now."

She sat up abruptly. "You know where she is!" Sharp girl.

"No, I don't."

She looked at me speculatively, then leaned back again, stubbing out her cigarette. "I don't want to get scooped, you know."

"Don't worry."

She sighed, and was silent for a while. Then: "Who's Cudjoe?"

Too damned sharp. "Cudjoe?"

"Patsy Baird told me Carol's with a man named Cudjoe. He was the Maroon leader."

"I know."

"So who's this one?"

"A beach bum," I said easily. "A package-tour gigolo."

She sat up again. "No, he's not. He's a big-league dope smuggler."

"Who are *you*?" I said sarcastically. "Mata Hari, trading sweet nothings for state secrets? The princess of pillow talk? I thought you loved me for my body."

"Don't be tacky. I'm tired of the runaround. Crandall, for example. When I asked him about Cudjoe he turned coy as a virgin on her first date. Evasive, like you're being now. Why?"

"Please," I said. "There aren't any virgins these days."

"Is Carol mixed up in a dope deal?" She wouldn't let it go.

"Of course not. Be patient, will you? I'll see you get your story. But only if you forget about Cudjoe."

She lit another cigarette and got up from the bed. "Promise?"

I nodded.

Apparently satisfied, Susan stretched and yawned, not at all self-conscious about her nudity. "I'd better have a shower, get back to the Sheraton and call Toronto."

"What's your schedule?"

"We're going to do some streeters. You know, ask people

about the announcement yesterday. And then, of course, there's a press conference at two. At least, Crandall told me there'd be one. We'll have to shoot that, I guess. The CBC will for sure. We also have the concert footage, so I should have a solid piece. But I doubt Richard will want me to go long tonight, unless there's a major development. I should be wrapped up early."

"If you are," I said, "maybe we can have drinks about six."

"Okay."

I poured some more coffee and reluctantly decided against joining her in the shower.


While I waited for Crandall at Tinson Pen, I studied a Jamaica Tourist Board road map, plotting our course to Black River. It was 110 miles from Kingston by road, but it would only be about seventy by air. I drew a straight line through Spanish Town and May Pen, south of the built-up Mandeville area and on to Black River, principal community in the parish of St. Elizabeth. The town is built beside swampy ground where the river slides into the sea after a roundabout route from the District of Look Behind. The map showed landing strips at a village called Middle Quarters and, farther upstream, at Siloah, so we'd have a place to put down if we got into trouble. It also showed a number of oddly named settlements: Quick Step, Maggotty, Lilliput, Retirement, Giddy Hall, Happy Grove, Speculation. Jamaica has a penchant for weird geographic nomenclature.

I'd made arrangements to rent a plane from Wings Jamaica Ltd., a small outfit making a living from flying lessons, sight-seeing flips and charters. Wings Jamaica had a mixed fleet – a Beechcraft Baron, a Champion Citabria, a few Piper Apaches and Cessna 150s and 172s. I chose a 172, a high-wing, single-engine, four-seater model I'd flown a hundred times. The agent checked my licence, noted I was fully qualified on instrument flight rules, and said I could pay by credit card.

Crandall arrived a few minutes after ten, looking pleased about something. He was carrying a Nikon camera fitted with an enormous telephoto lens.

"Karsh of Jamaica," I said, smiling.

"Morning, Shuter." He sounded almost jovial. "Great day for it."

"This is supposed to be the rainy season, but it hasn't rained since I got here. How was your meeting?"

"Routine. A lot of hand-wringing and the usual needling from Mr. Morgan."

"If we get a break this morning, you'll shut him up." I stepped closer and lowered my voice. "Any progress on Winston?"

He shook his head.

"I don't want to go back to Trench Town," I said evenly, "but I will—if you people don't crack that one. I'm serious, Crandall."

"Give us a chance. I don't want you going back there, either. It's too hard on my nerves."

"How's Sarah?"

"Recovering, I gather."

The agent announced our aircraft was fuelled and ready; we could take off any time. He led Crandall and me across the tarmac to the plane, handed me the keys, and wished us a pleasant flight.

I opened the door on the passenger side for Crandall, and then I did my walkaround, starting at his wingtip. "Cautious soul, aren't you?" said Crandall, as I climbed into the cockpit and secured my door.

"You know the saying: there are old pilots and bold pilots..."

"But no old, bold pilots?"

"Not very many."

At 2,000 feet I levelled off, throttled back to 2250 RPMs and adjusted the trim. We were cruising at an indicated speed of 135 MPH, headed almost due west. Five miles out, I picked up the mike. "Tinson Pen tower, Juliet Poppa Tango. Level at two thousand and leaving the control zone."

"Roger, JPT. Good day, sah!"

Crandall seemed relaxed. "May I smoke?"

"There's an ashtray in your door."

Off to the left, the Caribbean sparkled. Below us, the suburban tangle of Kingston was giving way to the greens and browns of the countryside. Visibility was excellent, the Cessna was running smoothly and I was enjoying myself. I love flying—as long as I'm the one at the controls.

"Here," I said, giving Crandall the road map. "I've marked the course. You can follow our progress."

"How long will it take?"

"Half an hour."

While we zipped along, Crandall and I swapped bits of personal history, an attempt to put some flesh on the bones of our acquaintanceship.

I told him about my time in the force, the watershed that Janet's death had been, the fat life with McGregor, and my occasional regret about leaving the RCMP.

He told me about his life in the Jamaican cops. He began as a cadet, in colonial times, and his career had continued uninterrupted through all the changes since: federation, independence, shifting government philosophy, economic disappointments, the beginnings of serious civilian unrest. The only constant, Crandall said, the only thing a man could count on was the idea of the law, which was majestic in its simplicity, however complicated the courts and the legislators tried to make it. The law was an easy master to serve; it had to do with right and wrong—period.

Not that he didn't have doubts. Everyone had doubts. Ganja, for example. Crandall wasn't sure that the weed was as bad as it was officially held to be; he had tried it two or three times, but disliked the feeling of lethargy it induced. Crandall was a man who liked to be in charge of things, including himself. Despite this, he had a hard time reconciling the official view of ganja with the official view of tobacco and alcohol, both of which he used and both of which, many doctors claimed, were more dangerous to personal health than cannabis. This didn't mean he was "soft" on the drug trade; far from it. Nor did he have anything but contempt for those members of the police force who were rumoured to be growing rich from ganja. He'd clap them into prison whenever he found them.

Another subject which made him uncomfortable was the trend toward the politicization of the police. It was a world-wide phenomenon, no longer peculiar to the dictatorships. But Crandall had been raised on the British model – as a boy at grammar school he had read and re-read the story of Sir Robert Peel, had absorbed the literature of Scotland Yard – and it had all seemed so *right* to him. Police had to function independently of politicians, just as the state had to be separate from the church.

Crandall, an only child, had always been a loner. If he'd been a Canadian, he said, he'd have been a Mountie. The idea of being a solitary policeman, ranging the wilderness in the name of the law, appealed to him. It was adventuring, by God, and essential; what more could a man ask?

"It's not like that any more," I said, wondering if it ever had been.

Crandall found it on our second sweep up the valley. I'd flown directly to the town of Black River, then swung inland and followed the river's meandering course. It was a substantial stream, fed by several tributaries, and it changed character radically as it moved from its source in the rugged interior through the coastal plain and into the sea. I'd kept the Cessna at 1,500 feet – low enough to see through all but the most professional camouflage but high enough that we wouldn't cause alarm on the ground.

Cudjoe's camp was about a mile west of the valley and four miles upstream from Windsor, the last settlement of any size on the Black River. If we hadn't been told where to look we'd probably have missed it; certainly, I couldn't fault the military and police pilots who'd been overflying Jamaica for a week, searching.

I pulled back on the wheel to gain some altitude and began a slow right turn, looking down. I noticed the strip first; it was strewn with brush, but I could see its outline. It was about 1,200 feet long and undoubtedly rough, but it would do – if a pilot had good nerves and a sturdy undercarriage.

Beside me, Crandall was focussing the Nikon, looking through the big lens.

"I can see four, five, no, six huts," he said excitedly. "They're camouflaged. Shrubs, branches, grass all over the place. And there's a bigger building, maybe a storeroom."

The camera began clicking, but we were quickly moving out of range.

"Can you see any people?"

"No."

"We'll come back a bit lower."

"Don't scare them," Crandall growled. "We don't want to lose them now."

"We have to be sure." I put the Cessna into a sharp downward turn. "I'll go by once, at about eight hundred feet. There's bound to be some air traffic in this area every day, and we're not official. We'll get away with it."

This time, I could see the camp clearly as we came up on it. There were eight huts plus the larger building. There were also a few people moving around. A field, covering perhaps two acres, adjoined the landing strip. There were no vehicles in evidence.

Crandall was firing away like Boris Spremo, the celebrated *Toronto Star* news photographer. I just hoped Crandall took as good a picture.

"Got it!" he said, as we zoomed over the camp.

"Look, I want to go up to about five thousand and make one more pass. That is, if you've got any more film."

"Plenty of film."

"A few high-altitude shots will enable us to pinpoint the location on a map."

No one in the camp appeared to have taken any notice of us. We might get away with a surprise attack, after all. While I took the Cessna up to 5,000, my thoughts were down on the ground, with Carol. If she was still alive, she was there, a mile below us and probably scared to death.

Crandall got his high-altitude shots, and there was nothing to do but fly back to Kingston and begin planning the raid. Typically, Crandall was already planning it. "A combined operation," he said, as I levelled out at 2,000. "The military and the constabulary."

"It's tough-looking terrain. It won't be easy putting a force in there."

"The army can come in by helicopter. The police will come up the river. A pincers."

"When?"

He looked at his watch. "This will take at least twenty-four hours to organize. First light Thursday."

It made sense. A dawn attack should catch Cudjoe and his men by surprise, maybe even sleeping. But it wouldn't be a cinch. Cudjoe was bound to have sentries posted, and with his ultimatum still unanswered and the deadline approaching, nerves would be taut. There was also the matter of the Kalashnikovs and the M-16s.

"Helicopters are noisy," I said, "but, provided we hit fast and in strength, they're probably best. We can expect a firefight, though. Probably a dandy."

Crandall lit a cigarette and glanced at me. "The government of Jamaica will always be grateful to you, Shuter."

"Sure."

"We owe you an enormous debt, and I'll make certain everyone knows it. There's no question that you're principally responsible for finding Jefferson. A terrific piece of work."

"That's all it is," I said uncomfortably. "Work. You don't

owe me anything. Just going in and getting Carol will be enough. Mind you, I wouldn't mind about five minutes with Cudjoe. Preferably in a dark alley."

"No," he said flatly. "We'll take it from here."

"You're joking."

But he wasn't. "It's an official matter, Shuter. There's no way a civilian can be part of it."

"Don't give me that crap. I've come too far with this thing."

"I know how you feel," he said, unmoved. "But you know that in a reverse situation a Jamaican civilian would never be allowed to accompany the RCMP and the Canadian army. So please, don't make it difficult for me."

"I'll make it difficult as hell," I said. "You owe me this, Crandall."

"Sorry." He stubbed out his cigarette and looked the other way. "I can't assume the responsibility."

For the rest of the flight, I badgered, cajoled, and threatened. But it was no use. Crandall was adamant. It was a job for the army and police, not a free-lance.

Furious, I called the tower. "Tinson Pen tower, Juliet Poppa Tango. I am due west of the field about fifteen miles, inbound at two thousand."

"Roger, JPT. Winds three hundred and twenty at ten, gusting to fifteen. Call on final at two miles."

Three miles out I pulled on the carburettor heat and reduced power to 1,800 RPMs. I established a rate of descent of 500 feet per minute and adjusted the trim. "Tinson Pen tower, JPT. Two miles out on final."

"Roger, JPT. Cleared to land."

I put on a couple of notches of flap. Over the threshhold, I reduced power again and set the Cessna down lightly on the numbers. Then I switched to ground control, got permission to taxi to Wings Jamaica, and signed off: "JPT, Roger. Thank you, sir, and good afternoon."

It had just turned twelve o'clock, and a developing friendship had just turned sour.

Crandall was in a hurry to see the Prime Minister. The PM, he said, would call Washington, London, and Ottawa with the news that the crisis was finally in hand. Jamaica had to head off the foreign governments before they issued warnings to their nationals.

"After I've finished with the PM," he said, "I'll go over the pictures and call a meeting of the task force. I can hardly wait to rub it in Morgan's nose. I'll ask Colonel Adams to come by a bit early. He'll have to be in on this."

We said a strained goodbye and Crandall rushed off to receive his prime ministerial pat on the back while I went up to the Wings Jamaica desk to settle my account.

There was another stack of telephone messages at the hotel desk: from Bishop, McGregor (two), Ras Daniel, and a half-dozen news operations including the Kingston *Daily Gleaner*. The concierge watched while I sorted through them, then cleared his throat. "Dere a lady waitin' here for you, too."

"Where?"

He pointed to the lobby where a young Jamaican woman sat, twisting a handkerchief and looking utterly forlorn. Of course. Ruth Llewellyn. What in the world was I going to say to her? Sorry? Anything but that.

"Ruth Llewellyn? I'm Michael Shuter."

She smiled uncertainly, her eyes red and puffy. "Good aftahnoon, sah."

"Thank you for coming."

"I dint know ... I wasn't sure ... But Winston, he tol' me 'bout you, an' he gave me all dat money, so I thought I say thanks."

*Thanks?* She was *thanking* me? I closed my eyes. "You have my deepest sympathy, Ruth. I liked your brothers very much."

She was near tears again, but managed to nod.

"The kids," I said. "Your children. Are they all right?"

"Dey jes' fine, thank you."

"Do you need anything? Is there anything I can do?"

She shook her head. "I'll manage, sah."

"I believe you will, Ruth." What now? God! "When is Winston's funeral?"

"Friday aftahnoon. It delayed because de police..." Her voice trailed off, then regained strength. "It all arranged."

At least I could do something about that. "Look, I'd like to look after the expenses. For the funeral."

She looked at me, puzzled. "Why you do dat?"

Instead of answering, I said: "If you'll just tell the undertaker and the florist to send their accounts to Holidair's office in Montego Bay, I'll see they're paid."

She didn't say anything, but went back to twisting her handkerchief.

"Why do you suppose Winston was killed?" I asked gently.

"I doan know. Maybe dey know 'bout de money."

"Maybe." Perhaps it was the best explanation, after all; I was the source of the money, too, so I wasn't completely ducking responsibility. "It doesn't make me feel any better to think Winston's dead because I gave him some money. Do you understand?"

"Yes, sah, I think so."

"Okay. So will you have the bills sent to the airline?"

She nodded, and dabbed at her eyes. We had a deal. I'd speak to Herb Johnson about it. I wrote down the name of the church and said I'd be there on Friday. In the meantime, if she needed anything she was to call me. Mr. Beckford would drive her back to Trench Town.

Ruth thanked me again at the car. Jesus!

I crumpled the sheaf of telephone messages and dropped them in a lobby ashtray. I didn't feel like talking to anyone at the moment. Upset, I went into the Surrey Tavern, a pseudo-English pub off the lobby. A few draft Red Stripes might improve my mood—but I doubted it.

# *Night Five (Tuesday) – 4:40 P.M.*

"Dawn it is," said Crandall, speaking from his office and avoiding direct references to Cudjoe, the camp in Look Behind, or our morning flight. "Thursday. A hundred troops, a hundred police."

"Good of you to let me know," I said sourly. "Will it be on television?"

"Buck up, Shuter. It's all in hand."

"Congratulations." I sipped my coffee wondering why I'd changed my mind about getting smashed; I'd been on the phone almost non-stop since coming up to the suite.

"The PM is very pleased," he went on. "He wants to express his gratitude in person."

"You haven't wrapped this up yet, Crandall. I'd hold off on the victory parade, if I were you."

"Colonel Adams and I have made allowances for everything."

I shuffled my pride to the bottom of the deck. "You won't change your mind?"

"About you coming? Sorry."

"Then good luck to you."

"Shuter, please. Put yourself in my position."

"Put yourself in Carol's," I said bitterly.

"So that's it. We'll see she comes to no harm. A special squad will be assigned to her."

"That's supposed to be my job. That's why I came to this crazy country."

He veered away from the subject. "The pictures we took are excellent. We're building a scale model of the target area, and using survey maps to plot our overland approach."

"Spare me the logistics," I said tightly. "We're going through a switchboard."

"Quite." He paused. "This may amuse you. Do you recall the field, beside the landing strip?"

"Yeah."

"Well, I didn't notice it at the time. We were busy. But the pictures show it clearly. It's ganja, ready for harvest. A bonus."

"I'm very happy for you."

He rang off with a dyspeptic grunt.

Earlier, I'd fielded several calls from reporters digging for a fresh angle. Was it true Holidair was going to scrap its Jamaica program? Was it true the Canadian government was threatening the airline's licence? Was it true Carol's father was posting a $25,000 reward? Was it true Carol and I used to be lovers? Was it true the earth was flat? God only knows *where* the press gets some of its ideas. I was as patient, polite and non-informative as possible. I denied the more outlandish suggestions, declined to speculate on Carol's whereabouts and promised one and all that the press would be informed the minute there was any solid news. But I was reassured on one point: from their questions, it was obvious the reporters had no idea of the real story. So far, the Cudjoe caper had been a masterpiece of news management.

After Crandall's call, I got out the road map again and studied the Black River area. The camp was a five-mile hike from the nearest secondary road. Crandall's men would have a tough time of it, especially after dark.

What surprises would Cudjoe have waiting? There were bound to be some, however thoroughly Crandall planned. Cudjoe might be a crude butcher, but his survival instincts would be scalpel-keen. He'd made very few mistakes. For a common dope dealer, he was operating like a sophisticated terrorist.

In terrorist terms, Carol was a hostage. So far, she hadn't been used that way; there'd been no need. But if Cudjoe found himself in a tight corner he wouldn't hesitate to use her as a shield – or as a bargaining counter. I closed my eyes and tried to picture the scene in the camp. Where would Carol be held? Or would she be held at all? Maybe she was still sharing Cudjoe's sleeping bag, hoping for a chance to escape.

The telephone intruded before my thoughts could grow any darker.

"We missed you last night."

"Daniel," I said, pleased to hear his voice. "You were terrific, even if you did steal that song off a downtown wall."

"We are all plagiarists," he laughed. "Did you like it?"

"Very much. Your speech needs work, though."

"You missed a great party after the show."

"So did you."

Daniel didn't press the point. "What news of our friend?"

"Which one?"

"Either one."

"There have been one or two positive developments," I said carefully, "and there has been a tragic one. Winston Llewellyn was murdered yesterday afternoon in Trench Town, shortly after I left him."

Daniel inhaled sharply, then uttered a long sigh. "I don't know what to say. *Both* brothers? It's beyond my comprehension."

"How do you think *I* feel?"

"Like Typhoid Mary, I suppose. My God, it's terrible!"

"It's no comfort," I said, "but his death stirred things up. I can't give you any details, but with a little luck Carol will be home for the weekend."

"I suppose I should be glad to hear it, but somehow it doesn't seem to matter any more. It's anti-climax. Two people dead, for no reason."

"Seven," I said quietly. "There are five you don't know about."

"*Seven?*"

"All innocent, just like Winston. It has to stop now, Daniel. It can't go any further."

"And you can stop it?"

"No. That's up to the police and the military."

"I just don't understand," he said slowly. "I can't grasp what's going on."

We didn't say anything for a few moments. Then he cleared his throat: "My news is trivial, by comparison. But..."

There was a sharp knock. "Hold on a second, Daniel. Someone's at the door." I put down the phone. "Who is it?"

"Me," said Susan.

She was standing in the hall, smiling. "Your phone's been busy and..."

"I'm still on it. Come in."

Susan kissed me lightly on the cheek, then walked across to an armchair and settled into it, searching her bag for a cigarette. I picked up the receiver again. "You were saying you had news?"

"Yes," he said, unable to keep the excitement from his voice. "We've been asked to do an album. Our own material. It's a tremendous opportunity."

"You're going to become rich and famous."

"I doubt it," he laughed. "But everyone else thinks so. They really like 'The Poor Can't Stand No More', and we have many other songs."

"You'll make it, Daniel. I'm certain. When are you going back to Negril?"

"Tomorrow. The rest of the band left this afternoon, but I have meetings here in the morning with lawyers and an agent."

"Don't let 'em skin you."

"Don't worry. I'll maintain a very dready expression throughout."

I told him I'd see him soon.

"Was that your reggae friend?" Susan asked.

"Yeah. He's going to make an album with the Lions."

"They're terrific."

"So are you. All finished?"

She nodded. "A thin piece. The press conference was a bust. Crandall didn't show. Some PR type from headquarters handled it, but he didn't have much to say. Search continuing, confident of a break soon, good co-operation from the public, blah blah blah. Hardly worth a clip. Richard wasn't impressed."

I looked at her sympathetically. "He's a hard man to please."

"He's also mad at you."

"Why?"

"Says you're refusing to return his calls."

"I'll make it up to him when I get home. A big lunch."

Susan laughed. "That'll do it."

"As for you," I said smiling, "you're to have a big dinner."

"I'll settle for a big kiss."

I patted the sofa cushion. "Here, then."

She shook her head. "Later, if you're good. Right now I need some advice. Richard wants us to go to Negril tomorrow and shoot a reconstruction. You know the sort of thing: 'This is the hotel where Carol stayed . . . This is the room she had . . . This is the beach she combed.' But I'm leery of getting caught, if something breaks. Should I take a chance?"

Nothing was going to break before Thursday, but I couldn't tell Susan that; she'd want to know how I knew. "I think you'll be safe," I said slowly. "Negril's only a little more than an hour away by air. You could get back in a hurry."

"That's what Richard says. Eric can stay here and backstop."

"Who's Eric?"

"My field producer. The cameraman and I can shoot a reconstruction without his help." She stubbed out her cigarette; I was going to have to start nagging her about that. "Okay, I'll go."

"I'll go with you," I said. "In fact, we'll go tonight."

Susan's eyes widened. "Tonight?"

"Sure. Your cameraman can fly down in the morning. You and I can have a good dinner and a morning swim."

She bit her lip, thinking. "I'm not on holiday, Mike. Maybe I'd better not."

"You're going anyway," I said. "If we go tonight, you'll be able to get an earlier start. Scout out your locations, or whatever it is you do."

"Why do you want to come?"

"Anything to see you in your bikini."

She laughed. "It's a bit late for that."

Before I could reply, the phone rang. "It's been doing that all day," I said, annoyed.

"Ahh, Michael! Mr. McGregor for you."

"Hi, Sam. What's new?"

"Precious little. The forecaster says it will snow tonight."

"Not in the Caribbean. Hold on, Sam. I'll take this in the other room." I turned to Susan. "It's my boss. Will you excuse me?"

"Sure."

"Would you mind hanging up after I'm on the extension?"

She nodded and I went into the bedroom, closing the door.

"I've been trying to reach you," McGregor said.

"Thank you, Susan." I heard her replace the receiver. "Hello, Douglas."

"Who's Susan?" he asked suspiciously.

"A friend." I've made it a policy not to discuss my female companions with McGregor.

"Oh. I was saying that I've been trying to reach you, but I couldn't get through."

"I'm not surprised. I've been running a journalism school all afternoon."

He chuckled. "You have my sympathy. We've been hounded to death." His voice became brisker. "Well, I gather there's good news."

"Perhaps."

"Alan phoned this afternoon. He'd had a quick word with the Prime Minister, just before the House opened. Apparently the Prime Minister had heard from Kingston that matters were finally in hand down there. As a courtesy, Alan informed me. What *is* the situation? Are we out of the woods?"

"I don't think we should discuss it on the phone."

He thought for a moment. "Are you aware of the latest developments?"

"Yes."

"I see." He paused. "You're quite sure?"

"Yes. In fact, I'm responsible for them."

"Ahh." There was another silence. "Alan seemed to think Thursday would see the end of it."

"With a little luck. They're going in for her then."

"And you're satisfied?"

"Not entirely. But it's out of my hands. The authorities have the ball and they're running with it. I've been grounded."

"You don't sound very happy."

"Look, I don't think we should say any more."

"Very well." He sounded disappointed.

"I'm going back to Negril tonight. I'll be at the Coconut Cove."

"All right. Do what you think best."

I looked at my watch as I broke the connection. It was almost five-thirty. We'd have to hurry, if we were going. *Do what you think best*, he'd said. Best for whom? Carol Malone? Douglas McGregor? Peter Crandall? Michael Shuter, for a change?

Susan was gazing out the window when I went back to the living room. Cloud patterns had formed over the mountains, great white puffs of cumulus barely moving across an azure sky. I put my arms around her from behind and held her close. On the pool terrace, a few stubborn sunbathers were angling their chaises to catch the last rays of the day. No one was in the pool and the pale blue water looked cool and inviting, fifteen floors below.

"Mike?"

"Uh huh?" I was nuzzling her hair.

"Negril tonight sounds like fun."

"Good," I said, releasing her. "If we can get there."

Trans-Jamaican said they had seats on their last flight to Negril. We could just make it, if we rushed.

Susan went to the Sheraton to pack a few things and try to find her crew; otherwise, she'd phone them from the Coconut Cove. I went through the suite quickly, gathering up my belongings. At the desk, while they were getting my account together, I debated whether to phone Crandall, but decided against it. Instead, I left a forwarding address with the Pegasus. Crandall could phone me, if he had anything to say.

Susan was in the hotel lobby with her typewriter and a smart over-the-shoulder bag, ready to go. Her field producer and cameraman were in the bar, swapping lies with other members of the press corps. The cameraman would fly to Negril in the morning and the field producer would cover for Susan in Kingston. Becky made it to Tinson Pen with minutes to spare. Susan went to the Trans-Jamaican counter to organize our tickets while I settled with Mr. Beckford. I'd kept my promise not to put very many miles on the old Buick.

We flew to Montego Bay in a Trislander, a three-engine British-built aircraft ideally suited to Trans-Jamaican's routes and passenger volume. Susan and I sat together, holding hands and chatting about tourism, Toronto, Bishop—anything but Carol.

At Sangster we transferred to a smaller, twin-engine aircraft for the fifteen-minute hop to Negril. There were no other passengers. The pilot, an old pro, made his approach to the short Negril strip by coming in low over the sea. He pointed down at the water and said: "Ganja runner. Came in a bit short." A Beechcraft Bonanza was sitting in about twenty feet of water. It looked to be intact. Whoever put it there had probably been able to swim away without a scratch. He'd been lucky. The battle of wits between smugglers and police is endless, with quiet little dramas unfolding almost every night. Sometimes one side wins, sometimes the other. The Negril strip, for example, is closed after dark and oil drums are set out to prevent illegal landings. But occasionally, the drums are removed and a seat-of-the-pants pilot makes a stab at it. The pay may be high, but so are the risks; you need steady nerves to fly for Air Ganja.

A solitary taxi was waiting outside the tiny terminal. The driver seemed happy to see us. He stowed our luggage and drove us the quarter-mile to the Coconut Cove, singing *sotto voce* all the way. The Mercedes was parked outside the hotel and I told Susan about the girl who'd run off with the tennis pro; Susan said the girl was probably right. The night clerk gave me my key and an envelope from Linda. The message read:

Dear Nelson Eddy,

Thank you for the lion. It's beautiful. And thank you for a lovely evening. The numbers are: 617-422-1559 (home) and 617-251-1600, ext. 243 (office).

Love,
Jeanette MacDonald

P.S. Could we see the Canadiens?

I put the note in my pocket, and led Susan to the suite, carrying our things. It was almost dark, and I was hungry again.

"It's very nice," said Susan, talking about the apartment. "You certainly travel well."

"Like a fine burgundy. Will you have a drink?"

She nodded. "Vodka, if you have it. I'm going to take a shower."

"I'm going to join you."

"We'll never get to dinner."


Unusually well-scrubbed, we dined on conch chowder and snapper, washed down by a barely drinkable Niersteiner; Gilly's cellar was drying up, and he didn't know when, if ever, he'd be able to get new stock. Ivan had found us a table near the dance area and we sat with our cognacs and coffee, listening to Silly and The Children of Jah. When the band eased into a Kristofferson standard, "Help Me Make It Through The Night," I asked Susan to dance. Normally, I'm not much of a dancer and I couldn't decide whether she brought out the best in me – or the worst.

We were moving slowly around the floor when Ivan came up and tapped my shoulder.

"Excuse me, Mr. Shuter."

"Go away."

"There's a call for you."

"Tell them to go away too."

"In the lobby. It's urgent."

I sighed. "Okay, Ivan, will you finish the dance?"

Susan held out her arms and Ivan grinned. "A pleasure, sah!"

"Just this one," I said to Susan, wagging a finger.


"What are you doing in Negril?" Crandall demanded testily. "You're meant to be in Kingston."

"Dancing, if you must know. And who says I'm meant to be in Kingston?"

"I don't want you playing the Boy Scout."

"It's a free country."

"It's anything but," he growled. "You won't like the Negril lock-up."

"I'm not going to see it."

"Don't be too sure."

"I want her out of there, Crandall. Before you guys hit."

"No. I mean it, Shuter. No."

I didn't say anything.

"I understand how you feel," he said, after a few moments. "But I have to consider the priorities. She's one person. We're worried about an entire country."

What could I say? That I thought his men would screw up? That I didn't trust them to do the job? That one civilian was more capable than 200 cops and soldiers? Obviously not. *Do what you think best.*

"Okay, Crandall. You're right."

"We just can't take the chance. If Jefferson's alerted, Thursday morning could turn into a bloodbath. We need the surprise element."

"When you put it that way..."

"The girl will be all right. You have my word."

Nobody could make that guarantee. "All right. I'll stay out of it."

His relief was almost tangible. "Good man. I think you'd be pleased with the way our plan is coming together. Final briefing's early tomorrow evening. You're welcome to attend."

"No, thanks. I'll sweat it out here. You can do me a favour, though."

"Gladly."

"When it's over, when you're out, would you phone me as soon as possible?"

"Of course."

Ivan had replenished our cognac and was sitting with Susan, enchanted. He stood when I approached the table but I waved him back to his chair. "Stay a while, Ivan. We haven't had much of a chance to talk."

"I'm sorry to have to tell you this, Michael," Susan grinned, "but Ivan's a much better dancer than you are."

"I'm not surprised. But can he skate?"

Ivan shook his head, laughing.

"Who was the call from?" Susan asked.

"Crandall."

"Anything I should know?"

"No."

"Ivan said it was urgent."

"Crandall thinks everything is urgent," I said, draining my cognac. "Let's have another drink."

We stayed on the terrace a while, then went inside to the bar.

Ivan asked to be excused; he had to prepare for breakfast. Shortly before one o'clock, I offered to take Susan next door to the Village where the disco stayed open till dawn.

"No," she said. "I'd sooner go to bed."

"You talked me into it."

# CHAPTER TWENTY

## *Day Six (Wednesday) – 10:50 A.M.*

It started to rain when I reached Bluefields, a resort area on the south coast halfway between Negril and Black River. Big drops tumbled warm out of a slate sky, as though they were determined to wash away all traces of the perfect weather I'd enjoyed for nearly a week. The wind swirled in gusts off the rumpled sea, and the beach was deserted – as empty as my stomach, but quieter.

The Mercedes moved smoothly over the rough pavement of Highway A-2. While I drove I listened to the radio in case there were bulletins. The ten-o'clock newscast had made only a brief reference to Carol. A police spokesman – probably the one who'd handled yesterday's press conference – told JBC listeners there were several leads and good news was expected soon.

I felt crummy about lying to Crandall and deceiving Susan but I'd make it up to them. Eventually they'd understand I had to look after business. With Susan, I'd had a bit of luck: she wasn't in the suite when I woke. Either she'd decided to go for a stroll on the beach or down for an early breakfast. Whichever, it spared me having to lie to her, face-to-face. I'd showered and shaved quickly, skipping my exercise again, and put on jeans, tennis shoes, and a sports shirt, carrying a pullover as insurance against a night in the open. I'd also written her a vague note, saying I had some work to do and wishing her good luck with her reconstruction piece and a safe flight back to Kingston.

It was overcast when I left Negril and started along the secondary road leading to Savanna-la-mar and the south coast. For the first few miles I kept checking the rear-view mirror. I was less concerned about being picked up by Cudjoe's men than I was about the police; but Crandall apparently had decided to accept my word. I had the road to myself.

I wasn't sure what I'd find in Look Behind or how I'd handle it, but Carol had to be given every chance. She might be indiscreet, wilful, even wanton; but she didn't belong in a shoot-out.

Black River proved to be a depressing town. It had a fishery and a market but little else of interest. I parked on the main drag in front of a clean-looking café that was open for business but not doing any. The woman at the counter greeted me with a smile to banish the clouds and served me two spicy meat patties which I washed down with a bottle of warm Red Stripe. My stomach continued to rumble, but whether in gratitude or complaint I couldn't tell.

When I'd finished eating, I walked a few doors to a general store where I bought a cheap haversack, a rubber poncho, a small first-aid kit, a penknife, and a compass. Next, I went to a grocery and picked up a brick of cheese, a baker's loaf, some jerk pork, a couple of tins of sardines, and four chocolate bars.

The cavalry was more or less equipped. Now, to the rescue.

After Black River the highway swung inland, running beside a broad, nasty-looking swamp for several miles. Traffic was still light and no one seemed unduly interested in me or the Mercedes. The rain had softened and the wind had dropped off, away from the sea.

Checking the map again, I decided to stay on A-2 through the section known as Bamboo Avenue, and to leave the main highway at a village with the rather grim name of Lacovia Tombstone. The map showed an alternative route over a secondary road from there to Maggotty which, in turn, was about five miles downstream from the hamlet of Windsor. At Windsor, road and river said goodbye for the last time.

Bamboo Avenue was a beautiful stretch of highway, even on a dismal day. For almost six miles, the road cut through a dense bamboo forest which grew so close that the tops of the trees formed a canopy for traffic. The forest was gloomy-looking and impenetrable; if I ran into anything like it on my way up the river, I'd have a problem hacking through with a penknife.

At Windsor, I crossed a narrow bridge and started up a tertiary road which, according to the map, simply petered out after about ten miles, on the far side of the village of Quick Step. Beyond, there was nothing but the wasteland known as Cockpit Country, a lunar landscape with trees, almost Karstian in places.

A half-mile beyond Windsor, I found a place to hide the car. The pull-off was little more than a cart track but it led to cover behind a tangle of shrubs and trees. The Mercedes would be safe there, secure from curious passersby. I turned the car around in case I needed a quick getaway, packed the haversack, put on the poncho, and got out.

The rain had all but stopped but the ground and bushes were soaking. So, within minutes, were my sneakers and jeans. I made my way slowly through tall grass to the edge of the river, which was fast and narrow and clear at this point. A faint footpath ran beside it and I decided to risk the path for a while. It seemed unlikely Cudjoe's men would be moving this far afield in foul weather. After taking a compass reading, I set off upstream, moving northwest. If the map was accurate the river would swing to my left in about two miles, then run due north to its source.

An hour later the sun was trying to break through the low clouds and I'd covered more than half the distance. I walked cautiously, not wanting to blunder into a sentry post or run into anyone coming down the path. If I could manage to get close enough to observe the camp without being seen, I'd have at least a chance of working out a plan; right now I was operating on blind faith.

I was sweltering under the poncho so I stopped to take it off and have a drink. The water was cool and delicious. The forest was dead quiet, except for the gurgle of the river and the intermittent scolding of a John Crow. The vulture seemed to resent my presence.

I was nearing the point where it would be prudent to leave the path and pick my way through the dense bush. After eating a chocolate bar I rolled up the poncho and stuffed it into the haversack. It was time to set off again.

Then I heard a new noise.

Someone was coming up the path behind me, and being sneaky about it. Quietly, I moved behind a thick clump of allamanda, its brilliant yellow flowers in glorious bloom. I decided that if the person on the path was one of Cudjoe's men – and he was armed – I'd take him out; a weapon would be worth the risk.

He was coming steadily closer and I held my breath, ready to pounce.

It was Susan bloody Quill, wrapped in a plastic raincoat.

"You stupid little idiot!" I'd seized her by the shoulders and was shaking her like you'd shake an apple tree in the fall.

"Don't be silly," she said calmly, when I finally released her. "I've got a job to do, too."

"How the hell did you get here?" I kept my voice low but I was furious. Furious and worried. In an attempt to extricate one woman from danger I'd managed to lead a second one directly toward it.

"I followed you, of course."

"*No* one followed me."

"Only for the last few miles." She began combing the

water out of her hair, utterly unrepentant. I could have cheerfully turned her over my knee. "I waited for you at Maggotty and followed you from there."

I glared at her, and struggled to recover my temper. "That's impossible. How did you know I was going to Maggotty? Or do I talk in my sleep?"

Susan put away her comb. "I'm Suzie Q, remember? The professional snoop."

"You're a professional pain in the ass! Goddamnit, Susan, this isn't a game."

She shrugged. "It doesn't make any difference, I guess. Not now. I knew something was going on yesterday morning, when you went flying. I was sure you were going after Carol."

"So?"

"So, yesterday afternoon I confirmed my suspicion."

"How?"

She smiled nervously. "I listened in while you talked to Mr. McGregor."

I stared at her, disbelieving. I'd heard her hang up the phone.

"And," she went on brightly, "there was the map on the coffee table. You'd circled Black River several times, drawn a line there from Kingston, and put a big X up here by the headwaters. It wasn't hard to guess what spot the X marked."

I was appalled by my carelessness, outraged by her deviousness. Susan had played me for a sucker.

Her eyes softened but her voice remained firm. "I think I know you pretty well. If the police were going after Carol and you were worried about her safety, which is what you told Mr. McGregor, then I just *knew* you'd try to help her somehow. I was certain you'd come here today, if the police were planning to come tomorrow."

"You may think you know *me* fairly well," I said, "but I don't know *you* at all. I can't believe you'd deliberately listen in to someone else's conversation. How did you get to Maggotty? Broomstick?"

"All right. You're angry. But there's no need to be insulting. I went by taxi. It was clear from the map that you'd have to go through Maggotty to get to the place marked with the X. I woke up early, crept out of the room, and got the desk to get me a cab. You came through the village about two hours after we got there. Then we just tagged along."

"Well, you can just turn around and go back."

"The cab's gone back to Negril."

"You can take my car."

She shook her head. "I'm not going back. This is a big story."

"Susan, you don't even *know* the story. Carol's nickels and dimes."

"If you make me go back," she said, "I'll go straight to Kingston and do a piece for tonight's news saying Carol has been discovered in a notorious dope dealer's hideout at the head of the Black River. I'll say the police and army are going to raid the place in the morning. And I'll say you're already on the scene." She looked at me shrewdly. "It may not be the whole story, but it will do. And I assure you, Richard will run it. Nobody loves a scoop more than Richard—except maybe me."

"That's criminal irresponsibility!" I stared at her, but she didn't blink: "You haven't even got a camera. What good's a TV reporter without a camera?"

"We can always get the pictures later. I want to see what happens."

"Look, Susan. I don't *know* what's going to happen. Cudjoe is a killer and he's got a lot of killers working for him. I don't want you getting hurt."

"You'll look after me," she said confidently.

Susan had me snookered. I couldn't send her back; she knew too much. And I couldn't take her back; that would leave Carol in the lurch. So I had to take her with me.

We left the river and started through the forest, our course dictated more by the terrain than the compass. Under a now-hammering sun, we moved carefully through some of the strangest countryside I'd ever seen. The vegetation was thick in places, non-existent in others. Weird formations of limestone stabbed into the sky, natural obelisks raised by capricious gods. There were sinkholes everywhere, some of them as deep and dangerous as mineshafts. No wonder eighteenth-century British troops had been ineffective here; whole armies could be swallowed up in Cockpit Country.

Susan kept pace without complaining and I was too busy concentrating on our route to maintain my anger. An hour after we'd left the river, we were picking our way up a fairly steep ridge when Susan lost her balance and tumbled backward with a short shriek. She landed with a thump on her butt, bounced once and lay back, winded. She'd only fallen about six feet, but the ground was hard.

Cursing under my breath, I scrambled down to inspect the damage.

Susan looked at me wryly. "I'll live," she said, sounding more embarrassed than hurt.

"Maybe." I reached down and took her hand, tugging her to her feet. She reached back and rubbed her rear end, grinning up at me.

Abruptly, her grin disappeared. "Mike..."

I wheeled and looked up the ridge to see two Sterling machine-guns, held steady by a couple of beauties wearing U.S. war surplus fatigues. Terrific. Their locks hung to their shoulders and they looked as wild and scary as anything Mau Mau had produced; Dedan Kamathi would have been proud of them.

Bloody Susan and her bloody cry of alarm!

The Mau Maus moved apart, keeping their guns trained on us. One of them gestured that we were to raise our hands. The other started down the slope, taking care to stay out of his partner's line of fire.

I took a half-step forward and the Mau Mau who was holding his position squeezed off a warning burst. The bullets chewed into the rock perhaps five yards to the left of my feet and whined off through the humid air while Susan gasped.

"Okay," I said, raising my hands. "Okay. Take it easy."

The one who'd come down to our level approached me cautiously, his expression grim. He took the haversack first, then patted my pockets and seized my penknife, compass and wallet. Next, he frisked Susan, his hands impersonal as they moved over her body. He removed a thin billfold from her jeans, briefly inspected her comb, cigarettes, lighter, and lipstick before returning them, and then stepped back.

"Let me guess," I said. "This is a stickup, right? You're Frank and Jesse James."

Neither man bothered to reply.

The one who'd searched us looked casually through both wallets, decided they were harmless, and tossed them at our feet, contents intact.

"My arms are getting tired," said Susan, sounding surprisingly calm. "May I put them down, please?"

The Mau Maus exchanged glances, then nodded. We lowered our hands and waited while the one who'd searched us went through the haversack. For some reason, he kept the poncho but dropped everything else carelessly to the ground. Finally, he let the haversack fall, too.

The other one jerked his head. "Dis way, mon. An' doan try to be clever, kind o' t'ing."

One thing about Sterlings, I thought unhappily; they're reliable, a lingering reminder of one-time British efficiency. I could forget any idea of making a play. Instead, I picked up our wallets.

Susan's eyes were too bright but otherwise she seemed more curious than worried. Submachine-guns and unkempt guerillas made a dramatic change from the police-blotter stuff she normally covered. "We may as well go with them."

She responded with a nod and a weak grin, stuffing her billfold back into her jeans.

We climbed to the top of the ridge, and this time Susan

made it without incident. Then we set off in Indian file, one gunman in the lead, the other at the rear.

Our position was bleak, but not hopeless. In less than fifteen hours, Crandall's men would arrive. The trick would be to stay alive until then, and the key to staying alive would be the way I handled Cudjoe.

"Let me do the talking," I said quietly, as we trudged along. "Forget all about tomorrow morning and the guy who phoned me last night."

She gave me a puzzled look, then nodded. "Okay."

"No talkin'," said the gunman at the rear.

A half-hour later, we emerged from the forest and entered the camp, watched curiously by several members of Cudjoe's gang. The Mau Maus ignored their shouted questions and marched us resolutely forward, past the larger building Crandall and I had spotted from the air, and then along a ragged line of huts.


"Not bad," said Cudjoe, looking lecherously at Susan. "Maybe not as foxy as this one here, but not bad at all. Shuter, you a thoughtful dude."

We were in Cudjoe's field headquarters, a crude hut perhaps fifteen feet square. The Mau Maus were standing tense at the door, keeping us covered. Cudjoe's lieutenant, Jimmy, was watching us narrowly, uncertain what our presence meant. Cudjoe himself was sprawled, naked to the waist, in a canvas director's chair. His thickly muscled torso and shoulders glistened in the hut's gloom and he was smoking the biggest spliff I'd ever seen. He appeared relaxed, confident, fully in control.

Beside Cudjoe, in shorts and a wrinkled T-shirt, stood Carol Malone.

She was dishevelled but still achingly beautiful. Carol was a fantasy in the flesh; no wonder Toronto art directors gave her assignments and dreamed of assignations. Her eyes were dull, though, almost vacant, as if she'd abandoned hope, resigned herself to endless humiliation. If she had, it was understandable: around her neck was a stiff leather collar connected to a leash which Cudjoe held loosely in his left hand. The collar and leash looked like something you'd find in the bondage section of the Pleasure Chest, the Beverly Hills sex shop patronized by jaded Hollywood potentates and their long-legged potentees.

"Very kinky," I said to Cudjoe, curling my lip in contempt.

"She tried to run away," he said, giving the leash a light tug. "I'm just showin' her how I treat bitches who try to run away."

Beside me, Susan was staring at Carol, taking shallow little breaths, shocked at seeing a fellow female being abused.

"So she's fine, eh?" I said tightly. "Enjoying her holiday, having a wonderful time? Jefferson, you're sick."

"I shoulda known," he said, frowning. "That's what bugs me. I shoulda known you wouldn't quit."

"I told you the tape wasn't enough."

Cudjoe nodded slowly, then glowered at Carol. "She been nothin' but trouble lately. Know what I mean, Shuter? I been thinkin' about givin' her to Jimmy." He glanced at his little lieutenant. "You'd like a taste, wouldn't you, Jim?"

Jimmy kept silent, gnawing his lower lip.

"She a pistol, brother," Cudjoe went on, amused. "A Satiddy-night special, every night of the week. And she digs it, you know?" He made an obscene gesture with his tongue.

Jimmy's eyes glittered at the prospect.

Carol, who hadn't uttered a sound or changed her expression from the time Susan and I were led into the hut, began to cry silently, tears coursing down her cheeks.

"You're disgusting!" said Susan, glaring at Cudjoe and darting sympathetic glances toward Carol.

Cudjoe shrugged. "Maybe you change your mind, sister, if I decide it your turn to get lucky." He took a deep drag on his spliff and leered. "I guess I oughtta thank you, Shuter. For bringing me the fresh, I mean." He nodded toward Susan.

"I'll cut your heart out," I said quietly.

He scratched himself and glared at me. "You forgettin', honky, you *my* prisoner, and you ain't cuttin' nothin'."

No one moved. Carol continued to stare at the ground; Susan seemed to be holding her breath; Jimmy appeared puzzled; finally Cudjoe laughed. "What am I gonna do with you, Shuter?" He looked at me curiously, as though I were an exotic specimen in his biology lab. "How'd you find this joint, anyway?"

"It wasn't hard." I made an impatient gesture. "Why don't you get wise? Give me the girl and I'll leave you alone."

"You a whole fistful of cards short of a full deck." Cudjoe shook his head in mock amazement. "I axed you a question. How'd you find this place?"

What the hell; he probably knew anyway. "A sensible girl, your Sarah. She decided she didn't want me mad at her."

Cudjoe nodded, then spat. "The bitch has disappeared."

"I stashed her," I said. "For her own good."

"Where?" he said softly. "Where did you stash her?"

"A safe place. You won't find her."

"I'll find her, Shuter. Don't you worry none about that. I'll find her, and then we see how sensible she is." When I didn't reply he continued. "I don't let people get in my way. It ain't healthy – for them or me. You could ask Winston Llewellyn, next time you're talkin' to him."

"Jefferson," I said, almost whispering, "you're a dirty rotten crazy murdering bastard and it's going to be my pleasure to beat the living shit out of you."

He seemed startled. "Like I said, you missin' a lotta cards. Whadda you think this is? The Y-fucking-MCA? We're gonna put on the gloves, go a few rounds? Lemme tell you somethin', honky. You about *this* close to a bellyful of bullets, 'cause I've had a bellyful of you."

I grinned at him, but resolved to be less pushy. I wasn't going to help anyone if I got killed. Cudjoe's spliff had gone out, which seemed to annoy him unduly. He made a face at it and flung it to the ground.

"Who else knows about this place?"

Match point. "No one. Why?"

"Who else, Shuter?"

"No one. I work alone."

He looked at me doubtfully, then jerked his head toward Susan. "Then who's this?"

"A reporter," I said. "She's been looking for Carol, too."

He frowned some more. "I thought you worked alone?"

"This was a mistake."

"Yeah, it's a mistake, all right. What I gotta figure out is how much it should cost you."

"Play it smart, Jefferson. Let me take Carol home and that'll be the end of it."

He yawned and shook his head. "Later, maybe. Not now."

"What's the difference? Later or now? You can't keep us here indefinitely and you're too smart to hurt us."

He didn't reply straight away. He seemed uncertain what to make of my arrival: was I playing from hidden strength or was I merely a resourceful loner who'd blundered into a situation he didn't understand? The silence stretched out while Cudjoe worked on the puzzle. It was uncomfortably warm in the hut and the air was stale, reeking of sweat and marijuana.

"It not indefinite," he said finally. "Only a few days now."

"What's only a few days?"

He studied my face. "You ain't as smart as I thought."

"I manage."

He let it go, turning to Susan. "A reporter, huh? You gonna do a story on Cudjoe?"

Susan looked at him coldly and didn't reply.

"I ain't sure I like the idea of a reporter," Cudjoe mused, frowning at Jimmy.

Jimmy shrugged. "What diff'rence it makin'?" It was the first time I'd heard him speak. His voice was guttural, as flat as Cudjoe's was high-pitched.

"What's your name, sister?" Cudjoe asked. "Who you workin' for?"

Susan glanced at me and I nodded. "I'm Susan Quill. I work for NTN."

"What's that?"

"A Canadian television network."

"A network," Cudjoe said, sounding almost impressed. "Where's your camera and stuff?"

"Kingston."

"But you here, with Shuter." He looked at her thoughtfully. "They makin' a lotta noise in Kingston about this one" – he tugged on Carol's leash – "on the radio and in the papers."

"Is it any wonder?" asked Susan.

Obviously, Susan's presence was bothering Cudjoe. Of course, even the heaviest criminals think there's something mystical about the press. At the height of his power, Al Capone used to tell his Chicago playmates they might be able to get away with killing a cop, but if they laid a glove on a reporter the heat would be instantaneous and intolerable. It would be ironic if Susan Quill wound up being my protector, rather than the other way around. How are you supposed to hide behind the skirts of a woman who wears jeans?

Cudjoe yawned again and closed his eyes, making me wonder how many spliffs he'd been through. "I wanna think about this," he said to Jimmy. "Take 'em next door and tie 'em up. Carol, too. Make sure they're watched."

Jimmy accepted the leash, holding it gingerly. Carol looked at Cudjoe with such loathing that I decided her spirit wasn't broken, after all; she was just a girl who didn't say much.

"Move," said Jimmy, glowering at Susan and me.

The Mau Maus backed away from the door and moved slightly apart, watching us all the while. Cudjoe began rolling another spliff, paying us no further attention.

# CHAPTER TWENTY-ONE

## *Night Six (Wednesday) — 4:45 P.M.*

After the interior murk, the late-afternoon sun was extra-bright. As we stumbled across the uneven ground toward the adjacent hut, several hoods watched us pass. The camp had a para-military look, with the men in odd-lot fatigues and carrying a wide assortment of weapons. There were shotguns and old Lee-Enfields, as well as the semi-automatic stuff I'd seen earlier. But discipline was less than absolute: most of the men lolled about, yakking, snoozing, or smoking dope. From the time the Mau Maus had first led Susan and me into the place, I'd been counting faces and I was in the mid-twenties when we reached the next hut. It seemed probable that Crandall's strike force would be big enough; Cudjoe's army was something short of formidable.

Our hut was slightly smaller than Cudjoe's. The walls were built of rough lumber and the roof was tin. There were no windows, no floor. Like all the buildings in the camp, including the larger one Crandall and I had seen from the air, it was camouflaged by ferns and branches.

Inside, Jimmy ordered the Mau Maus to guard us while he went off in search of some rope. One of the Mau Maus stood in the doorway, the other leaned against an interior wall, ready for anything.

We waited in silence, Susan apprehensive, Carol still looking angry. I decided that our session with Cudjoe had gone as well as I could have dared hope.

A few minutes later Jimmy came back carrying a machete, a length of sashcord, and three ratty-looking blankets. He dropped the blankets at our feet. "You need dese tonight."

He didn't waste any time, ordering Susan and Carol to stand aside and me to lie on my belly, hands behind my back. There was no point in arguing.

Jimmy knew his knots. I doubted he'd ever been a Boy Scout, so he'd probably spent some time at sea. Within two minutes I was securely bound, hand and foot. Cunningly, he'd run the cord through my belt which had the effect of pinning my wrists to the small of my back. The cord wasn't quite tight enough to cut off full circulation, but it was going to be an uncomfortable night.

The machete sliced cleanly through the sashcord and Jimmy turned his attention to Susan. She endured the experience in silent outrage. I watched closely, lying on my side, while his deft fingers tied and tested her knots.

Finally, it was Carol's turn, and for the first time Jimmy seemed uncertain, became hesitant in his movements. Carol, at least three inches taller than he, looked down at Jimmy expressionlessly as he stood before her. He let her stand while he tied her hands behind her back. I was surprised to see *his* hands trembling as he fumbled with the cord. Was he nervous? Until recently Carol had been Cudjoe's favourite; perhaps Jimmy wasn't sure she was in the doghouse for good.

But Jimmy was trembling with lust, not nerves. With an odd, twisted grin on his face, he put a tentative hand on Carol's breast. She went rigid but didn't utter a peep. Encouraged, Jimmy slipped his hand under the T-shirt and began fondling her in earnest.

Carol spat in his face.

Jimmy cursed and fell back, wiping his cheek. Then he slapped her, forehand and backhand. "White bitch! You gonna learn! You gonna be beggin' Jimmy!"

She spat at him again.

"Good shot!" said Susan, who'd been watching from the ground beside me.

Jimmy glared down at Susan, frustration burning deep in his eyes. Then, breathing harshly, he seized Carol by the shoulders and pushed her down, hard. For a moment I was afraid he was going to rape her – there was nothing to stop him – but he contented himself with tying her ankles, tightening the cord viciously.

Carol looked up at him calmly. "You pathetic little man." Her tone was haughty and, in the circumstances, should have sounded ridiculous. But somehow it sounded exactly right.

Jimmy stared at her for a moment, then shrugged and turned on his heel. "Stay lively," he said to the Mau Maus.

"Pig!" Susan snapped at Jimmy's retreating back.

"Carol," I said, "say hello to Susan Quill. I think you two will get along."

"No talkin'," growled one of the Mau Maus.


They changed the guard shortly after six o'clock, according to Susan's Timex. The ceremony owed little to the snappy ritual at Buckingham Palace, and Christopher Robin undoubtedly would have been disappointed by it. But I found the sloppiness reassuring; it augured well for morning. Or was I simply whistling past the crematorium?

A new hood, toting an AK-47, had sauntered up to relieve the Mau Maus. Cudjoe hadn't doubled the guard, he'd halved it. And where the Mau Maus had been all business, one of them sitting cross-legged in the doorway, the other propped unblinking against an inside wall, our new keeper virtually ignored us.

After glancing indifferently into the hut, he sat outside, leaning against the door-jamb with his back to us, yawning and occasionally scratching his head through his knitted cap. But the submachine-gun resting in his lap was a sobering reminder that we were in deep trouble.

Not that I needed external reminders; the sashcord was burning the skin on my wrists. After the Mau Maus left, I made one or two experimental manoeuvres to see whether Jimmy's knots would yield, but it was no use.

Because of the Mau Maus' ban on conversation, the first couple of hours of our detention had been a strain. We kept studying one another, communicating with frowns or smiles. The new guard, however, didn't seem to mind whether we talked and it was Carol who first understood that the rules had changed. She went through a series of contortions and shifted position so she could look Susan and me in the eye.

Carol, who seemed to know a lot about me, began with a whispered apology and ended with a general confession. "I guess I should thank you," she said, her green eyes flickering from my face to Susan's and back again, "and tell you how sorry I am that you're in this mess because of my stupidity."

"It'll be okay," I said softly. "Don't be too hard on yourself."

"I feel so ashamed," she said. "So foolish and ashamed. Everything just sort of got out of control, and the next thing I knew my status had changed." She smiled bitterly. "I'd gone from lover to captive, and you heard him – he's on the verge of making me the camp whore. I suppose some people would say it was an appropriate fate."

"It's not your fault," Susan whispered fiercely. "You were on holiday. Anyway, I can see why you were attracted to him."

"He's beautiful," Carol said wistfully, shaking her head. "A fabulous physique. I wanted to paint him. Now I want to kill him." She paused, and looked away. "I'm aware of how trite it must sound. Streetwalkers the world over tell the same story about their pimps..."

"Don't worry," I said. "You'll be home in a day or two. I think you've been very brave. And clever. The business about your sister, for example. If you hadn't done that, I might have taken the tape back to Toronto and been done with it."

Susan beamed at Carol, then frowned at me in puzzlement. "What do you think he'll do to us?"

"Probably nothing—before Saturday night. But we'll be out of here long before then."

"Why Saturday night?"

"Because that's the deadline."

"What deadline?"

Quietly, I outlined the scope of Cudjoe's ganja operation, described his challenge to the Jamaica government and explained why he'd been holding Carol.

"What a story!" Susan's cheeks were pink with excitement. "My God, it's the story of the year! Richard will go bananas. It's worth an hour special for sure."

"You're a long way from going to air," I said sourly. "We've got to get out of this, first."

"Crandall will get us out."


Jimmy arrived just before nightfall with three cups of soup. He asked our guard whether we'd been any trouble and was answered with a negative grunt.

"How you doin', mon?" Jimmy squatted beside me and checked my knots.

"It's not very comfortable, especially for the women." Neither Susan nor Carol had complained but I was stiff and sore so they had to be, too.

Jimmy nodded, but didn't offer to do anything about it. Carol refused the soup and Jimmy didn't argue the point. But Susan and I were starving. In turn, he helped us sit up and held the cups so we could drink. It was tepid and tasted only faintly of pumpkin, but it was better than nothing. I urged Carol to have some but she shook her head and looked away.

When Susan and I finished our soup, Jimmy put the blankets over us. "We let you walk around some tomorrow."

"There's no need to keep us tied," I said. "At least untie the women."

He shook his head. "Cudjoe's orders."

"I'm dying for a smoke," said Susan, giving him one of her Sunday smiles.

"You wanna do a spliff?" he asked uncertainly.

"Nope. But I've got some cigarettes in my pocket."

Jimmy thought about it, then nodded. "Okay, I let you have one." He worked a crushed pack of Rothman's and her lighter out of her jeans, lit the cigarette, and put it between her lips. Then he stuffed the lighter and cigarettes back into her pocket.

Susan inhaled gratefully, squinting to keep the smoke out of her eyes. I bit back a sarcastic comment; it was no time for one of my lectures. Instead, I asked Jimmy: "Where is Cudjoe, anyway?"

Jimmy looked at me steadily. "I tell you one t'ing, Shuter. So far, you bin lucky. Very lucky. Cudjoe say we not to let you go, but he doan wan' you hurt, either. So you lucky. But doan push it, mon."

When Susan's cigarette had burned down almost to the filter, Jimmy took it from her, stubbing it out carefully in the dirt. Then he stood back. "I check up on you later."

With that he turned and left the hut, telling the guard: "Stay lively, mon, or I cut off an ear."

Sleep was impossible and conversation required too much effort. I spent the next few hours stretched out in the dark, listening to the night sounds. There weren't many. Even nature accepted that this was a lonely part of the world, a place where quiet ought to reign. Occasionally, brief snatches of conversation or muffled laughter drifted in, but mostly Cudjoe's men seemed to be relaxing in their quarters.

Evidently there was a ban on open fires – probably as a precaution against night aerial patrols. The only light filtering into the hut came from the moon and the occasional passing torch being carried by someone on his way to or from sentry duty.

That there was any organization at all was a tribute to Cudjoe. He didn't have much to work with: a collection of cutthroats brought together by greed and held together by fear. In a way, Cudjoe was a straight-line descendant of the old-time buccaneers, a black Henry Morgan – albeit without any of the romance usually associated with pirates. Morgan, of course, had prospered at the expense of the Spanish to the point where an English King had felt obliged to knight him. Somehow I doubted Cudjoe would ever show up on the Queen's birthday honours' list.

Susan had shifted so she was half-lying against me, her head burrowed into my shoulder. The contact seemed to reassure her. We stayed that way a long time, listening to Carol's deep, steady breathing. If Carol was asleep, she belonged on the honours' list: "For Valour," as it says on the Victoria Cross.

They changed the guard again shortly after midnight, two men taking over from the guy who'd been so bored. Before settling down, the new men came into the hut to inspect what they were supposed to watch. One of them carried a flashlight, which he played across our faces. The other carried a double-barrelled shotgun.

After satisfying their curiosity, the new guards went outside and took up position on either side of the doorway, prepared to wait until dawn. Occasionally they exchanged a few words but mostly they sat in silence, drowsing.

Susan stirred against me and muttered something about a cigarette but I didn't reply. Instead, I shifted my position and stretched, trying to keep my shoulders, back, and legs loose, and the circulation going. Carol's breathing pattern had altered after the guards' visit and I decided she must have been sleeping, after all.

About an hour later there was a burst of activity. Men

were rousted from their quarters and there was a series of shouted commands.

A plane was coming in.

I could hear Cudjoe's voice, ordering brush removed from the landing strip and torches to be lit. Soon, there was a dull orange glow outside and I could see our guards clearly. They were watching the activity off to the right, where Cudjoe was directing operations. He had more nerve than an abcessed molar. In the midst of a national takeover bid, it was still business as usual.

The pilot overflew the camp once, getting his bearings. He came past very low. The plane's engines were shockingly loud in the quiet of the night. Then they faded as he moved away to make his turn and start his final approach.

There was silence for a few minutes and then I heard him again, throttled back and on his way down. He made it, taxiing up close to the camp and cutting the engines.

For the next ten minutes or so, while Cudjoe's men were evidently loading the plane, I could hear a succession of grunts and curses. The plane itself would be a stripped-down piece of junk, with only a single seat for the pilot and a minimum of avionics. Ganja-runners utilize every inch of space and they don't spend a lot of money on frills or maintenance. Crashes are common and planes are frequently abandoned, sometimes after a single trip.

I watched, impressed, as several men passed our hut carrying jerrycans of gasoline, presumably from the storage shed. With full tanks, the Florida keys would be within easy range although it wasn't a flight I'd like to try.

Eventually I heard the engines again. The plane bumped along to the end of the strip, turned, and then surged forward, engines snarling. Seconds later, it was up and another shipment of grass was on its way to the schoolyards and living rooms of middle-class North America.

Less than twenty minutes had elapsed between touch-down and takeoff, turnaround efficiency worthy of Holidair's top crew.

I called an escape conference at four-thirty. Our guards appeared to be fast asleep and hadn't stirred for at least an hour. Whispering so softly that I could barely hear myself, I told first Susan and then Carol that we were going to try to get away.

Susan argued briefly, saying it would be safer to wait for Crandall. But I told her I wasn't prepared to take the risk. Cudjoe's men had too damned many guns. There'd be chaos when the raid began and I wanted to be long gone. Carol said escape sounded like a fine idea – the sooner the better.

"How are you going to get free?" Susan whispered.

"I'm going to untie you."

We lay back-to-back while I groped and picked at Susan's knots, trying not to make any noise. My fingers were numb, almost useless, and it was slow, awkward work. I couldn't see what I was doing and could barely feel.

The sashcord was smooth, almost slippery, and I couldn't seem to get any purchase on the knots. Within minutes, I was drenched with sweat and all but exhausted – merely from lying on my side and wiggling my fingers. It wasn't easy on Susan either; she had to concentrate to remain still.

Eventually, I managed to loosen the first knot. This small triumph arrived just in time, because I'd grown discouraged and frustrated and was on the verge of abandoning the attempt. Only the thought of what was going to happen in about an hour's time kept me going; that, and Susan's whispered encouragement.

There were five knots altogether, and none of them came easily. But, eventually Susan's hands were free and I rolled away from her, drained.

"My hands sting," Susan whispered.

"Rub them," I said. "That's the circulation returning."

"What now?" she whispered after a few moments.

"Rest a bit. Then untie me. But not a sound, okay?"

I felt her hands on my wrists. It took her several minutes, working in the dark, but she managed to undo my knots. When I was free I sat up and untied my ankles, trying to ignore the stinging sensation in my hands. Then I slumped back and rested. The guards hadn't moved.

"What about me?" Carol whispered impatiently.

"Wait." I looked at my watch: five-thirty. Crandall's men should be on their way by now. We were cutting things close. Very close. But my strength was returning and my body wasn't as stiff and sore as it might have been. All I had to do was figure out a way to overpower our guards without waking up the camp. Carol would probably be the most effective bait; until recently, she'd enjoyed VIP status.

"Carol," I whispered into her ear, "I've got to get one of those goons in here, and everything has to look exactly right when he comes through the door."

"What do you mean?" She sounded nervous.

"When I'm ready, I want you to call one of them."

"What do I say?"

"Tell him you've got to go to the bathroom. Make it sound good."

"It will," she said. "I *do* have to go to the bathroom. In fact, I'm bursting."

I leaned across and told Susan to lie back as though she were still tied and I arranged her blanket so she was covered from the chest down. Next, I took Carol's blanket off, so her bonds were in view. Finally, I covered myself and lay back.

"Go ahead."

There was a pause. Then she said: "Excuse me."

Neither guard responded.

"Louder," I whispered.

"Excuse me!" We'd been whispering so long that Carol's normal voice sounded like a shout. One of the guards stirred.

"Please," she said. "Can you help me?"

The guard peered around the door-jamb and switched on his flashlight. I squinted against it, giving my eyes a chance to adjust.

"Please," Carol said urgently. "It's an emergency."

304

"What you wan'?" He was suspicious.

"I have to go to the bathroom."

The guard muttered something to his partner and there was a coarse laugh.

"No problem," said the one with the flashlight. "You can go dere."

"No!" she snapped. "You help me outside."

There was more discussion, and more laughter.

*Come on! One of you get in here!* I was wound up tight, as edgy as a junkie whose connection was hours overdue.

"Please," Carol pleaded.

They both came, which made it easier. The one with the flashlight glanced at Susan and me, then bent over Carol, a broad grin on his face. His partner looked on, shotgun pointed carelessly toward the ground.

Now!

I surged to my knees and hit the first one as hard as I could, the heel of my hand smashing into the sinew and gristle behind his ear. He crashed down onto Carol with a groan and lay still.

The other one made an amateur's mistake; he tried to bring the shotgun into play, which kept both his hands busy. An armed man is actually at a disadvantage against an unarmed one, at close quarters.

I didn't give him any chance at all. I brushed the shotgun aside, kneed him in the groin, seized his throat, and got round behind him, clamping a hand over his mouth to stifle the yell that was building in his lungs.

Then I broke his neck.

It snapped like a piece of kindling and when I released him he crumpled like Raggedy Ann, dead at my feet. I'd had no choice: another second or two and he'd have squeezed the trigger and awakened the world.

Gasping, I inspected the first one, who remained sprawled across Carol. He was breathing unevenly, unconscious. To make sure he stayed out for a while I whacked him on the temple with the butt of the shotgun, breaking the skin. He'd live, but he wouldn't be too lively for a few days.

I turned off the flashlight and began untying Carol while Susan glared at me.

"You killed them!" she whispered, sounding outraged.

"Just one."

"You didn't have to do that!"

"Be quiet! We'll discuss it later."

Carol rubbed her hands and ankles and then got unsteadily to her feet. It was five-fifty now, barely half an hour from first light. I handed the flashlight to Carol, took a machete off Sleeping Beauty's belt, and picked up the shotgun, breaking it open. The shells were slugs, not birdshot.

"Here," I said to Susan, giving her the machete. "Don't lose it."

"What now?" asked Carol.

"We go."

Cautiously, we stepped outside and stood in the shadows of the hut, listening and looking hard for any sign of activity. No one was moving in the camp. So far, so good.

There was heavy moisture in the air, but it wasn't raining. Fog? Surely not. But definitely a low ceiling. I hoped the choppers would be able to find the place. A postponement would ruin my entire day.

The best immediate cover was the ganja field. The plants were as tall as a man, and we ought to be able to make our way through it unseen. There was open ground at the far side of the field, but after that the forest was dense. If we made the forest, we'd make it all the way.

Carol and Susan followed me, walking on tiptoe, as I moved away from the hut and headed for the field. We got there without incident and I stopped. The low ceiling had me worried.

"You two stay here."

"Where are you going?" Carol asked.

"There's something I want to try. But if there's any trouble, run. Don't wait for me. Go through the field and don't stop."

They both nodded solemnly. I checked the time again: it was six and counting. "Susan, give me your lighter."

She dug it out of her jeans.

"Okay," I said, taking the flashlight from Carol. "I'll be right back."

"Be careful," said Susan.

Hunching low, I crept back into the camp, moving as stealthily as possible over the damp ground. Where would the sentries be posted? On the perimeter, apparently; no one challenged me as I moved through the gloom.


The storage shed wasn't locked.

I stepped inside, closed the door, and switched on the flashlight, surprised to discover that Cudjoe's larder was well-stocked. There were dozens of cases of food—beans, Irish stews, ackees, even tinned bacon—and several cases of ammunition. There were also two cases of overproof rum, in mickeys, and one of them was open. I shoved a mickey into my hip pocket; before the morning was out, the women would need a bracer.

Where the hell was the gasoline? I shone the light around, puzzled. Then I found it, under a tarpaulin. There were at least fifty ten-gallon cans of high-octane; enough to make a beacon to light up the world. Or at least guide a few helicopters.

Working quickly, I began unscrewing the caps. When I'd removed a dozen, I picked up one of the cans and started sloshing the fuel around. The fumes were overpowering in the confinement of the shed, making me want to gag. The stuff smelled even worse than rum.

I took another full can and began spilling a trail across the dirt floor and then out the door. It was past six o'clock and I was just about out of time.

Twenty yards outside the shed I stopped. The can was empty. I reached for Susan's lighter; time for another *son et lumière*.

"Hey!"

It was one of the Mau Maus, only ten yards away. He snapped on his torch, stared, and then dropped it, swinging up his Sterling.

Both slugs caught him in the chest, knocking him backwards a dozen feet. Not bad for snap-shooting. The shotgun's boom made my ears ring. I had just blown a two-note *reveille* for Camp Cudjoe. Or was it "The Last Post" for me?

Cursing, I flicked Susan's lighter and watched the flames race toward the shed. Then I was running hard as sleepy-looking men began to stumble out of their huts.

Behind me, there was a series of thumping explosions as the gasoline cans began going up. The fire lit up the camp like a television studio. I'd advanced the dawn by a few minutes and I hoped Crandall would understand why.

# CHAPTER TWENTY-TWO

## *Day Seven (Thursday) – 6:10 A.M.*

Flames climbed fifty feet into the air and some of the ammo in the storage shed was beginning to crackle like deadly popcorn. The fire and explosions caused enough confusion that I was able to make it back to the ganja field without stopping a bullet. No one was doing any shooting yet, unless you counted the shed. Bullets exploded by heat are supposed to lack the velocity and kill-power of those fired through a rifled gun barrel, but I wasn't keen to prove it this morning with my own flesh and blood.

Carol and Susan were rooted where I'd left them, stunned, their faces ashen in the gloom as I galloped toward them.

"Run!" I yelled, startling them into action. Carol wasn't a very good runner, but Susan moved like Terry Metcalf after taking a screen pass and breaking into the secondary.

We crashed blindly through the ganja. The plants were mature, of the Kali variety, a particularly potent strain of marijuana. But I was less interested in their hallucinogenic properties than in the temporary protection they offered. The ganja grew dense and tall and it tugged, scratching, at my clothes and face as I ploughed through it.

Behind us, pandemonium continued. The ammo went on exploding and Cudjoe's men, understandably confused, took cover, shouting and cursing. Lead was whizzing around indiscriminately. When we were well into the field I shouted at the women to stop and get down. We huddled, gasping, on the damp ground, safe enough for the moment, protected by the darkness and the weed.

It hadn't been one of your classic, Ambassador Ken Taylor-style escapes—stealthy and absolute, *à la* Teheran—but it would do. We were on the loose, which was the most important thing, although I'd have been happier to be a lot farther from the camp.

Above the chaos, I could hear Cudjoe's distinctive tenor, choked with rage as he shouted orders. The fire was still too hot to fight, and nothing in the shed would survive it anyway, so he was free to concentrate on us.

Cudjoe knew we were in the field, but he didn't know exactly where. Quickly, he sent two gunmen scampering around the field's border to guard the clearing beyond, thereby sealing us in. Next he screamed at the rest of his men to assemble where he stood. If they were smart, they'd keep their heads down; bullets were still popping in the fire.

"My God!" Susan panted. "What did you do?"

"An impromptu exercise in air traffic control," I said, grinning. After our long frustrating night of enforced inactivity, the burst of action had left me exhilarated, pumped up.

"What the hell does that mean?" She was glaring at me, half-frightened, half-angry.

"It's a lousy morning for flying. Poor visibility. Low ceiling. I wanted to make certain the army choppers could find the camp."

"The blind and the deaf could find the camp," Carol muttered. She was trembling and grim-faced.

Susan had managed to hold onto the machete and I took it back from her. It was better than having no weapon at all. I'd abandoned the empty shotgun and the flashlight before setting off on my mad dash down the line of huts, but for some reason I'd held onto Susan's disposable lighter. I returned it. "Reliable little piece of equipment. No air traffic controller should be without one."

"If we get out of here," Susan said, "I'm going to have this lighter gold-plated."

"When we get out of here," I replied, "I'll buy you a jewel-encrusted Dupont. Hell, I'll buy you two of them."

"And I'll buy you an exploding cigar," Carol said, as a ricocheting bullet whined overhead. It was the first light-hearted remark I'd heard her make, but she was still trembling. I took the mickey of rum from my hip pocket and wrenched off the cap. "Here," I said, offering it to Carol. "Drink some."

She took a sip, then coughed and shuddered. I passed the rum to Susan, who knocked back a mouthful with the panache of a long-service Royal Navy rating downing his daily ration of grog. She offered the mickey to me, but I shook my head. "You look after it."

"What now?" Susan asked.

"Now we wait. Crandall's attack should start soon."

Unless, of course, there'd been a screw-up or a change of plans. Well, it was too late to worry about that; we were fully committed.

In the eastern sky, the first blush of morning was visible, ghostly pale in contrast to the vivid light cast by the fire. It was still coal-black on the ground and the ganja, which grew haphazardly rather than in neat rows, continued to provide good cover. But as the sky became lighter we'd become increasingly vulnerable.

"He'll search the field," Carol protested.

"It's a big field," I said. "Let's wait and see."

"Shuter!" Cudjoe's voice pierced the murk like an icicle plunging into a spring snowbank—clear and cold and dangerous. "Come outta there!"

Susan and Carol looked at me worriedly, but I just shrugged. "The hell with him. Let him come in."

"Shuter! If you don't come outta there—*right now!*—you're dead!"

The ammo had stopped popping and the fire was starting

to die out. The sky meanwhile was growing perceptibly lighter. I grinned at the women. "No sweat. Every second we hold out improves the odds."

"You got one minute!" Cudjoe was running out of patience with me.

The minute raced by and he was shouting again. "Know what I'm gonna do, honky? I'm gonna give the bitches to the men!"

"Sounds interesting," Susan said, not quite achieving the light tone she'd tried for.

"Not to me," muttered Carol.

"Quiet!" I told them. "Something's happening."

At the edge of the field a debate was under way between Cudjoe and Jimmy. I strained to hear but couldn't make out what they were saying. However, they were definitely arguing about something and the argument was becoming heated. Finally, I heard Cudjoe scream: "Do it! Do it or I'll waste you right here!"

Moments later, the first machete bit into a ganja plant and I understood. Cudjoe had decided to cut down the field, and I doubted it was solely because the Kali was ready for harvest.

We didn't react immediately. Instead the three of us lay there, almost mesmerized, listening as a group of men got into the rhythm, swinging their big knives in unison.

Time to move. "Come on," I said to the women. "Follow me."

We began crawling deeper into the field, angling away to the left, putting distance between us and the line of machetes. The cutters kept coming, urged on by Jimmy and Cudjoe. We couldn't retreat indefinitely, of course; sooner or later we were going to run out of field and there were gunmen in the clearing, blocking the way to the forest.

When I estimated we were about twenty yards from the clearing I stopped. It would take the cutters at least ten more minutes to reach this point, although I'd have to make a decision before then. Where was Crandall? I looked up at the dark-grey sky, then down at my watch. It was past six-thirty. Where the hell was he?

The crawl had been hardest on Carol. She was in shorts and her knees were scraped raw. She was also badly frightened. "What are we going to do?"

I didn't say anything.

For the next few minutes we lay back listening to the *chunk! chunk! chunk!* of the machetes, coming closer. The cutters were mowing down the ganja like a combine in a prairie wheatfield.

*Come on, Crandall!* Bloody Jamaicans and their "soon-come" mentality. Dawn probably meant high noon.

The cutters were very close now. We could hear their grunts as they worked. Susan reached out and took my hand, squeezing it hard. I was at the point of standing and running, to try to draw everyone away from the women, when there was another sound. It was faint but familiar, and it was rapidly growing stronger.

Helicopters, coming fast and low; their harsh clatter sounded sweeter than Ras Daniel on his best day. Hell, at that moment the choppers made the Vienna Boys Choir sound like a tone-deaf mob of undisciplined ragamuffins.

"Typical," I muttered to Susan. "The thirteenth hour."

"Jamaica time," she grinned.

The machetes stopped advancing as, one by one, the men heard the helicopters too. There were a few puzzled shouts and then Jimmy was yelling orders, telling the men to get their weapons.

Cudjoe's troops went scrambling back over the new-mown ganja, running toward the camp and their guns.

They were also running toward Crandall's guns. Off to the right, automatic weapons began to chatter. Crandall's police were laying down covering fire so the choppers could land on the strip. The police fire was devastating, thick as summer hail and a lot deadlier. Some of Cudjoe's men never made it into the camp, but most did and within a minute or two the firefight I'd expected was under way.

"Stay down, for God's sake!" I shouted at the women. We hugged the ground but the angle of police fire was steadily swinging away from us and after a few moments I couldn't resist the temptation to stand and take a look.

Three of the helicopters were already on the ground, their rotors still churning. They were disgorging soldiers in full battledress, the men firing as they emerged from the khaki machines. It was a stirring sight. When the last two choppers were on the ground, Crandall's pincers began to close—brutally.

Cudjoe's men were trapped in a semi-crossfire and the troops and police were pouring so much lead into the camp that I wondered whether anyone would survive. One thing about Crandall: when he did something, he did it. There were no half-measures this morning in the District of Look Behind. Thank God the women and I weren't still in our hut, waiting to be rescued.

"Shuter!"

He was almost on top of me, approaching from an angle, his eyes even wilder than his hair. Cudjoe was grinning like a lunatic, ignoring the battle behind him.

Carol uttered a terrified moan as Cudjoe slashed his way toward us, his machete scything through the plants as smoothly as a straight-razor cutting teenage peach-fuzz.

I stared at him, awed by the spectacle of his powerful arms and huge shoulders working so effortlessly, so tirelessly. We weren't in an alley, but I was finally going to get my time with him.

"You did this, you mother!" Cudjoe was screaming at me from less than twenty feet. Something had snapped in him; he was like a man possessed by unimaginable demons. His men, his grand design, were forgotten now; all he cared about was killing me.

I hefted my machete uncertainly. It was sharpened on

314

both sides and pointed at the tip, but it didn't feel comfortable in my hand. The handle was slippery with sweat. However, it was all I had, so I waved it at him. "Come and get it, sucker!"

Cudjoe grinned maniacally and kept coming, eager to oblige.

I moved off at a slight angle, pushing my way through the standing plants until I gained a clear area. We faced each other, glaring across a space of less than ten feet.

He didn't waste any time but closed with a rush, aiming a mighty swing at my head.

I held up my machete to parry. There was a loud clash of steel. The force of the blow almost tore the knife from my hand. I was dimly aware of Carol sobbing and Susan staring, silent and horrified.

Cudjoe swung again, and again I managed to block. He had an advantage in height and reach, not to mention at least fifty pounds in weight. I'd have to stay outside and hope he made a mistake.

He swung again, and this time I simply twisted my body out of the way, countering with a thrust of my own. It missed but it slowed him, made him think.

We crouched, exchanging murderous looks, and then closed once more. Our knives clashed and we both pulled back.

My chest was heaving and my knees felt like gelatin. Cudjoe wasn't even breathing hard. But his face was contorted with anger, an intense primitive rage. He'd become a killing machine, programmed to destroy.

Holding his machete directly in front of his body, he started forward again. This time he didn't attempt a wild swing but simply moved steadily closer.

I began to retreat, taking care not to trip. I'd only taken two steps when Cudjoe lunged ahead, feinting at my belly. When I lowered my machete to parry, he stepped in close and banged me on the side of the head with his big left fist.

The blow knocked me flat.

I was down, and any second I was going to be out.

My ears rang and I was seeing everything in slow motion: Cudjoe towering over me, cackling in triumph, raising his knife, getting ready to close my file.

I tried to scramble up but I was far too slow and his machete was already starting down.

Then his hair caught fire.

Flames blazed about his head and he let out a roar of pain and surprise.

Susan, bare to the waist, stood behind him, holding her lighter and staring expressionlessly at what she'd done.

What she'd done was take off her T-shirt, drench it with the rum, set it ablaze, and hurl it in Cudjoe's face. *Terreuriste flambée*.

It spoiled his aim.

Things were still happening in slow motion, but I managed to roll slightly to my left and, as Cudjoe's knife continued down, I struck up as hard as I could. There was a searing pain in my side as his machete sliced through my shirt and bit into the flesh just above my right hip.

But there was also a satisfying jolt through my arm and shoulder as my knife drove into Cudjoe's broad trunk. It went in deep, missing his rib cage but penetrating upward into his chest cavity.

Cudjoe collapsed on me heavily, cursing and coughing. The T-shirt, still ablaze, had fallen to one side. There was a terrible stench of rum and singed hair.

Desperately I pushed him off and scrambled away, drawing my machete clear. I got to my knees, then to my feet, and looked down at him. Blood was pumping from his wound; my machete had hit his aorta and probably a lung.

There was no fear in Cudjoe's eyes, no pleading. Only rage and bitter hatred. "Shuter..." he gurgled, "...you honky bastard...I wanna..." He coughed again, and the blood spurted harder.

His machete lay red on the ground by his outstretched arm. I kicked it away, and then seized him by his hair, raising my own knife and taking aim at his corded neck. Winston, Lucky, the degradation of Carol, were reason enough.

I tensed, ready to swing.

"Mike, no! For God's sake!" Susan's voice sliced into my consciousness.

She was right: we were men, not animals, and I wasn't a licensed executioner. Slowly, I lowered the machete, releasing Cudjoe and watching him slump back.

He coughed again and a few seconds later he died — alone, the way all of us must.


For a while, Carol, Susan and I stood huddled together, propping one another up, weak and wobbly survivors. We avoided looking at Cudjoe's body and initially we didn't talk. There was nothing to say; there was everything to say.

Up by the camp, the battle was over. Crandall's security forces had routed Cudjoe's men, with the expenditure of a staggering amount of ammunition. The smell of cordite hung heavy in the muggy air and we could hear the excited voices of officers, shouting commands. A handful of Cudjoe's men had fled into the forest but pursuit teams were already after them.

I looked down at Susan, who was still going topless, and tried to tell her what I thought. But the words wouldn't come; there'd be time for that later. I let my machete fall to the ground and slowly unbuttoned my tattered shirt.

"Put it on," I said.

"You're bleeding!" she whispered, looking at the cut in my side.

"I'm alive."

She inspected the wound. "It looks serious."

"It's okay. Put on the shirt, or Crandall will run you in for indecent exposure."

Carol was staring at us, in deep shock. "You two...I...I don't know what..."

"It's okay," I told her. "Everything's fine now. It's over."

Susan put on my shirt, then looked at me through eyes that were brimming but somehow refused to overflow. "Mike...Mike, I..."

"Later."

A single tear finally rolled down her cheek and then she smiled – too brightly. "Aw, Shuter – what a story! What a goddamned story!"

I didn't have enough strength left to carry Cudjoe's body, but I didn't want to leave it in the field. So I reached down and seized his dreadlocks, wrapping them around my right hand.

Dragging him, I started slowly, painfully, across the field while Susan and Carol stumbled along behind.

On the way I counted nine bodies. They'd never made it to their guns. When we came up on the first helicopter, the pilot, who was relaxing with a cigarette, stared at us in astonishment, then shouted something. I shook my head and kept moving.

With me naked to the waist and dragging Cudjoe's body, with Carol scratched and bruised and wearing her revealing shorts and tight T-shirt, with Susan wrapped in a bloody rag, we presented an unlikely sight to the policemen and soldiers who watched us mutely as we struggled up the line of huts.

Finally, an army officer stepped forward. It was Colonel Adams. He looked at me oddly and then, for some reason, he saluted. "Mr. Shuter! Sah!"

"Get Crandall," I said. "I've got his man."


The army medic was trying to be as gentle as possible as he bathed my wound and prepared to stitch it closed. The cut wasn't deep, but unless it was stitched the scar would be ugly. Not that I cared. I've got my share of scars, not all of them on the flesh.

Crandall was less gentle. He had given me an extended lecture, complete with fist-pounding and vague threats about obstruction charges and breaches of Jamaica's Official Secrets Act. But there'd been a faint twinkle in his eye while he roasted me.

The twinkle faded when I invited him to cut the bull. "Have you had a look around, Crandall? This place looks like the O.K. Corral."

He nodded sourly. "We fought a battle here."

"Do you think the girl would have had a snowball's chance?"

"We knew you were out, Shuter." He lit another cigarette and smiled coldly when I winced; the medic was applying a stinging goo to my side. "When we saw the pillar of flame, we knew you were out."

"You didn't even know I was in."

"Of course I did. When you disappeared from Negril, it was obvious you'd broken your word."

I looked at him steadily. "I'll make it up to you one day."

"Yes," he said, "you will." He paused. "May I ask you? Why did you bring the reporter?"

"For protection."

He thought about it for a while. "I see."

"How did your men fare?" The medics had been busy, but mostly they'd been patching up members of Team Cudjoe.

"One dead," Crandall said quietly. "Seven wounded. A big price, but we won a big prize."

"Congratulations," I said, meaning it this time.

He frowned briefly, then smiled. "Shuter, you may be irresponsible, unreliable, foolhardy. But I, Jamaica, the Prime Minister . . ."

I cut him off. "Tell him hello. I got what I came for."

He shook his head. "If . . . if there's ever anything I, we can do . . ."

"There is. You can organize me a seat on one of those choppers. My boss will be wanting a report."

"That's right. I'd forgotten. It's just a job to you, isn't it?"

I looked at him bleakly, but didn't reply. The medic had finished with his needle and thread, his gauze and tape. Crandall nodded abruptly and held out a friendly hand. "I'll see about your helicopter," he said gruffly.


"She sounds," said McGregor, during our third conversation of the afternoon, "like a remarkable young woman."

"Yeah," I said, swirling some of Gilly Byles' vodka around in my glass and trying to ignore the throb in my side.

"And she's certainly attractive, at least on television."

"Yeah," I said again, wishing he'd drop it.

"When everything settles down," he went on, "I want you to bring her here for dinner one evening. Sam will outdo himself."

"We'll see, Douglas."

"We could all do with a little feminine company from time to time," he said softly.

"From time to time," I sighed. "But it may take a while. She's mad at me. I don't know. Maybe I'm mad at her, too."

"Whatever for?"

I drained my vodka before answering. "Bishop and half his newsroom are on their way to Kingston. They're going to originate an hour special out of there tomorrow night. I've told Susan I won't appear on it."

McGregor was silent for a few moments. "Well, I won't advise you either way. But I want you to bring Miss Quill to dinner."

"We'll see."

"Are you sure," he said, after a moment, "that Carol is going to be all right?"

"It'll be hard for a while, until all the noise goes away, but she'll be okay. Tell Malone he's got quite a daughter."

"I will, I will."

I spilled a little more vodka into my glass. "Okay then?"

"More than that. You've done a magnificent piece of work."

"You haven't seen the bills yet."

McGregor chuckled; once a Scotsman....

# CHAPTER TWENTY-THREE

## *Day Eight (Friday) – 7:40 A.M.*

It was agony, but I forced my body to finish the entire program. There was nothing wrong with my arms or stomach muscles, so the pushups weren't bad. But the wound in my side shrieked with every situp and a little blood seeped through the dressing. I didn't care; I'd be damned if I'd let the rot take hold. I'd gone three days in a row without a proper workout and at my age three days is too long.

After a shower, I changed the dressing and put on a swimsuit and a T-shirt. Daniel was waiting at the stables, getting acquainted with a bay gelding that had seen better days. Most of us had.

"Good morning, Mike," Daniel said, sounding concerned about something. "Did you sleep well?"

"Yeah. As untroubled as a millionaire." It was true; I'd killed three men yesterday but I was without remorse. Death sometimes goes with the territory.

"Good mornin', sah!" Nigel, grinning, led a saddled Molasses from the stable. She seemed glad to see me, butting my shoulder and snorting with pleasure while I stroked her nose and fed her an apple from her private stock.

"I suppose she's already gone through a half-year's supply of treats?"

"No, sah! I don't spoil her."

"You can spoil her just a little," I said, putting my foot in the stirrup. "She's a very good horse."

Daniel swung aboard the bay and we walked, side-by-side, out of the paddock. We didn't say much; we'd done our talking last night.

It was another flawless morning. The sea was flat-calm and the sky cobalt. Off shore, the *Calico Jack* rode up on her anchor chain while a couple of ambitious deckhands slapped black paint on her freeboard. At the water's edge, an attractive Swiss couple who'd been at the Coconut Cove for the past two weeks were adjusting their snorkels and getting ready for a lazy, pre-breakfast swim.

But mostly the beach was empty, which was fine with Daniel and me.

We walked slowly past the Sundowner Hotel, where the waiters were setting tables, and then we let our horses trot as far as the Negril Sands Club, where Molasses and I had made our stand with the speargun. There was no sign of Trevor and his young scuba-diving friends, and that was fine, too. It wasn't a morning to be with strangers.

"Let's walk a bit," I said to Daniel. We dismounted and took off our tennis shoes, enjoying the warm water and soft sand. The horses plodded along behind, apparently content.

"This is a great beach," I said unnecessarily.

Ras Daniel grinned. "Haven't you seen Jamaica's ads? 'We're more than a beach. We're a country.' They help your airline sell tickets."

"There are a lot of countries, professor, but there are few beaches to match this one. No wonder you'd sooner sing for your supper in Negril than try to run Jamaica from Kingston."

"At last," he said, "you're beginning to understand. We'll make a Rasta of you yet."

"That's me. Ras Michael, the born-again Rasta."

Daniel laughed. "Locks wouldn't suit you. Mr. Byles would probably ask for your room."

A kid drifted out of the palms, full of early-morning optimism and midnight guile.

"How are you, mon?" he said with an insincere smile.

"Fine," I said. Daniel didn't say anything.

"You wanna buy some good smoke?"

I shook my head and we kept walking.

"It dynamite stuff," he persisted, falling into step beside me. "I make you a good price."

"Not today."

"Maybe tomorrow?"

"No, not tomorrow, either."

He gave up then. He nodded to Daniel, turned and ambled back toward the trees. There'd be other prospects before the sun got much higher. No problem, mon.

"I've been wondering all night," said Daniel, when the kid had moved out of earshot, "what do you think about Cudjoe? Really think about him, I mean. Was he the disease that afflicts Jamaica—or only the symptom?"

What could I tell Daniel about his Jamaica, his beautiful Jamaica, with its laughter and its pain? That someone was going to have to come to grips with the country's fundamental problems or there'd be another Cudjoe, another crisis? That sunshine and blue water, reggae and slogans aren't enough to sustain a country? That they never are?

I walked on in silence. Then I stopped and started putting on my shoes.

"Well, Mike?"

"He was the symptom," I said. "The disease is elsewhere."

"I don't understand."

"Cudjoe was an entrepreneur, trying to serve a market. That market is not here. It's a state of mind, not a matter of geography."

"But he was a killer," Daniel said slowly, "not a businessman."

"Yes, he was a killer." I let the rest of it go unsaid.

We got back on our horses. Molasses felt like a run and I let her canter a while, then pulled her up and we waited for Daniel.

"How did your negotiations with the lawyers and the accountants go?" I asked, when he drew up alongside.

"We are going to record the album next month."

"You'll be rich and famous," I grinned.

"Fame and fortune," he said solemnly, "are an illusion."

"You stole that from *Evita*."

"I told you before, Mike: we are all plagiarists."

"Well, let me know when you play Maple Leaf Gardens. I'll want tickets."

Daniel didn't reply. We walked along, comfortably. The sun was higher now, warm on my back. A big breakfast and then I'd pack and fly to Kingston.

I had a funeral to attend, and then a late-afternoon flight to catch—scheduled, north-bound, first class. I'd explain it to McGregor another time.

After eight days and seven nights on the road, it was time to go home and feed the fish.

# ACKNOWLEDGMENTS

Many people helped develop Shuter and waited patiently for him to appear. They know who they are and they know I am grateful. But three deserve special mention: Andrew Cochran, television genius; Scott MacCulloch, pilot-extraordinary; and Alan Murphy, Irishman.

Lew Anthony
Toronto
January, 1981